GUERRILLA

remix

MARKETING

D0503353

JAY CONRAD LEVINSON
AND JEANNIE LEVINSON

Entrepreneur
Press

Entrepreneur Press, Publisher
Cover design: Andrew Welyczko
Composition and production: Eliot House Productions

This publication is designed to provide accurate and authoritative information in
regard to the subject matter covered. It is sold with the understanding that the
publisher is not engaged in rendering legal, accounting, or other professional
services. If legal advice or other expert assistance is required, the services of a
competent professional person should be sought.

Library of Congress Cataloging-in-Publication Data
Levinson, Jay Conrad.
        Guerrilla marketing remix: the best of guerrilla marketing/by Jay Con-
rad Levinson and Jeannie Levinson.
        p.   cm.
        ISBN-13: 978-1-59918-422-7 (alk. paper)
        ISBN-10: 1-59918-422-2 (alk. paper)
        1. Marketing 2. Marketing—Planning. I. Levinson, Jeannie. II. Title.
HF5415.L4768 2011
658.8'02—dc23   2011028811

Printed in the United States of America

19 18 17   10 9 8 7 6 5

Dedication

With pride, gratitude and real love—we dedicate this *Remix* to the guerrillas who were part of the mix—part of the lore that has become and is becoming guerrilla marketing. Those guerrillas are the guerrilla co-authors whose names appear in this book and whose gleaming words of advice and knowledge generously flow from these pages.

—Jay and Jeannie Levinson

Contents

PART 2

Guerrilla Wisdom from Guerrilla Co-Authors

Contents

Foreword

JAY INVENTED IT.

You don't get to say that very often (not the "Jay" part, of course, the "invented" part). Jay invented modern marketing. Jay invented the guerrilla mindset. Jay invented the notion that advertising and marketing weren't the same thing. Jay figured out how to take this brilliant idea and turn it into hundreds of brilliant ideas and dozens of books.

This book is just the tip of the iceberg. It's not a short book, but it's ultimately too short, because there's too much to cover.

The world of marketing is a better one because Jay made it that way.

—Seth Godin
Author, *Poke the Box*

Seth Godin
45 Main Street 3R
Hastings on Hudson, NY 10706
http://www.sethgodin.com (click on my head!)

part 1

INSIGHT INTO GUERRILLA MARKETING

chapter 1

What Marketing Really Is

I T'S THE PRECIOUS CONNECTION between you and whoever buys what you sell.

The connection is made online, in person, by phone, by mail, at a show, on a sign, by hearing, by reading or by seeing. It lasts from the moment the customer learns about you until he or she gets enticed away from you by a cagier guerrilla. But if you're a guerrilla, that probably won't happen to you.

You know what guerrillas know—that you knock yourself silly winning a customer, and you don't lose that customer no matter what. That means you realize that the precious connection comprises what marketing really is—an entire experience.

Your job as a guerrilla: Make every single moment of the experience satisfying, simple, and worthwhile for the customer. When you do that, you're truly a practitioner of guerrilla marketing.

> *Marketing is—the precious connection between you and whoever buys what you sell.*

It isn't easy to be that good. To give you a powerful competitive advantage, we're giving you the pure gold we've mined from the treasury of guerrilla marketing. In our opinion, it's all gold, but in these pages appear the nuggets that are purest and newest, the most leading edge and timeless of all.

> *Marketing really is—an entire experience.*

Marketing begins the second that you know you've got a product or service to sell to a person. In that second, crucial questions pop up: What is the name of what you'll be selling? Where can people buy it? How much will it cost? How will people pay? How much will it cost you to produce it? What color will be on the website and the shelf?

The answers to these questions change like the wind because marketing changes the same way. That ability to change is part of the DNA of guerrilla marketing.

There are two other parts to that DNA: The first is the ability to operate according to a very simple plan. Everybody can do that.

The second part is committing to that plan. Not everybody can do that. Most people expect quick answers, which don't happen; instant results, which don't happen; and high profits at the outset, which don't happen. So they abandon their plan, making certain that it won't happen. And then they complain that marketing doesn't work for them.

But marketing works for everyone—if they do it right. This *Guerrilla Marketing Remix* exists to help you do it right.

Guerrilla marketing has made the transition from a maverick kind of marketing to mainstream marketing. It has taken its message from a single place in California to the majority of the world. It has been embraced by both small and large businesses on our planet for two straightforward reasons:

> *Marketing without a plan is like going into battle under a commander who says: "Ready . . . fire! . . . aim."*

1. It simplifies a seemingly complex topic.
2. It works every time if you do it right.

Guerrilla marketers have mastered the craft of doing it right. The purpose of this remix is to transform you into a guerrilla marketer. After the transformation, you'll understand that marketing is all contact anyone representing your company has with anyone who does not represent your company. Marketing is not just the blaring trumpets. It's also the easily overlooked details. But guerrillas don't overlook them.

> *Marketing is— the truth made fascinating.*

Guerrillas understand that today, marketing is the truth—always the truth—made fascinating—always fascinating. In the past, much of marketing was not the truth. And certainly, most of it was not fascinating.

What a lot of people fail to understand about marketing is that it is a process. It is not an event. Guerrilla marketing has a beginning and a middle but rarely an end—unless you sell your business. Even then, it should not have an end, unless you sold your business to a half-wit.

Marketing is also a business more than an art. Sure, It embraces all art forms—music, writing, acting, dancing, video, painting, illustrating, photography, singing—but don't delude yourself thinking that you're an artist. You're a guerrilla, and your focus is on the profits of your business. If there's any emotional gratification involved, it's because of the steady and robust rise of those profits, not because of any awards or compliments you receive along the way.

> *Marketing is— a process, not an event.*

A great artistic performance is often followed by applause and cheering. A great marketing performance is often followed by apathy and inaction. Why is that? That's because it is marketing and not an artistic performance. Yet, many non-guerrillas, failing to hear the applause, figure that their marketing isn't working. Marketing hardly ever works instantly. If you need instant results, go into farming. Often, that works faster than marketing. But even the best farmers can't rush the process of planting, fertilizing, and harvesting.

Marketing is—an opportunity to educate prospects and customers on how to succeed at achieving their goals.

Guerrilla marketing works consistently and eventually. It hardly ever works immediately. We're glad we're clearing that part up right at the outset. We don't want to see any long faces on business owners who have everything it takes to succeed except for patience.

Here's what else marketing is: It's a big chance for you. It's your sparkling opportunity to educate your prospects and customers on how to succeed at achieving their goals. Whether those goals are to earn more money, grow a business, shrink a waistline, play better golf, attract a mate, or lose weight, marketing is your chance to show people how to make their dreams a reality. We're living smack-dab in the middle of the Information Age, so you can give away free information to help your target market hit their own bull's-eyes.

Perhaps you can do it with information. Or marketing success might lie in the products you offer or the services you render. Whatever it takes, your product can probably solve the problems of your audience. So consider yourself a problem solver. When you do, you're well on your way to being a guerrilla marketer.

Of course, in addition to being a craft for a problem solver, we must admit marketing also involves an element of art. Truth be told, marketing is the art of getting people to change their minds; it's a way to persuade them to see it your way, to stop doing things the way they've been doing them and begin doing them your way because doing them your way will make their lives easier, will help them achieve their goals, will help them be happier—whatever that takes. So one of your jobs as a guerrilla is to see what it really does take.

GOLD RUSH

In 1853 a man went to the California gold rush hoping to make his fortune by selling tents to the miners. However, the weather was fine, and the miners slept out in the open, so the man could sell no tents. But he was creative; he made his fortune anyway, and his name is famous to this day.

How did he become rich? . . . And who is he?

He used the tough tent cloth to make trousers for the miners. His name was Levi Strauss.

Let's stop here for a moment just so you can be clear on one thing. Are we telling you that guerrilla marketing is easy? We are not. Because it is not easy. There are many good things about it, including effectiveness, certainty, efficiency, freedom from stress, and the pure joy of doing things right. But it is not about ease. One would think that to be a guerrilla marketer, you've have to work your tail off. And you do have to work hard.

But we've created this Remix so that you don't have to work your tail off. Jay has worked a three-day week from our home since 1971, so we don't want to lead you down a garden path toward overwork. No guerrilla is a workaholic.

Marketing is— the art of getting people to change their minds.

Excellence in hiring, training, and delegating protects guerrillas from that malady. What do hiring, training, and delegating have to do with marketing? They have everything to do with it because they are integral parts of the experience your customers will have with you.

Guerrilla marketing is a realization that a galaxy of details affect the power of your brand, the experience your customers have with you, and the size of the smile on your face when you review your profits.

'Nuff said. Let's just do it.

HUMAN RESOURCES HELPFUL HINTS

Take the prospective employees you are trying to place and put them in a room with only a table and two chairs. Leave them alone for two hours, without any instruction. At the end of that time, go back and see what they are doing.

- If they have taken the table apart, put them in Engineering.
- If they are counting the butts in the ashtray, assign them to Finance.
- If they are waving their arms and talking out loud, send them to Consulting.
- If they are talking to the chairs, Personnel is a good spot for them.
- If they are wearing green sunglasses and need a haircut, Computer Information Systems is their niche.
- If the room has a sweaty odor, perhaps they're destined for the Help Desk.
- If they mention what a good price we got for the table and chairs, put them into Purchasing.
- If they mention that hardwood furniture DOES NOT come from rainforests, Public Relations would suit them well.
- If they are sleeping, they are management material.
- If they are writing up the experience, send them to the Technical Documents team.
- If they don't even look up when you enter the room, assign them to Security.
- If they try to tell you it's not as bad as it looks, send them to Marketing.

WALT DISNEY AND RAY KROC

Both Walt Disney and Ray Kroc were said to have been neat freaks, to the point of OCD (obsessive-compulsive disorder). The story is told that one day both were attending the same event and found each other in the restroom at the same time. Neither one of them wanted to touch the restroom door handles, so they struck up a conversation that lasted for more than 20 minutes, as they patiently waited for someone else to enter the restroom, which allowed them to both scurry quickly out the door before it closed.

NEATNESS

Neatness is not something that occurs on a Monday morning. Neatness is something that should go on every second that you're open. If people see that your premises are sloppy, they're going to assume that's the way you run your business. If they see your premises are neat, they're going to assume that's the way you run your business.

While we were visiting Disney World, we spent some time at Epcot, and we sat down on a bench and watched people litter for about half an hour because we wanted to see how long the litter would stay on the ground. It never stayed there longer than 10 minutes. People would appear from behind shrubbery or drop from a cloud and pick up the litter and restore the neatness. Disney employees clean the restrooms twice every 30 minutes. Disney knows the importance of neatness.

What's the main reason people patronize McDonald's? 1) Clean restrooms. 2) Good French fries. Hamburgers don't really factor in it at all. McDonald's executives know clean restrooms are a free marketing weapon and that people make purchase decisions based on the neatness or sloppiness of premises.

Walk into a Nordstrom department store—see if you can find any hint of sloppiness. You never will because Nordstrom managers realize neatness is a marketing weapon.

chapter 2

What Marketing Is Not

HOWEVER IT APPEARS TO THE PUBLIC, don't kid yourself into thinking that marketing is show business. It is not. There's no business like show business, and that includes marketing.

Think of marketing as sell business, as solve-a-problem business, as create-a-desire business, but don't think for a moment that you're around to entertain the throngs. Someone else got there before you. You're here to provide those throngs with positive purchase experiences. You're a guerrilla.

Guerrillas know that no matter how much they may advertise, marketing is definitely not advertising. There are 200 weapons of guerrilla marketing. Advertising is one of them. Whatever you do, don't overlook the other 199. Your customers won't appreciate it if you do.

Sure, advertising is seen by a lot of people. And there was a time when it worked. But it certainly doesn't work now nearly as well as it used to.

Marketing is NOT show business. Think of marketing as sell business, as solve-a-problem business, as create-a-desire business, but don't think for a moment that you're around to entertain the throngs.

If you have a website, don't expect it to work. Planning an ad campaign? Expect grief. How about PR? Doesn't work as well as it used to. So what does work?

Marketing combinations work. If you have a website and you advertise it vigorously and you run a publicity program to tie in with it, they will all work—each part of the formula contributing its own particular magic. The guerrilla marketing weapons actually help each other work, which is why guerrillas are ever mindful that individual weapons can't win battles all by themselves.

That's why advertising is not marketing, and email is not marketing, and telephone calls are not marketing—not alone they're not. But as part of a combination, they're lethal. Marketing is not any single one of the 200 weapons. It's the wise use of many of them.

Everyone knows that people look online first before making a purchase. So is being online the trick for your business? It is part of the trick, but being online is not marketing. It also needs a lot of help. We hope you're beginning to see that it's the guerrilla who provides the help that the weapons of marketing need.

The guerrilla helps with information and with action. One without the other hardly does the job. Together, they pack an awesome punch. We're here with this Remix to provide the exact information that you need.

The action is up to the person whose name is on your driver's license. All the information that exists is meaningless without that person taking action.

Marketing is not any single one of the 200 weapons. It's the wise use of many of them in combination with each other.

TELEPHONE DEMEANOR

Once, we were called into Midas Muffler Shops because they were dismayed at their inability to make appointments with callers. Midas was getting 100 percent of its initial contacts by the phone, which is wonderful, but employees were converting only 71 percent of those callers into appointments, which is terrible. It meant they were dropping the ball 29 percent of the time.

While surveying the shops in person, we couldn't help but notice that most of the time, the ringing telephone was answered by a person who obviously didn't want to be on the phone. That person was too busy, in a conversation with a customer, in a bad mood, or an introvert.

Whatever the reason, the person answering the phone didn't want to be doing that—and it showed. No wonder so many callers failed to make an appointment for a new muffler.

We suggested Midas undertake a telephone training program. It would take only half a day. Midas was so warm to the idea that it instituted a new rule: "You can't answer the phone at a Midas Muffler Shop unless you've taken this telephone training."

Within six months, Midas began converting 94 percent of all callers into finished appointments. That represents more than a million dollars in profits, yet the cost was negligible.

For many companies, there was a time when marketing was direct mail. But now, it's known that direct mail needs a lot of help. Companies using this technique need to employ some guerrilla imagination.

Many people continue to think that marketing is telemarketing, or couponing, or social networking. All of those actions are part of marketing, but none of them are the whole deal. Don't ever think we're still in an age of single-weapon marketing. If you do, you may be the only one left who thinks that way.

Guerrilla marketing embraces 360 degrees of communication, reaching target audiences in as many ways as are affordable and possible. Your task as a guerrilla is to be aware of all the marketing

POSTAGE STAMPS

Guerrillas know that people are assaulted with a blizzard of direct mail every day. Most of those direct mailing pieces get thrown into the wastebasket without the envelope ever being opened.

So guerrillas facing up to this reality put 11 stamps on each letter. They decide to pop for first-class postage, but rather than a single stamp, they'll put on 11 stamps. They'll put a six-cent stamp, two four-cent stamps, two three-cent stamps, and six two-cent stamps, and then they'll mail the letter because they know the recipient has never received a letter with 11 stamps on it.

That letter's going to be noticed. That envelope is going to be opened, and the contents are going to be read because it's the first time in the person's life they ever received a letter with so many stamps upon it. This is the true essence of guerrilla marketing. It does not cost more money, but it does take time, energy, and imagination.

Another application of this in direct mail is if you're going to do a mailing from Dallas, where you live, first have your mailing sent to someplace like Portugal, then have it mailed from Portugal because then your prospects will be receiving an envelope for the first time in their lives with a Portuguese postmark and a Portuguese stamp. That's what we mean by imagination.

MARKETING COMBINATIONS

We know a guerrilla bed seller with a mom-and-pop store who chalks up more than $1.5 million in sales each month and uses only four marketing weapons.

1. Radio commercials direct people to his website and his showroom.

2. His website answers questions and directs visitors to his showroom.

3. Trained salespeople capitalize on the momentum created by the radio and website.

4. The free gift of a comforter, a set of sheets, two pillowcases, and two good pillows ensures healthy word-of-mouth marketing after the sales.

How expensive is that combination of marketing weapons? Not very expensive—but extremely effective. That should be your goal as a guerrilla: marketing that is not very expensive but extremely effective.

Sounds almost too easy, but it isn't easy to come up with the winning combination. Yet guerrillas have learned that what they sacrifice in ease, they make up in profits.

weapons available to you, to experiment with many of them, and then to identify the combination of weapons that provides the highest profit to you.

Here's something else that marketing isn't: brochures. People rush out to produce a brochure, thinking that's all the marketing they'll need. It probably is a very important link in the chain that leads to success, but a brochure certainly is not marketing all by itself. Maybe it used to be, but this is not your parents' generation. It's yours—especially if you're a guerrilla marketer.

Pay close attention here because many failed businesses just didn't get this. Marketing is not a stage for humor. If you use humor in your marketing, people will recall your funny joke but not your compelling offer. If you use humor, it will be funny the first and maybe even the second time. After that, it will be grating and will get in the way of what makes marketing work: repetition. Humor sabotages your marketing right from the outset, but some misguided people think that marketing is supposed to be funny.

> *Marketing is not a place for humor. If you use humor in your marketing, people will recall your funny joke but not your compelling offer.*

Those same people most likely think that marketing is their invitation to be clever. Get that notion out of your mind. People remember the most clever part of your marketing but it's your offer that they should remember. Think of cleverness as a marketing vampire that sucks attention away from your offer.

MIXED MESSAGE

An anti-drug organization distributed material to children in school. However, this had the opposite effect to what was intended.

Why?

The group distributed pencils with the printed message: "WAY TOO COOL TO DO DRUGS."

As the children sharpened the pencils down, the message became: "COOL TO DO DRUGS,"

and eventually just "DO DRUGS."

Attention to details can make or break your campaign message.

Think of cleverness as a marketing vampire that sucks attention away from your offer.

Also dismiss the notion that marketing is complicated. Marketing becomes complicated for people who just cannot grasp the simplicity of marketing, but it is most assuredly user-friendly to guerrillas. They begin with a seven-sentence, guerrilla marketing plan, then they commit to that plan. That's certainly not complicated.

We've saved the best for last. We've saved it for last because it's the number-one misconception about marketing. More money has been lost due to this misconception than due to any other factor in marketing. We see people who do everything right until they actually start marketing—and that's when they fall right on their keister or their face. Neither one is an option for guerrillas.

LOCATION, LOCATION, LOCATION!

There are two important things for you to know about location.

1. Many bankrupt businesses in America at one point had the best location in town, but they relied so much on it that they ignored the other 199 weapons. Location isn't enough. It's important but not enough.

2. The best location in the United States and the best location in your town is on the internet.

America is learning how to buy things in a new way in a new place. They're learning to buy things in a new way by buying online. And the new place is the internet. And unless you're there, you're missing out on a location that's only going to improve in time.

2 / What Marketing Is Not

Marketing is not a miracle worker. Fortunes are lost regularly by people who expect miracles from marketing. But the marketing business is not the miracle business. It's the patience business. It's the planning business. If you expect miracles, you're going to get ulcers.

Marketing is an opportunity to earn profits with your business, a chance to cooperate with other businesses in your community or your industry, and a process of building lasting relationships. But a miracle worker, it is not.

> *The marketing business is not the miracle business. It's the patience business. It's the planning business. If you expect miracles, you're going to get ulcers.*

chapter 3

The Birth of Guerrilla Marketing

I FIGURE THAT GUERRILLA MARKETING was born in 1957 when, as a U.S. Army counterintelligence analyst, I was required to write reports of investigations in one and one-half pages, single-spaced. That taught me the importance and the challenge of being concise.

It also led me to begin a career in advertising, first as a secretary because I could type 80 words per minute, and then as a copywriter when I had written so many ads and commercials that never saw the light of day that I finally learned how to make them good enough to run.

Eventually, I had the blessed experience to be able to create advertising for famed brands like Green Giant, Pillsbury, Chrysler, Procter & Gamble, Kellogg's, Sears, and Quaker Oats. I got to see, hands-on and

> *I figure guerrilla marketing was born in 1957 when, as a U.S. Army counterintelligence analyst, I was required to write reports of investigations. That taught me to be concise. It also led me to begin a career in advertising.*

firsthand, what worked for the big companies with the bottomless bank accounts.

Then I ventured off on my own and created marketing materials for then-little companies in new industries: computers, solar energy, waterbeds, fast-food chains, plus a little-known men's magazine called Playboy. These enterprises had empty wallets but big ideas. I quickly learned what they needed and could afford on the marketing front. It was different from what the big guys used. So were the pressures. The smaller companies couldn't afford to make mistakes and had to get everything right the first time.

I got to see firsthand what worked for big companies with bottomless bank accounts. Then I ventured off on my own and created marketing materials for then-little companies in new industries.

By this point, I had written a couple of books about earning money without the necessity of holding a job. The first, *Earning Money without a Job*, led to my being invited to teach a class at the extension division of the University of California—Berkeley.

The second book, *555 Way to Earn Extra Money*, was the result of my yearlong research—without Google's help—of how other people get it on without a job. In it, I had a chapter on how to market with a limited budget. Both books helped my class at Berkeley to be filled to the brim.

One day in class, one of my students raised his hand and asked, "Jay, most of us in this room have long hair, Levi's, empty pockets,

"I have always believed that writing advertisements is the second most profitable form of writing. The first, of course, is ransom notes . . ."

—Philip Dusenberry

> *I knew that, in business, my students wanted the conventional goals of financial independence, freedom from stress, balance in their lives, and companies they could grow to their heart's content. But they couldn't achieve those goals with marketing unless they used unconventional methods.*

great ideas for businesses, and zero ideas on how to market those businesses. Can you recommend a book for us to read?"

Stupidly, I said, "Yes, I promise I'll be back to you with book recommendations next week." After class, I went to the library to find good books to recommend but found none. I went across San Francisco Bay to the library at Stanford University but came up empty once again. Same sad story in the public libraries for Oakland, San Jose, Sacramento, and the city of San Francisco.

All the existing marketing books I found seemed to be written for readers running companies with $300,000 monthly budgets. These were certainly not the kids in my class. Plus, the books had an uncanny ability to make me yawn and confuse me.

But I had made a promise to my students to recommend a book. So I did what I had to do: made a list of ways that companies can market without investing much money in the process. My list, "527 Ways to Market without Much Money," was exactly what my students needed but was not exactly a winner in the book title department.

I knew that, in business, my students wanted the conventional goals of financial independence, freedom from stress, balance in their lives, and companies they could grow to their heart's content. But they couldn't achieve those goals with marketing unless they used unconventional methods.

It's the same situation faced by guerrillas in wartime. They want the conventional goal of victory, but because they lack the financial resources, they need to employ unconventional methods.

Guerrilla Marketing. That was an apt title for the book I was going to write for my class. The subtitle stated the premise and the promise: *Secrets for Making Big Profits from Your Small Business.*

When I sat down to write the book, which I did for my students, I had no idea that the book would become a series and take on a life of its own. I had no clue that it would sell more than 21 million copies in 62 languages, making me one of the world's first authors not to understand 61 editions of his own book.

The rest of the series came from the same spark that ignited the first guerrilla marketing book. Every book I write does not come from inspiration, or even perspiration, but from my own need to write books that fulfill the needs of others.

Entrepreneurs are in the same situation faced by guerrillas in war-time. They want the conventional goal of victory, but because they lack the financial resources, they need to employ unconventional methods.

The long-haired kids in my class? The ones with tiny businesses nobody had heard of? They used guerrilla marketing to build enormous companies almost everyone has heard of now: Apple, Microsoft, Adobe, Hewlett-Packard, Oracle, and a pack of other Silicon Valley leaders. Some later brought me to their headquarters to deliver a series of guerrilla marketing seminars.

While this was happening, the largest businesses in the world realized that they, too, could and should use guerrilla marketing to

"Ideas are like rabbits. You get a couple, learn how to look after them, and pretty soon you have a dozen."

—John Steinbeck

power up their profits. Many members of the Fortune 100 had me deliver presentations to their entire companies, not wanting to miss out on the chance to earn higher profits while investing less money. That's nice work if you can get it, and you can get it with guerrilla marketing.

You can't create superstar businesses all by yourself. A man who conducted seminars for the California Department of Probation heard me speak and asked if he could represent me as my speaking agent. "My speaking agent?" I asked. He answered, "You're probably too busy giving talks and writing books to have a person whose

FURNITURE STORE

There was once a man who owned a little furniture store. One day he got to work and noticed that there was new construction going on at the lot on his right. Later in the week he noticed that it was a competing furniture store, much larger than his own.

Then a month later he noticed that there was new construction on the lot to his left, and to his dismay he soon realized that it, too, was another large furniture store.

If that weren't bad enough, one day he got to work and noticed that the store on his right had unfurled a huge banner outside announcing, "Grand Opening Sale—prices slashed 50 percent." He looked to the left and saw that the other store had also unfurled a banner saying, "Monster Clearance Sale—prices slashed 75 percent." Worse yet, each banner was larger than his own store.

The little store owner, being a guerrilla, and knowing he couldn't compete with those kind of prices, responded by creating and displaying his own banner, which simply read:

"MAIN ENTRANCE."

sole responsibility is getting you more speaking engagements. I can do that for you, including the countless details, as your speaking agent if you pay me a percentage of each engagement I book."

And so was born Guerrilla Marketing International, and so spread the word about guerrilla marketing. It grew a lot because of the efforts of my late speaking agent, Bill Shear, and now by my new speaking agent, daughter Amy.

> *Guerrilla marketing has grown because it is astonishingly simple and because it works so well.*

Our company is presided over, thank heavens, by my wife, Jeannie, also my favorite co-author. So you can see that as the brand has grown so have our opportunities for nepotism, which we unabashedly pursue.

After all, guerrilla marketing reminds you never to do what you can delegate. I always want to expend my energies writing and speaking. As new things such as the internet and social media enter the marketing world, I team up with experts on those things to help create a new guerrilla marketing entity.

Guerrilla marketing also has grown because it is astonishingly simple and because it works so well. You'll see.

chapter 4

The Spread of Guerrilla Marketing

R IGHT FROM THE START, guerrilla marketing ignited possibilities in the entrepreneurial imagination.

Guerrilla marketing flourished and gained fans for 10 straightforward reasons, not the least of which is that it really and truly does help guerrillas generate higher profits.

1. It is simple and not complicated.
2. It works every time if you do it right.
3. It has an enticing name that attracts experimentation.
4. It fits small business, which grows at a record pace.
5. It is affordable no matter how dismal the economy.
6. It embraces new forms of marketing.
7. It eliminates most of the stress about marketing.
8. It is ideal for the internet and connected world.
9. It helps big business as much as small business.
10. It grows profits for businesses around the planet.

Luckily, I lived in the San Francisco Bay area, one of the cradles of modern civilization. It was a fertile ground to nourish the infant guerrilla marketing. And it was in the 1970s, lush, historic terrain for robust marketing escalation, with a tsunami of knowledge and technology happening in my own backyard.

An explosion of wisdom! But most of it was ineptly masterminded by individuals who knew everything about technology but nothing about marketing. The original computer marketing was created by nerds for nerds, understandable only to nerds. I was seriously considering the purchase of a computer but was overwhelmed

Original computer marketing was created by nerds for nerds, understandable only to nerds.

by the marketing, which sent me scurrying to the medicine cabinet in pursuit of two or even three aspirins to calm my techno-babble-created headache.

I'm not saying that all wisdom comes from nerds, but I do consider them to be at the helm of a lot of progress. The clients I encountered were either old-world business types brainwashed about marketing by their fuddy-duddy education or new-age, techno types befuddled about marketing by their analytical instruction. They were forming companies in industries that hadn't existed when I—or they—were born. It was a golden age for guerrilla marketers.

That intense need screamed out for practical, usable, understandable information about marketing. Walking the walk so I could more justifiably talk the talk, I disseminated that information in books, talks, seminars, radio and TV interviews, newsletters, articles, coaching programs, subscription websites, online forums, and presentations at conventions for all sorts of marketers who just plain needed to become guerrilla marketers. Everybody did.

Everybody could understand it. Everybody could afford it. Everybody could profit with it. Everybody could learn how to do it right. Everybody could experiment with it. Everybody liked how it removed the stress associated with marketing—non-guerrilla marketing, that is.

COMPUTER INDUSTRY VS. CAR INDUSTRY

Bill Gates reportedly compared the computer industry with the auto industry and stated, "If GM had kept up with the technology like the computer industry has, we would all be driving $25 cars that got 1,000 miles to the gallon."

In response to Bill's comments, General Motors issued a press release stating, "If GM had developed technology like Microsoft, we would all be driving cars with the following characteristics:

1. For no reason whatsoever, your car would crash twice a day.

2. Every time they repainted the lines in the road, you would have to buy a new car.

3. Occasionally your car would die on the freeway for no reason. You would have to pull over to the side of the road, close all of the windows, shut off the car, restart it, and reopen the windows before you could continue. For some reason you would simply accept this.

4. Macintosh would make a car that was powered by the sun, was reliable, five times as fast and twice as easy to drive—but would run on only 5 percent of the roads.

5. The oil, water temperature, and alternator warning lights would all be replaced by a single "General Protection Fault" warning light.

6. The airbag system would ask: "Are you sure?" before deploying.

7. Occasionally, for no reason whatsoever, your car would lock you out and refuse to let you in until you simultaneously lifted the door handle, turned the key and grabbed hold of the radio antenna.

8. Every time GM introduced a new car, car buyers would have to learn to drive all over again because none of the controls would operate in the same manner as the old car.

9. You'd have to press the "Start" button to turn the engine off.

One of the more amazing aspects to the movement was how this new marketing discipline—created to help small businesses and devised to give them leverage against the big businesses—began to capture the fancy of those big businesses.

Invitations poured in for me to address the national conventions of one behemoth company after another. They were hiring me to train their people about how to benefit from guerrilla marketing. After all, they wondered, why shouldn't we be able to get more for our marketing investment, the same as the little companies? Why shouldn't we cuddle up with this maverick marketing, which is obviously becoming mainstream marketing?

Guerrilla marketing holds to the highest standards of ethics, and goes out of its way to offend no individuals, no groups, no communities.

Each time I would address a giant convention audience, I was gratified to see that my guerrilla speaking agent had seen to it that each member of that audience was holding a new copy of my latest guerrilla marketing book.

Those books came out at the rate of two per year from my Underwood typewriter, then my Royal typewriter, then my Remington Selectric typewriter, then an Epson word processor. I'd write one book by myself. I'd write the next with a co-author.

When social media loomed large on the horizon, I could conscientiously study it for a year and write a book about it alone. Or I could co-author it with Shane Gibson, a recognizable presence on Facebook, a well-known tweeter on Twitter for a long time, and a speaker on the social media before I knew what they were about. Decisions like that are easy to make. That's why the spread of guerrilla marketing information has been so prolific and books about it so abundant.

I learned early from Howard Gossage, one of my two mentors—Leo Burnett was the other—that you shouldn't try to say everything to

NEW-AGE OFFICE TERMINOLOGY

Adminisphere: The rarefied, organizational layers beginning just above the rank and file. Decisions that fall from the adminisphere are often profoundly inappropriate or irrelevant to the problems they were designed to solve.

Alpha Geek: The most knowledgeable, technically proficient person in an office or work group.

Blamestorming: Sitting around in a group, discussing why a deadline was missed or a project failed, and who was responsible.

Chainsaw Consultant: An outside expert brought in to reduce the employee head count, leaving the top brass with clean hands.

Chips & Salsa: Chips = hardware; salsa = software. "Well, first we gotta figure out if the problem is in your chips or your salsa."

CLM (Career Limiting Move): Used to describe ill-advised activity. Trashing your boss while he or she is within earshot is a serious CLM.

Cube Farm: An office filled with cubicles.

Dilberted: To be exploited and oppressed by your boss. Derived from the experiences of "Dilbert," the comic strip. "I've been Dilberted again. The old man revised the specs for the fourth time this week."

Flight Risk: Used to describe employees who are suspected of planning to leave a company or department soon.

GOOD Job: A "Get-Out-Of-Debt" job. A well-paying job people take in order to pay off their debts, one that they will quit as soon as they are solvent again.

Idea Hamsters: People who always seem to have their idea generator running.

Mouse Potato: The online, wired generation's answer to the couch potato.

NEW-AGE OFFICE TERMINOLOGY

Ohnosecond: That minuscule fraction of time in which you realize that you've just made a BIG mistake.

Percussive Maintenance: The fine art of whacking the heck out of an electronic device to get it to work again.

Prairie Dogging: When someone yells or drops something loudly in a cube farm, and people pop their heads up over the walls to see what's going on.

SITCOMs (Single Income, Two Children, Oppressive Mortgage): What happens to yuppies when they have children and one of them stops working to stay home with the kids.

Stress Puppy: A person who seems to thrive on being stressed out and whiny.

Tourists: People who take training classes just to get a vacation from their jobs.

Treeware: Hacker slang for documentation or other printed material.

Umfriend: A personal relation of dubious standing or a concealed intimate relationship, as in "This is Dylan, my . . . um . . . friend."

Uninstalled: Euphemism for being fired. Heard on the voicemail of a vice president at a downsizing computer firm: "You have reached the number of an uninstalled vice president. Please dial our main number and ask the operator for assistance." (Syn: decruitment.)

Xerox Subsidy: Euphemism for swiping free photocopies from one's workplace.

Yuppie Food Stamps: The ubiquitous $20 bills spewed out of ATMs everywhere. Often used when trying to split the bill after lunch, "We each owe $8, but all anybody's got are yuppie food stamps."

404: Someone who's clueless. From the World Wide Web error message, "404 Not Found," meaning that the requested document could not be located. "Don't bother asking him; he's 404, man."

everybody because you will end up saying either everything to nobody or saying nothing to everybody. Instead, you should try and succeed at saying something to somebody. The guerrilla marketing books, increasingly specialized as they are, try to say many somethings to many somebodies. That seems to work.

So does opening my mind to the constant changes that take place in marketing. When I wrote the first guerrilla marketing book, there was no internet. But now, if guerrilla marketing did not include the internet, it would become obsolete in a hurry. But now, if guerrilla marketing did not include the internet, it would become obsolete in a hurry. That's why guerrilla marketing today includes technology,

OUTWITTING THE COMPETITION

A man went to a TV station and bought one minute's worth of advertising time. He handed a DVD to the station manager and learned the exact second when his one-minute ad would be on the station.

Just before the scheduled time, the man turned on his TV set, tuned it to the correct channel and waited. At exactly the time for his ad, a test pattern went on. The sound, an intense, pure tone, did not change for one full minute. The picture stayed the same, too. The man, very pleased, smiled and turned off his TV set.

What just happened to make him so happy with his ad?

The man was a political candidate running for a local office on a very limited budget. He had been tipped off that his well-funded opponent had just bought a very expensive, 30-minute infomercial time slot.

Being a guerrilla, the less-funded candidate bought the minute just before the infomercial and broadcast a test pattern, hoping to induce TV viewers to turn off their sets or change the channel.

social media, memes, psychology, ecology, nonprofit growth, and networking. It will continue to change with the times. Like the technocrats who remind us that "there's an app for that," we can envision saying, "there's a book on that." We can almost say that already.

I wonder how widespread guerrilla marketing would be if there were no internet; no power-packed mobile devices; no generously accommodating broadband. Guerrilla marketing works hand-in-hand with technology. It pairs up well with the small-business explosion. And it's easy to love during a recession. No wonder it has spread.

Many non-guerrillas erroneously thought that guerrilla marketing meant ambush marketing. It doesn't. Or sneaky marketing. It doesn't. Or marketing with graffiti. It doesn't. Or unethical marketing. No way. Guerrilla marketing holds to the highest standards of ethics, and goes out of its way to offend no individuals, no groups, no communities. The only people guerrilla marketing is designed to offend are your competitors. You have our blessing when you do that.

chapter 5

The Simplicity of Guerrilla Marketing

A LOT OF MARKETING THEORY confuses people because it's more complicated than it has to be. One of the reasons guerrilla marketing has been so warmly welcomed by business is because it's not complicated and is very straightforward. While wondrous new technologies can help you in your mission of raising your profits, guerrillas don't let those technologies blur that mission. Keeping it simple is a guerrilla goal and a powerful competitive advantage when it comes to speed and profitability.

The seller is happy when the buyer is happy. So make as many buyers happy as you can. That requires quality and service, but that's why you're here—and it's not complicated.

The entire process is made up of five broad strokes. Take those strokes and add as many bells, whistles, systems, technologies, apps, and economic doodads as you want—but be sure that all five broad strokes are taken. Do that and you'll never think that marketing has

> *A lot of marketing theory confuses people because it's more complicated than it has to be.*

"Know where to find the information and how to use it.
That's the secret of success."

—Albert Einstein

to be anything that Simple Simon couldn't handle with his right hand tied behind him.

The first broad stroke doesn't require any of your hands—only your ears. The first broad stroke is your ability to listen. Be alert for problems. Be alert in social situations and the social media. Be alert in the attention you pay to the mass media. Are people talking about problems they have, problems that need solving?

Zero in on the problems that don't yet have solutions. Pick a problem that you can solve. That's how you respond to opportunity. The first broad stroke begins with your ears. Don't tell me that it's complicated to listen.

GREATER EFFICIENCY

A store owner was receiving complaints from customers about not being able to find anyone in the store to ask for help.

How did the owner achieve greater efficiency by using nothing but simple cones?

At the water cooler, drinking cups in the shape of paper cones were provided. Since the cones couldn't be set down on any surface, employees had to drink the water more quickly. This simple strategy caused the employees to speed up their breaks and increase their productivity—allowing more time on the floor for customer service.

Keeping it simple is a guerrilla goal and a powerful competitive advantage when it comes to speed and profitability.

The second broad stroke is determining how much it will cost you to solve that problem. Maybe you can solve it with information and with service. If not, how much will it cost you to make it or buy it? Be very careful with this step as with all the broad strokes, to overlook nothing. Broad strokes tend to magnify errors, so you don't want to make even the most minor mistake. Savvy manufacturers, led by Japan, now hire mistake counters to help reduce errors they don't want to make in the daunting world of mass production. Guerrillas are their own mistake counters, and their favorite number is zero. Avoiding errors is hardly a complicated chore.

> "Talk to people about themselves and they will listen for hours."
>
> —Benjamin Disraeli

The third broad stroke is the entire subject of this book. When you tally the costs of producing your offering, don't overlook the costs of marketing it. And don't overlook the necessity to market it.

If you build a better mousetrap, the world won't beat a path to your door unless they know about that mousetrap. They learn about it from your marketing, especially if it's guerrilla marketing.

Marketing is the KEY to selling an idea. It's not a bailout—it's a rescue plan.

If you've come up with a truly nifty solution, the marketing for it will catch wind and fan out to others who have long been

Marketing is the KEY to selling an idea. It's not a bailout—it's a rescue plan.

STICKY SITUATION

A man and his dog went for a walk in the woods. When the man returned home he invented something now worth millions of dollars.

What was it?

During his walk in the woods, the man picked up several burrs on his clothes. When he returned home, he examined them under a microscope and discovered the mechanism whereby they stick on.

He went on to invent Velcro.

---

searching for a solution. It's nice work if you can get it, and you can get it if you market.

In prehistoric days, marketing was not part of the cost of goods. You had some delicious and nourishing nuts and berries, and if a hungry caveman came by, you probably traded several handfuls of those nuts and berries for one of those soft and furry animal skins he was carrying across his shoulder.

Today, the best, most delicious and nourishing nuts and berries most likely come from your local supermarket, a dynamite nut and berry website, and advertisements in *Gourmet* magazine. That kind of marketing costs money. So you'd better prepare for it before offering your wares to the world. Yes, marketing is part of the capitalism deal, but it's not complicated.

It is now pretty much understood why people patronize the businesses that they do. It's known that they favor products and services that they trust, a human characteristic that has given rise to a phenomenon called "branding." Branding helps people trust you. One of the jobs of a guerrilla is to convince customers to trust his or her offering.

Of course, quality is one of the factors that earns trust. And that's why it's part of the third broad stroke. Another factor that gains gobs of trust—and gives the little guy an edge over the big guy—is the ability to service what he sells. Don't forget that one of your sacred goals is make your customers happy. Terrific service does just that.

Terrific service is not necessarily free for you to provide. And yes, it does require effort. In particular, it requires a person who wants to deliver it and doesn't do it just because he's supposed to. Hire people who want to deliver mouth-drop-open service and you're well on your way to becoming a blue-ribbon guerrilla.

Factor in the cost of service right along with the cost of marketing and cost of goods. But remember that if you do it as the guerrilla does it, that investment in superb service pays off far beyond the promise of its cost.

You can render that sort of service if you really understand the importance of service in this century. It's not what it used to be or what your teacher or your papa told you it was. It's not what you—or, fortunately for you—most of your competitors think it is. The true definition of service is this: "Service is whatever the customer wants it to be." Know that, and you won't ever have to kid yourself into thinking that service has to be complicated. That's the fourth broad stroke.

Service is whatever the customer wants it to be.

The fifth broad stroke is what guerrilla marketing is all about. Not sales. Not store traffic. Not turnover. Not responses to an offer. Not hits to a website. Not conversion ratios of visitors to the site. Not awards. Not sales records. Not any metric you can name. That fifth broad stroke is profits, what's left over after you've deducted the cost of everything else in your business. No matter how glowing the other numbers in your business may be, it's the profits that should glow, that keep you in business, that enable you to grow your business, that attract investors, that entice buyers of companies, and that ought to be the prime reason you went into business.

It's your job to grow healthy profits every year. You owe that to yourself, your employees, your family, and your future. That's why profits best reflect your success. Profits are elusive. Profits are honest. Profits are hard-earned. But profits are not complicated.

They are the fifth of the five broad strokes of success, and they are crucial to your company's health. But earning them is not a winding road. Instead it is a straight road, possibly uphill, but always leading to exactly where you envision going.

The entire marketing process is made up of five broad strokes:

1. You must be able to listen. Pick a problem that you can solve.
2. Determine how much it will cost you to solve that problem.
3. Don't overlook the costs and necessity of marketing your solution.
4. Service what you sell.
5. Earn profits (what's left over after you've deducted the cost of everything else in your business).

chapter 6

The Monumental Secrets of Guerrilla Marketing

THERE ARE 20 SECRETS, each only one word, each word ending in the letters "ent." Be mindful of the 20 secrets revealed as you operate your enterprise and you'll exceed your most radiant projections. It is slightly amazing to me that these are secrets at all. They are not secrets to guerrillas.

1. Commitment

The first secret comes from a flashback in my career when I worked for an advertising agency that serviced a cigarette company with a brand in 31st place. Worse yet, it was perceived as a feminine cigarette in an era when more women smoked than men, but men smoked more cigarettes. Our plan was clear: Use marketing to change the identity of the brand from female to male while increasing sales of the brand.

There are 20 secrets, each only one word, each word ending in the letters "ent."

This would not be easy. "Cathexis," a word with Greek roots, relates to the degree of emotional attachment people feel to something. Cigarettes are a very high cathexis product. Getting women to switch shampoos because of marketing is easy because the majority of women do switch shampoo brands during the year. Shampoo is a low cathexis product. But smokers rarely switch.

The agency where I worked sent two photographers and an art director to the ranch of a friend of a staff member in west Texas. They were told to spend two weeks shooting unposed pictures of cowboys doing what real cowboys do on a real ranch. Each photo was to have beautiful Western scenery, horses, and men. No cows. No women.

While the shooting was taking place, a team of Leo Burnett ad agency creative people in Chicago dreamed up a fictional place. It was called "Marlboro Country." They came up with a theme line: "Come to where the flavor is. Come to Marlboro Country."

TAXI

We were riding to an ad agency presentation and spoke excitedly about the presentation we were about to make.

The cab driver turned his head to ask, "You guys really believe that advertising stuff works?" He was definitely not an ideal customer. Or was he? "It doesn't work for me." He added, "I never would buy a product because of advertising. Never have. Never will."

One of our people asked him, " What kind of toothpaste do you use?" "Oh, I use Gleem," he said, referring to the top-selling toothpaste at the time, "but it has nothing to do with the advertising. It's because I drive a cab and I can't brush after every meal." Such is the power of branding—to him—to you—to me.

The photographs were developed, then enlarged. Each showed the beauty of the American West, a cowboy and a horse, plus a pack of Marlboros. On each, the theme line of Marlboro Country capitalized on the research that showed flavor was what cigarette smokers wanted most in their cigarette.

The Marlboro brand group in New York was so psyched by the campaign that they agreed to invest $18 million in it the first year. That Marlboro man was seen on TV, magazines, newspapers, and billboards across the land, in addition to being heard on the radio to stirring Western music, the theme music from the movie *The Magnificent Seven* (which is my favorite film).

Within that year, the Marlboro man became a cultural icon. Everyone knew who he was, what he symbolized, and of the existence of Marlboro. At the end of that year, that cigarette brand, once the 31st-best selling in the country—was still the 31st-best selling. Focus group interviews showed that the brand, once thought of as a feminine cigarette—was still perceived as a feminine cigarette.

Here we'd been showing macho men in macho surroundings, working their tails off on a ranch, and the brand's sales hadn't budged. But now let's switch to today—right now.

Today, Marlboro is the number-one selling cigarette in the United States—number one to men and number one to women. It is now the number-one selling cigarette in the world. One of every five cigarettes sold on planet Earth is a Marlboro.

But nothing has changed with the marketing, other than cigarette advertising being banned from radio and TV, and the price of cigarettes soaring. The same marketing campaign that appeared to fail has succeeded to the point that Marlboro is now known as the best-marketed brand in history.

How did that happen? It happened because of the power of the first secret of guerrilla marketing. It's the same secret as the secret of a good marriage or a great golf game or a successful business. The word is "commitment."

COMMITMENT

Two frogs fell into a large cylindrical tank of fluid, and both fell to the bottom. The walls were sheer and slippery. One frog died but one survived.

Why?

The frogs fell into a large tank of cream. One swam around for a while but then gave up and drowned.

The other frog kept persistently swimming until his movement turned the cream into little lumps of butter on which he safely floated.

Your level of commitment and perseverance can determine if your marketing campaign sinks or swims.

I don't like saying this in print, but I don't want you to miss the point here: brilliant marketing without commitment isn't nearly as profitable as even medium marketing with commitment. It's the commitment that makes it happen. The hero of the Marlboro campaign was not the creative who dreamt up the marketing, but the chairman of the board of Philip Morris, parent company of Marlboro, who stayed with the campaign from day one, reminding us that we had let him know that the marketing might not work immediately. Thank you, Joseph Cullman IV, for being a guerrilla.

2. Investment

The second secret reminds you what marketing really is—an investment. It's the best investment you can make if you do it right. It's less risky than the stock market and pays off better than other kinds of investments, but again—only if you do it right. This *Remix* of guerrilla marketing exists to help you do it right.

Leonard Lavin, founder of Alberto-Culver, the VO5 people, always described marketing as a conservative investment. The success of his company attests to the accuracy of his observation. Don't expect miracle results from marketing. Few conservative investments result in miracles. Instead, expect eventual success. Knowing these secrets can lead to that success.

3. Consistent

The third secret reminds you that restraint will be your ally in guerrilla marketing. The first people who tire of that marketing will be the people who love you most but offer the worst possible advice.

These people are your employees, co-workers, family, and friends. They spend a lot of time paying attention to your marketing, so they become bored with it before the public, which barely pays attention to your marketing. That's why your closest allies counsel you to change your marketing.

Your job is to make sure your marketing is consistent—the third secret. That means when those well-meaning cohorts of yours suggest that you change your marketing, you've got to give them a warm hug, then send them on their way, realizing that they probably are not guerrillas. Staying the course is what guerrillas do.

4. Congruent

Up next is the secret that alerts you to the problems that can arise when some people create your website, others do your PR, others write your email copy, others design your graphics, and still others create your brochure.

This is not a healthy situation. Marketing is like a tug of war, and you can't win one of those with different people all pulling in different directions. You can only win with people all pulling in the same direction.

> "To pull together is to avoid being pulled apart."
>
> —Bob Allisat

You're in charge of practicing the fourth secret—making sure all your marketing is congruent, helping to make all the marketing more powerful. Tug-of-war battles and Super Bowls are won not by individuals but by teams. Winning teams are congruent in their efforts.

5. Content

Your mother knows the fifth secret. She doesn't spend money buying razzle-dazzle and special effects. She knows the difference between the sizzle and the steak. She almost always opts for the steak, for the real thing.

That's why that fifth secret is content. It used to be taught that the intelligence level of the public is on par with that of a 12-year-old. Now it's known that the intelligence level is akin to that of your mother. She has grown too wise to buy style over substance. The same is true for your prospects. They want the substance of your offering and not just the style. Don't think for a second that they don't know the difference.

6. Assortment

The sixth secret reminds you that advertising doesn't work as well as it used to. Same for PR. And millions of people have learned that a website can be a path to financial oblivion. So what does work?

A combination of marketing weapons is what works for guerrillas. Their ads make their PR stronger, and both make their website more effective. No wonder the sixth secret is assortment, for the days of single-weapon marketing have passed, and marketing needs a 360-degree effort to thrive.

PRICE TAGS

Many shops have prices set just under a round figure, for example, $9.99 instead of $10 or $99 instead of $100. It's assumed that this is done because the price seems lower to the consumer. But this is not why the practice was started.

What was the original reason for this pricing method? The practice originated to ensure that the clerk had to open the cash register to give change for each transaction, thus recording the sale and preventing him from pocketing the bills.

Why do you suppose people buy the brands they do, the products they do, and the services they do? An ambitious study, reported in *Advertising Age*, revealed that of all the factors motivating a purchase, price came in number five. That means 86 percent of them felt there were more important factors than price.

One of those factors was selection, which came in at number four. People want to feel that they are in control—not you—which is why they appreciate the choice they get with your selection.

Service came in third. These days, remember, the only definition of service is "anything the customer wants it to be." Service is not what you learned in school or were taught by your boss or your father. It's so important that it ranks third on the list of why people buy what they do.

"Don't tell people how good you make the goods;
tell them how good your goods make them."

—Leo Burnett

Second place went to quality. If you don't have quality, guerrilla marketing will kill your brand faster because more people will learn about it quicker. Don't mistakenly think that quality is about you. It is not. The definition of quality to guerrillas is "what customers get out of your offering" and not what you put into it.

Of course, people care about the quality you give them, but they care far more about the quality they get. Guerrillas well know that it's always about the customer and rarely about you.

7. Confident

First place in this study went to something that shouldn't surprise you if you've read this far. People said they tend to buy from businesses in which they are confident—the seventh secret. Your commitment makes them confident. So does your ability to be consistent, to treat your marketing as an investment, to present a congruent message, and to provide honest content.

Who do you suppose can make a commitment to an investment and be consistent enough to make people confident in what you are offering?

8. Patient

The answer to the question above is the eighth secret of guerrilla marketing: patient people. If you aren't patient, you'll have trouble making a commitment, be too shaky to hang in there with an investment, and constantly be tempted to tamper with your marketing, which is hardly being consistent. If you don't have patience, perhaps you should explore another line of work. It's a sign that as sweet as you are, you just may not be a guerrilla.

9. Amazement

Here's a true, but disturbing fact: People do not pay much attention to marketing or advertising. What do they pay attention to? To whatever

> ## TRUTH
>
> A woman named Truth wandered into a village and knocked on the door to a home. The door was opened, then immediately slammed shut. She went to another house and knocked on the door. Again, it was opened, then instantly shut in her face. The same thing happened again and again. Finally, Truth went to the house of Fable and asked, "Why do people take one look at me then slam the door?" Fable answered, "Because most people can't handle the nakedness of truth. Try cloaking yourself in story."
>
> Truth did just that and began to tell a story to whoever opened the door when she knocked. Invariably, she was invited to come inside, to sit and get comfortable, even to stay for dinner.
>
> Forget everything you've heard about kids and attention spans. We're told that kids have short attention spans. But if you tell a kid a story, what's the first thing the kid wants you to do when it's over? "Tell it again!" Kids love stories, and adults are just grown-up kids.
>
> Amaze your prospects with true stories. Don't give them bare facts. Give them fascinating stories. Then they'll pay rapt attention to your marketing.

attracts their attention. Sometimes that's marketing or advertising, but usually it isn't. That's why you've got to capture their attention with the ninth secret—making sure there's an element of amazement in your marketing.

10. Convenient

In order for us to tell you the 10th secret, we've got to tell you a lie. We tell it to you because it is damaging to your business, your family and yourself, but mainly because you've probably been buying into it all your life.

Here's the lie: Time is money.

That is not true. The Harris Poll, the Gallup Poll, The Roper Poll, and the Universities of Pennsylvania and Maryland conduct studies to see what people cherish the most. Back in 1988, time went to number one on the list. It is been there ever since and will probably stay there for the rest of your life.

People now know that time is not money; time is life. That's why the 10th secret is being convenient. You dare not waste any of your customers' or prospects' time. You've got to orient everything in your business to being convenient, to saving time for those who do business with you.

Make it easy to learn about you, to contact you, to park, to pay, to get service, to obtain information. Don't waste one precious second of a customer's time or you'll probably never hear from that customer again. Customers know that time is life, and now, you do, too.

11. Consent

Halfway through the 20 secrets, we encounter one that we hope will not shatter your dreams. But somebody has got to tell this to you if you're to become a guerrilla marketer.

Realize that you can no longer make the sale with marketing. In the past, you could make the sale strictly with marketing. But the past is hardly the present. Now we live in a time of nonstop media. It's a bear to try to make a sale with marketing. So savvy guerrillas, led by guerrilla Seth Godin in his breakthrough book, *Permission Marketing*, go not for the sale but for consent to market to individuals. That consent is the 11th secret of guerrilla marketing.

Most people will withhold their consent. Others will gladly consent to receive your marketing materials. It's estimated that at any given moment, 4 percent of people want to buy your product right now, another 4 percent need to know one or two more things before buying, and 92 percent just don't care about you and your

CONSENT MARKETING

Awoman who runs a highly successful summer camp in the northeast United States runs tiny ads in the backs of magazines. She says one good thing about her camp, then asks parents to call, write, or email for a free DVD. Does that tiny ad sell the camping experience? It does not.

She has a booth at the inevitable camping shows that pop up each winter. She posts a smiling counselor or two there, exquisite photographs, and a collection of DVDs, free for the taking. Does that booth do the trick of getting the kids' parents to sign up for the next summer session? You know it doesn't even come close.

The parents view the DVD, see happy campers, trained counselors, luscious scenery, and superb equipment. Does that sell the camping experience? Not nearly. The only purpose of the DVDs is to get parents to sign up for a free in-home consultation.

Eighty-four percent of people who have the consultation register their kid for the next summer. The kid's brother or sister may also get signed up. Maybe cousins get involved, and classmates. And they sign up not just for this summer, but for the one after that and the one after that.

The guerrilla camp owner makes a very high-profit sale without investing much money—only by getting consent, then broadening that consent.

stuff. Love them for it. They are letting you save your time and money.

Instead, focus your efforts on those who are the most torrid of prospects. Broaden the consent they gave to you.

The whole idea of consent is why "opt-in" is now in the dictionary. You may not be able to make the sale with marketing, but when that marketing is merely a door opener, you probably can make the sale. Guerrillas are rarely in a hurry.

12. Involvement

Involvement is the difference between hollering something to somebody across the street and whispering that same thing in the person's ear. You know what a huge difference that is. That's why involvement is the 12th secret.

One of the best things about the internet is its ability to involve. Instead of a radio commercial, TV spot, or print ad that just sits there, a website has the impressive ability to involve: to get someone to send for a free report, a newsletter subscription, a contest entry—to take those first steps toward a relationship.

Guerrillas take full advantage of the internet's ability to involve, that same ability offered by the Twitters and Facebooks of the world. Why do you suppose those new media are taking the marketing universe by storm? It's because of their ability to involve, an ability that you have as a guerrilla.

> "True interactivity is not about clicking on icons or downloading files. It's about encouraging communication."
>
> —Edwin Schlossberg

It wasn't easy to establish a warm, caring relationship before the advent of the internet and social media. But it's very easy now—if you're a guerrilla. Nobody proposes after the first date, though that is what I did with Jeannie. But millions of people enjoy a courtship. If you think about it, that's just what marketing is.

13. Subsequent

Non-guerrillas think that the big money is made at the time of the sale. In some cases, such as jet planes and pricey houses, that's the truth. But in most cases, the big money comes from the long relationship you have with the customer and with all the follow-up sales after the first one.

It's no surprise that the 13th secret is that serious money arrives subsequent to that initial sale. Nearly 70 percent of business lost is due not to shabby quality or careless service but due to customers being ignored after they've made the purchase. Guerrillas work hard to win a customer. You can be sure they won't risk losing that customer due to indifference. Once a customer gets on that customer list, he or she becomes a member of the family and is treated like a family member. You'd never ignore a newborn baby, would you?

14. Dependent

The age of the lone-wolf entrepreneur is now a part of history. It's just not happening now the way it used to. One of the main reasons for that is the phenomenon called "strategic alliances." Two or more businesses join forces, at least on the marketing front, and share the costs. They also reap the benefits of spreading the word.

Business is learning the value of being dependent upon each other. That's why being dependent is the 14th secret of guerrilla marketing.

Guerrillas have a name for being dependent: "fusion marketing," where companies share the costs of spreading the word. Another name for it is "affiliate marketing," a concept we hope you'll check out for yourself on Google. And these days, the secret is being popularized as "performance marketing."

That phrase sums it up: People who are not on your payroll try to sell your products or services. They only get paid if they perform—actually make sales for you.

Millions of people around the world are supplementing their income by becoming affiliates. Millions of companies are delighted at this way of increasing sales without increasing costs.

A LESSON FROM GEESE

Have you ever wondered why migrating geese fly in formation? As each bird flaps its wings, it creates uplift for the bird following.

In a V formation, the whole flock adds at least 71 percent more flying range than if each bird flew alone.

Whenever a goose falls out of formation, it suddenly feels the drag and resistance of trying to fly alone . . . and it quickly gets back into formation.

Like geese, businesses who share a common direction and sense of community can get where they are going quicker and easier than those who try to go it alone.

We are no longer living in the age of the lone-wolf entrepreneur, independent and proud of it.

When a goose gets tired, it rotates back into the formation, and another goose flies at the point position.

If businesses had as much sense as geese, they would realize that success depends on fusion marketing partners working as teams, taking turns doing the hard tasks, exchanging leads, and sharing their marketing budgets.

To help affiliates help their businesses, guerrillas provide a host of sales materials, especially for websites. They train their affiliates on how to succeed, knowing they'll benefit as well. Naturally, most affiliates do not succeed, but the best of those who do are termed "super affiliates" and bring in several thousand dollars a year. You can just imagine how well the company fares if they have a ton of affiliates earning that kind of money.

It all boils down to the "I'll scratch your back if you scratch mine" idea. The better you are at scratching, the more income you'll earn by being dependent.

FUSION MARKETING

Fusion marketing is based on the "I'll scratch your back if you scratch my back" idea. Fusion marketing used to be called "Tie-Ins with Others" or "Collaborative Marketing" or "Co-Marketing."

Fusion marketing means I'll put up a sign for you in my place of business if you put up a sign for me in your place of business. I'll enclose a circular for your business in my next mailing if you enclose a circular for my business in your next mailing.

There's a lot of fusion marketing going on in America, indeed, in the world today. You see a commercial you think is for McDonald's, but midway through you think it's for Coca-Cola, and by the time it's over, you realize it was really for the latest Disney movie.

A lot of fusion marketing is going on for small businesses. We just mentioned big businesses that are doing it, but lots of small businesses are doing it, too.

15. Armament

The dictionary defines "armament" as "the equipment necessary to wage and win battles." This is hardly a secret to guerrillas who know that the armament of guerrillas is technology—easy-to-use, easy-to-afford technology. Knowing that secret enables guerrillas to market and service just like the big spenders without needing to spend big.

A remix should not be dated, which is why we're not recommending specific technologies for your business. The speed of change and improvement is dizzying—and exceptionally beneficial to those who embrace the armament of guerrillas today. It's no secret that the internet enables better communication and that auto-responders set the stage for better service. Everyone and their cousin are aware of the impact of the social media.

WHO ELSE DOES MY CUSTOMER PATRONIZE?

A restaurant opened in my community, which is very competitive when it comes to restaurants. And the restaurant asked this question: "What other businesses do my customers patronize?"

The answer it came up with was hairstyling salons. So the restaurant gave all the salon owners within a two-mile radius a coupon for two free dinners. Now, I mean two free dinners—no strings attached. This is not one of those things where you've got to buy one to get one free or use the free meal coupon between 5:15 and 5:30 on a Wednesday.

This was two free dinners, anything included, no strings attached. Well, the salon owners would go to the restaurant, enjoy their meals, go back to their salons and talk up the quality of the restaurant to their customers.

The restaurateur had properly identified the styling salons as the "nerve centers" for the community, and by tapping into that nerve center the restaurant got a lot of word-of-mouth marketing in a very short time. Within six months, that restaurant had a longer wait for reservations and a longer line out the door than restaurants that had been around for 10 years.

You ask yourself, "Well, how much did they invest in that marketing campaign?" And then you realize the restaurant invested hardly anything—only the cost of free meals for the salon owners within a two-mile radius. So you've got to ask that question, "Who else do your customers patronize?" And then do a favor for those people.

Go to Times Square in New York. There are enormous, illuminated signs wherever you look. They're expensive to construct and expensive to maintain, yet the biggest marketers in the world constantly utilize them.

But we're not recommending that kind of armament to you. Instead, we want to call your attention to the thousands of people in

---

TECHNO-SAVVY SPORTS BAR

Elmer had a sports bar—one with several TV screens hooked up to a satellite receiver and tuned to receive popular sports events.

One day, there was a ballgame in a stadium nearby. The game was blacked out from the local satellite receivers, but Elmer, being a guerrilla, made it possible for all his customers to see the game anyway.

How?

Satellite signals are generally scrambled. To receive them in usable form, you must buy an electronic device called a transponder and pay royalties to the satellite company, which in turn sets your transponder to unscramble the appropriate signals.

Elmer's accomplice ran a sports bar in a distant city and also had a transponder. To obtain unscrambled signals of locally blacked-out games, they merely swapped transponders.

Times Square. They're not looking at those gorgeous signs as much as they're peering at their handheld armament—their mobile devices. As the world changes and technology is at the forefront of change, guerrillas increase their profits.

16. Experiment

Here we are, extolling the power of commitment in marketing, but how are you going to know what to commit to? By availing yourself of the 16th secret of guerrilla marketing: Be willing to experiment so you will know what is worthy of your commitment.

To guerrillas, the three most important words in marketing are test, test, and test. You can easily risk inexpensive failures in your quest for glittering success. The more you test, the more you'll know.

The process of guerrilla marketing is relatively simple: Be aware of all the weapons of marketing available to you, experiment with the ones that sound the best, then commit to the marketing combination that works best. Commitment comes from a patient leader and the lessons you learn as you experiment your way to financial glory.

NANOCASTING

Nanocasting is a new word coined by Errol Smith, a brilliant guerrilla marketing associate of ours.

To understand nanocasting, let us tell you about a businessman who sold the product Viagra. One day he decided to advertise his Viagra on national television. That is called "broad-casting." He didn't have much success with that particular ad campaign.

So he decided to experiment a little bit. He went to the station manager and told him, "I only want to advertise it on a cable channel that is geared toward men, let's say SPIKE or ESPN for example." What he engaged in is considered narrowcasting. The spots pulled a little better, but not by much.

The businessman went back to the station manager to experiment further, and decided to refine his marketing to be shown on TV during shows that are geared toward men's health; this is referred to as microcasting. The spots did much better, but he was still not totally satisfied with his results.

Finally he discovered the most precision type of marketing: By targeting his advertisements to men's TV, on health channels, on episodes that are dealing specifically with the problem of erectile dysfunction. Everyone watching that show was in his target market, and his marketing campaign ended up breaking the bank.

Now, that's nanocasting.

17. Measurement

This secret of guerrilla marketing can actually double your profits: measurement. Face up to the reality that some of your marketing weapons will hit the center of the bull's-eye while others will miss the target entirely. Your task as a guerrilla is to know the difference.

Famed millionaire John Wanamaker said, "I know that half the money I spend on advertising is wasted; the trouble is I don't know which half."

By paying rapt attention and by conscientious experimentation, you'll soon learn which half you are wasting; you'll know the winners from the losers. That's not an easy job, but to guerrillas, it's mandatory. Instruct everyone who works for you to ask every single customer, "Where did you hear about us?" and then keep careful records on your guerrilla marketing calendar.

Be sure to think short and long term when assessing the wins from the losses because some things you think aren't working are really working very well. It just takes them longer to work. Measuring is no job for amateurs.

SEAGULLS

Seagulls fly in ceaseless circles in the sky, constantly looking for food. They keep flying in circles, constantly looking for that food, and when they find it, they land, eat their fill, then rise into the sky again—only to fly in circles again looking for food because that is their strongest instinct.

The strongest instinct in the mind of a guerrilla marketer is constant learning. Guerrillas listen to tapes, view DVDs, attend seminars, and read books. Then, instead of thinking they've learned everything, guerrillas absorb all that they've learned and go and learn more because new information is constantly coming down the pike. That's why guerrillas are constant learners.

18. Enlightenment

What you're doing this very moment is exactly what we mean by this secret. You're getting wiser and more informed about marketing. The secret of enlightenment is one of the most valuable of the secrets.

19. Augment

Let's say that you actually do practice the concepts revealed to you with these secrets. Suppose you quickly learn that your new insights result in new and impressive profits. What to do next?

Here's a hint: It's not lean back and rest on your rewards. The real secret of what to do next is the 19th secret of guerrilla marketing: Augment your marketing attack.

Believe us here—your competitors are getting smarter every day. They're keeping an eye on you while remaining alert for ways to match you, even surpass you. You can't just kick back and grin. You've got to augment your attack, making it more effective, more powerful, more profitable.

LADIES' NIGHT

There were once two bars situated across the street from each other. The first bar was getting most of the business because they were offering "FREE DRINKS" to all the single ladies. The owner of the second bar thought hard about what he could possibly offer as a competitive advantage.

Being a creative guerrilla, he mounted a prominent sign out front. Soon all the single ladies were racing over to his bar instead. What did his sign say that caused such a mass migration?

It simply read: "FREE CHOCOLATE."

> "The average person has four ideas a year which, if any one is acted on, would make them a millionaire."
>
> —Brian Tracy

It's tempting to pat yourself on the back for a marketing job well done, but guerrillas don't waste their time patting but instead devote their time to improving. If you had no competition, things might be different. But you do have competition, and the marketing wisdom out there is more available than ever before. A guerrilla marketing attack has a beginning and middle, but if you're a guerrilla, it has no end.

20. Implement

The other secrets of guerrilla marketing fall by the wayside if you don't practice the 20th secret—which is that you must implement those ideas in your daily life and not just learn the ideas for academic reasons.

The world belongs to the doers and not to the thinkers. Guerrilla marketing isn't, wasn't, and never will be a spectator sport. It is all about action, and that's just what you must be—a person who takes action to breathe life into these priceless secrets.

Sadly, the majority of people reading these words—yes, the majority—won't do anything about them. But a small minority will turn them into real-life deeds, running their businesses by them, and seeing how their action results in the profits the majority only dream

> "All our dreams can come true—if we have the courage to pursue them."
>
> —Walt Disney

THE 20 SECRETS OF GUERRILLA MARKETING

1. Commitment	11. Consent
2. Investment	12. Involvement
3. Consistent	13. Subsequent
4. Congruent	14. Dependent
5. Content	15. Armament
6. Assortment	16. Experiment
7. Confident	17. Measurement
8. Patient	18. Enlightenment
9. Amazement	19. Augment
10. Convenient	20. Implement

about. Guerrillas are dreamers, too. But more than dreaming, they take the action that gives wings to those dreams.

An invaluable marketing tool is the ability to learn about marketing, and then to translate what you learn into profits. One of the keys to marketing online is to begin by learning about marketing. If you don't know about marketing, your chances of success on the internet are dim indeed.

But if you do know about marketing as it is today you'll have a commanding competitive advantage over those who would dare to woo your customers and prospects away from you. These 20 secrets provide you with the momentum you need to prevail in any circumstance. Memorizing

These 20 secrets provide you with the momentum you need to prevail in any circumstance. Memorizing them is not necessary, but living by them is compulsory for guerrillas.

them is not necessary, but living by them is compulsory for guerrillas. The more you know about marketing and the more you keep up with the advances and breakthroughs, the better you'll be at marketing.

chapter 7

The Guerrilla Marketing Strategy

THERE ARE COUNTLESS DETAILS to attend to if you're going to be a practicing guerrilla. We're counting on you to attend to every single one of them because your competitors are probably going to overlook several. Lucky for you.

Lucky, too, that you now get to explore seven areas that just cannot be overlooked. These are the seven areas upon which you must concentrate. In fact you'll be able to state your entire guerrilla marketing strategy in these seven statements. Each is only one sentence long, and all but the fourth one are short sentences.

Use your guerrilla marketing strategy to guide your efforts for the next year, three years, five years—or forever. Create it to last as long as possible. Every six months, look at it with an eye toward improving it or leaving it alone. The good marketers improve it regularly. The great guerrillas never change

Use your guerrilla marketing strategy to guide your efforts for the next year, three years, five years—or forever.

GUERRILLA MARKETING PLAN

In business, it's crucial to know the difference between a strategy and tactics. Many business owners, confused about the difference, wander around and end up lost.

Strategy is the guiding light that illuminates the path.

Tactics are the specific steps you take along that path.

it because they were smart enough to get it right the first time. In the fool's mind, there are many options. In the wise person's mind there is only one.

> *Seven sentences are all you need to enter the fray as a guerrilla.*

Seven sentences are all you need to enter the fray as a guerrilla. In my presentations, I give audience members five minutes to create their strategies. That's all it takes. In more than a quarter of a century of giving this exercise, I've never seen anyone take longer than five minutes—and that includes many leaders of Fortune 500 companies. I give five minutes because I don't want overanalysis to diffuse focus. I want people to trust their instincts. Not easy, but many guerrillas do it.

The first sentence states the purpose of your marketing. After being exposed to your marketing, what single, physical act do you want individuals to take? Do you want them to click to a website, click on a hyperlink, call a phone number, send a fax, send an email, text their friends, look for your product the next time they're shopping, come into a store where they can buy it? What physical act do you want them to take? This is the act where the momentum starts. How do you create this momentum? With the nudge you give people in the first sentence.

COMPETITIVE ADVANTAGE

Question: What feature of the *Old Farmer's Almanac* made it vastly more popular than all its rivals for more than 100 years in the rural U.S.?

Answer: The *Old Farmer's Almanac* had a hole in the top left corner that made it ideal for hanging on a nail in the outhouse.

The second sentence states the single, best competitive advantage you offer to motivate people to take the act you nudged them toward in that first sentence. We assume you offer several benefits to purchasers. So do your competitors. If you offer any benefits that those competitors don't offer, those are your competitive advantages. Pick the best and shine a bright light upon it. If you focus here, you'll help your target market to focus upon your advantage and what that means to them. When they do that, your momentum increases.

The third sentence is where you list that target market. The smaller it is, the more clearly you'll be able to focus. Give your target market members the unmistakable feeling that you'll be talking directly to them and not to someone over their left shoulder somewhere. Marketing is a process akin to courtship, and your target market is the person you're courting. Perhaps you have more than one target market. Probably, if you're into it for profit motives. Probably not, if you're into it for courtship. Check it out.

Momentum flourishes in those markets; read on to find out why.

The fourth sentence is not really a sentence but a list. It's where you list the marketing weapons you'll use. You'll probably use so many that instead of a sentence you'll have to put them into list form. You'll find all the 200 guerrilla marketing weapons at your disposal starting on page 81. It's a lush selection for a guerrilla. Now the momentum really picks up steam. Hang on.

APARTMENTS

A series of apartment buildings in Los Angeles had a 70 percent occupancy rate. But one of the buildings had a 100 percent occupancy rate. It was near the same neighborhood, same churches, same schools, same smog, and yet, in this building, all the apartments stayed rented. How did this happen?

That particular building manager put up a sign that said, "Sign a lease . . . get free auto grooming." What the devil is auto grooming? That meant they hired a person to wash the tenants' cars once a week.

The salary they paid the car washer was easily worth the difference between a 70 percent occupancy rate and a 100 percent occupancy rate. The building management simply asked themselves, "What might our tenants appreciate?"

The answer was simple. And their generosity in regularly performing the simple act of a weekly car wash was the difference between a highly profitable building and a so-so profitable building. No rocket science here, only common sense and a spirit of generosity.

The fifth sentence of your strategy tells what you stand for. It's your niche, your positioning. If you're not brand-new to business, we can guarantee that you already stand for something. Is it what you want to stand for in the minds of your prospects and customers? When people hear the name of your business, do they think of economy, quality, speed, service, innovation, professionalism, experience, or something else? You're in charge here. Whatever you select, make certain that it shines brightly from all of your marketing. The importance of your positioning cannot be overestimated.

The sixth sentence states your identity—your company personality. We're not referring to some phony image but to your honest identity. An image is defined as a façade. Façades misrepresent the truth. Honest identities stem from truth.

COPY CENTER

We were consulting with the largest copying company in the San Francisco Bay area, a firm serving a population of close to 8 million people.

I asked the owner of the company which industry churns out the most copies. "The legal industry," he told us. "Do you have any marketing strictly addressed to them?" we asked.

"Not really. Should I budget some of my marketing budget to that industry?" he asked. "No, don't budget more—just direct some of your budget that goes to the small-business audience to the legal industry," we suggested.

He did that and his profits—not just his sales but his profits—rose by 31 percent the next year. He didn't have to invest one extra penny in marketing to that industry; he only had to recognize that he had more than one target market.

If people respond to the image you portray, as soon as they begin dealing with you, they'll realize that you misrepresented yourself to them. No bond can be created under that circumstance. Almost everyone has been stung by shady marketing. That's why the world takes much marketing with a grain of salt. But if you're communicating the truth and it feels like the truth to people who interact with you, a bond will begin to be created. It will intensify the momentum that results in a lasting relationship. Phoniness in marketing will come back to punish you. Total honesty will come back to reward you. It energizes your momentum.

The seventh sentence states your marketing budget as a percentage of your projected gross sales. Since the start of this century, the average business in the United States, Europe, and Asia invested 4 percent of its gross sales in marketing. But we both know that the average business is not a shining example to follow.

PROCTER & GAMBLE

We do a lot of work with Procter and Gamble, who we consider one of the most sophisticated marketing companies on the planet Earth. Here's how good Procter and Gamble is: 97 percent of the homes in America have at least one Procter and Gamble product in them. So P&G must be doing something right. One of the things they are doing right: They have a very brief marketing plan for every single brand they offer to the public.

When we used to present to Procter and Gamble marketers, they'd also have ultra-brief strategies. They might have had 200 pages of documentation, but they would have created a very brief marketing plan for each one of their brands. Boiling down that documentation forced them to focus, which enabled everybody who worked with the product people to understand what they were trying to accomplish.

That meant the plan would be simple to understand and wouldn't put any readers to sleep. The P&G people were streamlined enough to winnow their strategy to a concise length.

Concise and understandable are two hallmarks of good strategies. That's where it begins.

Typically, companies invest more than that, especially at the outset, to establish their brand. Once established, they're able to cut back on that percentage. But don't forget that guerrilla marketing is not about decreasing the percentage of your investment as much as about increasing your return. That means your profits. Guerrillas know that there are really only two kinds of marketing. Expensive marketing is the kind that doesn't work. If you invest $100 in a full-page, full-color advertisement and it nets you $50 in profits, that's expensive marketing. If you invest $10,000 and it nets you $100,000 in profits, that's inexpensive marketing. It has nothing to do with your cost. It has everything to do with your profits.

SEVEN-SENTENCE GUERRILLA MARKETING PLAN

1. State the physical purpose of your marketing.
2. State the single, best competitive advantage you offer.
3. State your target market.
4. List the marketing weapons you'll use.
5. Tell what you stand for—it's your niche, your positioning.
6. State your identity, your company personality.
7. List your marketing budget as a percentage of your projected gross sales.

chapter 8

Guerrilla Marketing to the Unconscious Mind

PAUL HANLEY WAS A FRIEND, a guerrilla marketing master trainer in England, and the co-author of *The Guerrilla Marketing Revolution—Precision Persuasion of the Unconscious Mind*. After taking enormous strides for guerrilla marketing in the United Kingdom, Russia, and the Middle East, Paul died in the crash of the plane he was flying in 2006.

These pages he originally wrote for *The Guerrilla Marketing Revolution* have helped many guerrillas.

The Brain Uses Images to Help the Conscious Mind Understand

Every word in your natural language is represented in your mind by an image. Every sound you ever hear is associated to an image in your mind. Every feeling you have ever experienced or can imagine experiencing is also represented by an image, or images, in your mind. The ways in which you experience the image, and indeed the absolute contents of the image, are what make it personal to you.

Traditional marketing acknowledges that people have images in their minds but doesn't truly understand how or why, or indeed know how to use that critical information. There have been marketing campaigns designed to create wonderful visualizations in people's minds.

Many advertisements actually ask that you "imagine" something. The only way to imagine anything is to create an image in your mind. So in fact, traditional marketing is part of the way there. However, what traditional marketing has failed to understand is that nobody will have the same visualization that the advertisement designer experienced. No two people will have exactly the same images, regardless of how specific your creation of the visualization may be. Therefore intentionally implanting images in your prospects' minds should be a part of the message, but not the message.

The next essential reason that guerrillas should market to the unconscious mind may hurt your feelings a little until you've read the explanation.

The Unconscious Mind Is Much Smarter Than the Conscious Mind

As you are reading this, your unconscious mind is looking after you, monitoring and controlling your body temperature, your immune system, your balance, your spatial awareness, your breathing, your heartbeat, your circulation, your bodily fluids, and your five senses.

Most importantly, it does all this without bothering your conscious awareness. It tells you when to blink. It tells you when your body needs more oxygen or water or carbohydrates. How often are you aware of these messages? Not very often. Anything that you have ever considered to be instinct or a reflex action is actually unconscious system management.

The unconscious mind recognizes its superior performance over the conscious mind, and as a result it tends to protect it by only providing information that the conscious mind demands or requires for comprehension. Even then, the unconscious mind is often selective in the data transfer, regularly choosing to "drip feed" the information to prevent overload. This may be because the information challenges existing beliefs or simply because the nature of the data is complex.

Although the unconscious mind is more intelligent than the conscious, it rarely overrides decisions made by your conscious. For example, when a smoker picks up a cigarette, the unconscious mind says, "Cigarettes are not good for your health. They're going to kill you." Then the conscious mind argues, "But I like them." There are women who are regularly beaten by their partners, yet they stay with them. Their unconscious might say, "You are going to get seriously hurt one day. He doesn't respect you. You should leave him." Then the conscious mind pipes up, "But he might change, and it was probably my fault."

This type of interaction between the conscious and unconscious is called internal dialogue. It is when you actually hear voices in your head, which brings us to reason number three.

The Unconscious Mind Controls Your Internal Dialogue

Let's clarify something right now: everyone hears voices in their head. It isn't schizophrenia or any other psychological problem. It's how your brain manages thinking. We call it internal dialogue. Even now as you read this page, you can hear yourself reading it. Your brain is making you sound out each sentence because the majority of the language that you use is verbal, and writing is only a representation of a word.

Internal dialogue is perfectly natural, and recognizing its influence on the decision-making process is an excellent marketing weapon.

Guerrillas seek to utilize every advantage offered, and the opportunity offered by utilizing language to stimulate positive, internal dialogue is a powerful advantage.

Your goal as a guerrilla should be to bring about positive states in your prospects, because people in poor or negative states make bad decisions.

If a prospect is in a positive state when he or she makes a purchasing decision, he or she is much less likely to experience buyer's remorse. A study was conducted to identify how many customers would buy from sellers again if you offered a similar or related product at a similar price. The answer was 34 percent. Have you any idea of the expense in marketing to an audience two-thirds the size of your existing client base? It's substantial, especially when you recognize that you can market to your existing clients for free, and 34 percent are likely to purchase from you!

We now know that there are ways to motivate the purchasing decision, and the majority of these methods require that the prospect is in a positive state, rather than buying to avoid discomfort. Indeed the question should be whether a person avoiding a consequence is being motivated to purchase or forced to do so? It's a thin line.

Guerrillas focus not only on satisfying customers, but also on retaining customers. A customer who feels that he or she has been backed into a corner to make a purchasing decision is less likely to buy from you again when compared to a customer who was given many options and freedom of choice. Guerrillas present options and respect the customers in their ability to make informed decisions.

To move prospects to positive states and keep customers in those states, guerrillas use language, imagery, and the guerrilla marketing weapons that produce constructive messages, which in turn bring about positive, internal dialogue.

Propulsion is a more powerful marketing weapon than aversion. For example, traditional marketing might offer the very negative: "Without a security alarm, your home and family are at risk." Guerrilla marketing prefers the more positively motivating: "Sleep soundly in the safe knowledge that you have protected your home and family."

Ask yourself, when you last made a purchase of sizeable value, what were you saying to yourself afterward? If you were still questioning whether you should have made the purchase or not, then the marketing process was not complete and your internal dialogue had not been considered. If you were happy and excited about the purchase, your internal dialogue would have sounded different. When you suffer buyer's remorse, the tonality of your internal dialogue is very different from what it would be when you are in a positive state.

If you have told your friends and family about a purchase you are about to make and they tried to discourage you, did their voice tonality sound particularly enthusiastic? Did they use a supportive tone when they said, "That is such a terrible waste of money. Are you on drugs?" Did you feel the heady grip of eagerness to get to the store? Of course not. The same is true of internal dialogue. If the dialogue is not positive and fails to build excitement, the purchasing decision is not ready to be made.

The Unconscious Mind Can Understand and Link Multiple Messages

Over the past 30 or 40 years, many scientific research papers have been published on the abilities of conscious awareness. Although various opinions have been offered, they generally all agree that the conscious mind struggles with more than three or four issues at any given time.

Your unconscious mind can manage millions of functions, and in this respect is very much like a supercomputer. There is a huge difference, however, between the human brain and any computer on Earth. The brain can associate datastreams based on relevance, disregarding unimportant information, and make a decision based on historical data, possible future outcomes, and experience. A computer can only make decisions by evaluating all available information as it can't decide what is relevant and what is not.

Guerrillas choose to market to the unconscious mind because they can simultaneously appeal to several parts of the mind with multiple messages. This, in turn, helps speed the decision-making process.

Guerrillas also know that the unconscious mind can construct even the most tenuous of links, associating information sets to build a more detailed understanding for the conscious mind. As a rule of thumb, allowing the unconscious to create links for itself is more productive than giving direct instructions. In order to accept direct instructions, the brain requires trust in the sender of the message—rapport. Creating rapport can take days, weeks, or even months.

Giving the unconscious a set of marketing messages that it can then assemble to produce a coherent marketing overview results in a rapidly devised and committed decision. After all, the unconscious trusts its own judgment better than any direct instruction from someone else. Typically, when marketers present marketing messages as a direct instruction, the conscious mind will second-guess the decision, and the conscious mind isn't that smart.

The Unconscious Mind Makes Decisions Before Consulting the Conscious

Guerrillas know that it is possible to enable a prospect to make a decision before he or she is consciously aware that a decision has been made. This is done by marketing to the unconscious mind.

This is one of the most important lessons you will ever learn about the human brain; the unconscious mind cannot work slowly—it can only work at high speed.

The unconscious mind is most comfortable, and indeed efficient, when working at high capacity. Furthermore, it actually tries to find shortcuts when processing so that it can speed its data management and decision strategies. When seeking shortcuts, the unconscious mind

FIRE

A fire crew was called to a large warehouse fire. Upon arrival, the crew surveyed the warehouse, and the order was given to enter the premises to fight the fire. After two or three minutes, the officer had an uneasy sensation about the whole event and ordered his team out of the premises. They argued that everything was OK, but he insisted that they immediately vacate the building.

Within 30 seconds after they had cleared the warehouse, there was an enormous explosion, and the area where the firemen had been working became a ferocious inferno. Without doubt, the team would have been killed if they had remained in the building—and they owed their lives to the unconscious mind of their officer.

When the officer was interviewed an hour after the event, he still could not explain why he made the decision that he did. However, the next day he was able to detail exactly why he had instructed his team to vacate the premises.

Without being consciously aware, his unconscious had noticed that the smoke coming from the fire was orange, not black, and he could see air being sucked back into the fire.

His unconscious mind also noticed that the fire was very quiet and that there were few of the familiar crackling noises associated with regular burning. These unconscious details set off an important comparison process in the officer's brain.

It considered the hundreds of fires that the officer had previously experienced, added the material collated in training, and compared all this data with the situation it faced. The result was that the officer's unconscious mind identified a backdraft—one of the most dangerous types of fire, known for violent explosions.

Due to the urgency of the situation, the unconscious did not give the conscious mind all the details or the chance to argue. Instead, the conscious was simply told, "There is danger. You must remove your men." The officer was not aware why, but due to the intensity of the message, the conscious complied without question.

Guerrillas seek the understanding and compliance of both unconscious and conscious minds.

makes multiple attempts to identify relevant associations in any or all of the data sets. Why is this important to guerrillas? Well, we know that when marketing to the unconscious mind, we can be more subtle than when using traditional marketing. We can make use of language patterns including presupposition, generalization, ambiguity, and deletion.

Since the unconscious mind works at such high speed and is so much more sensitive to subtlety than the conscious mind, it always recognizes models, associations, and patterns ahead of the conscious. This is an insight that very few marketers seem to understand. It is now accepted that mental processes are essentially unconscious, and the conscious mind responds to these processes. Knowing this, why would we want to target the conscious mind for marketing purposes? Traditional marketing has failed to identify that all decisions are first made by the unconscious. Yet many successful advertising campaigns appeal to the unconscious mind, usually by accident.

Have you ever made a decision which proved to be incorrect, and suffered "I knew it" remorse? If you knew it, then why did you make the decision you made? In the most basic terms, your conscious mind decided to override the decision made by the unconscious. Frankly, considering the greater resources available to the unconscious mind and its processing abilities, it's incredible that we ever allow our conscious to make a decision at all.

As guerrillas, we know that we must market to the unconscious mind. However, we also need to keep the conscious mind actively involved. It is rare that the conscious mind is happy to

Guerrillas know that marketing to the unconscious mind is the route to rapid, yet stable, purchasing decisions. Ordinary marketers don't know this— which is why they are ordinary.

be a passenger. This is due to ego. Guerrillas know that marketing always needs to be mindful of ego, and occasionally needs to nurse an ego. The unconscious regularly battles with the ego, so ideally, guerrillas seek the understanding and compliance of both unconscious and conscious minds. Guerrilla marketing has produced success after success throughout the world because guerrillas know that marketing to the unconscious mind is the route to rapid, yet stable, purchasing decisions. Ordinary marketers don't know this—which is why they are ordinary.

THE UNCONSCIOUS MIND

- The brain uses images to help the conscious mind understand.
- The unconscious mind is much smarter than the conscious mind.
- The unconscious mind controls your internal dialogue.
- The unconscious mind can understand and link multiple messages.
- The unconscious mind makes decisions before consulting the conscious.

chapter 9

The Guerrilla Marketing Weapons

AS THE GUERRILLA MARKETING STRATEGY is the brains of a marketing program, the guerrilla marketing weapons are the muscles. You certainly won't need all the weapons about to be suggested here, but you also can't remain oblivious to any of them. As times change, perspectives widen. A guerrilla marketing attack is a 360-degree assault. A 359-degree attack has a weak spot.

As one who may be just starting with a guerrilla marketing campaign, this is unquestionably the best time to learn about the weapons, about their plentitude, about their potency, and about their economy. For us, just having you know the range of your selection lets us breathe deeply: 200 weapons, 200 choices, countless combinations.

You can't help but be aware of your relationship with each of the weapons as you

As the guerrilla marketing strategy is the brains of a marketing program, the guerrilla marketing weapons are the muscles.

Unless you're in business for laughs over profits, you've got to become familiar with all of these 200 weapons. It's the grown-up thing to do. Guerrilla marketing is fun, but is not child's play.

read its name. Either you know it intimately and are expert in its usage, or . . . you've tried it and may still be using it but know in your heart that your expertise is limited, or . . . you've never tried it, or . . . you know what it's about but don't feel that it's the ticket for you at this junction. No prob. Nowhere is it written that you must use all 200 weapons. Hall of Fame guerrillas have achieved marketing greatness with only a handful.

Unless you're in business for laughs over profits, you've got to become familiar with all of these 200 weapons. It's the grown-up thing to do. Guerrilla marketing is fun, but is not child's play. You should experiment with several of the 200 weapons, being ultra-careful not to waste your precious marketing investments by not learning how well a weapon fared. If it cost more than it earned, eliminate it unless you've got a good reason not to. If it earns more than it costs, use twice as much of it next go-round. Do other weapons produce even more profits for you? Experiment and find out. That was not a rhetorical question.

After dabbling with several methods as you search for the magic formula, it will be time to ruthlessly cut all the weapons that aren't proving their worth, leaving you with an arsenal of lethal combinations of weapons that have proven their merit to you in action. The phrase to remember is "lethal combinations." That's what you want a lot of. You get it by knowing all the contenders, eliminating the losers, and doubling up on the winners. You learn which is which by experimenting.

Don't worry; we're not going to throw a wagonload of weapons into a pile in front of you. We've neatly categorized the weapons to make things as clear and simple as possible.

Mini- and Maxi-Media

Some of the weapons fall into the category of "mini-media" because they certainly aren't major media, but they definitely are media. Enormous companies have been built with the mini-media alone.

Another option for you are the maxi-media, the logical category of larger, costlier, splashier, and more traditional media. These are 19th- and 20th-century weapons, still effective, but lots of their luster has gone.

E-Media

The newest category, the e-media, is new because most of the weapons within it are new, most of them not being even a gleam in a software engineer's eye at the time *Guerrilla Marketing* turned up in bookstores and libraries. Nonetheless, the e-media merit a category of their own, and a hefty one it is.

The Info-Media

Most media imparts information, but some media are all about information, rather than it being merely a peripheral reason for their existence. Some of these media are old. Some are new. All are capable of turning a business around. And some can do that for free.

The Human Media

Many media are things. Others are people. So many are people that we decided to create a category solely of these media. When we say the human media are about people, we're really saying that they're about you. You are the one who can breathe life into some of these media, and you are the one who actually is the media. These overlooked weapons of marketing are too powerful to be overlooked.

The Non-Media

The past category about human beings was indeed about human beings. And this upcoming category, about the non-media, is definitely not about the media. The non-media can make substantial contributions to your profits, but they won't do so as standard media. Because they are not officially "media," we don't want them to escape your notice. In fact, we're shining a bright light upon them with every one listed here.

Company Attributes

People are naturally attracted to companies that demonstrate specific attributes. The more of these attributes that you can claim for your company, the rosier our prediction of fame and fortune in your life. If your company comes up empty when assessing all these attributes, remind your broker to sell short on your business. The truth is that the more of these attributes you have, the more poised you are for success. It's obvious right from the start.

Company Attitudes

The company attributes we mentioned were about your company. The company attitudes we list are about your mind. All of these attitudes ought to be descriptive of your company, but in reality, they are descriptive of you. They begin with you. They flourish because of you. They win sales and profits because of you. Maybe 5,000 people help you do these things. But we know these attitudes come from your brain

> "Your attitude, not your aptitude, will determine your altitude."
>
> —Zig Ziglar

and rest on your shoulders. And we know how much they can mean to your company.

Always keep in mind that a bound-for-glory guerrilla marketing attack begins with your awareness of the 200 weapons. Then it progresses to the realm of experimentation, where by trial and error and tracking, you learn which of the weapons are lethal and which are duds. Finally, you discover the combination of weapons that produces the most profits for you. When that happens, we pity your competitors.

THE 200 GUERRILLA MARKETING WEAPONS

Maxi-Media

1. Advertising
2. Direct mail
3. Newspaper ads
4. Radio spots
5. Magazine ads
6. Billboards
7. Television commercials

Mini-Media

8. Marketing plans
9. Marketing calendars
10. Identity
11. Business cards
12. Stationery
13. Personal letters
14. Telephone marketing
15. Toll-free number
16. Vanity phone number
17. Yellow Pages
18. Postcards
19. Postcard decks
20. Classified ads
21. Per-order, per-inquiry advertising
22. Free ads in shoppers
23. Circulars, fliers
24. Community bulletin boards
25. Movie ads
26. Outside signs
27. Street banners
28. Window displays
29. Inside signs
30. Posters
31. Canvassing
32. Door hangers
33. Elevator pitches
34. Value story
35. Back-end sales
36. Letters of recommendation
37. Attendance at trade shows

THE 200 GUERRILLA MARKETING WEAPONS

E- Media

38. Computer
39. Printer, fax
40. Chat rooms
41. Forums boards
42. Internet bulletin boards
43. List-building
44. Personalized emails
45. Email signatures
46. Canned emails
47. Bulk emails
48. Audio/video postcards
49. Domain names
50. Websites
51. Landing pages
52. Merchant accounts
53. Shopping carts
54. Auto-responders
55. Search-engine rankings
56. Electronic brochures
57. RSS feeds
58. Blogs
59. Podcasting
60. Own ezine publications
61. Ads in other ezines
62. Ebooks
63. Content for other websites
64. Webinar productions
65. Joint ventures

66. Word-of-mouse marketing
67. Viral marketing
68. eBay, other auction sites
69. Click analyzers
70. Pay-per-click ads
71. Search-engine keywords
72. Google AdWords
73. Sponsored links
74. Reciprocal link exchanges
75. Banner exchanges
76. Web conversion rates

Info-Media

77. Knowledge of your market
78. Research studies
79. Specific customer data
80. Case studies
81. Sharing
82. Brochures
83. Catalogs
84. Business directories
85. Public service announcements
86. Newsletters
87. Speeches
88. Free consultations
89. Free demonstrations
90. Free seminars
91. Published articles

THE 200 GUERRILLA MARKETING WEAPONS

92. Published columns
93. Published books
94. Publishing-on-demand items
95. Speaker at clubs
96. Teleseminars
97. Infomercials
98. Constant learning

Human Media

99. Marketing insights
100. Yourself
101. Your employees and reps
102. Designated guerrillas
103. Employee attire
104. Social demeanor
105. Target audiences
106. Your own circle of influence
107. Contact time with customers
108. How you say hello and goodbye
109. Teaching ability
110. Stories
111. Sales training
112. Use of downtime
113. Networking
114. Professional titles
115. Affiliate marketing
116. Media contacts
117. "A" list customers
118. Core story

119. Sense of urgency
120. Limited offers
121. Calls to action
122. Satisfied customers

Non-Media

123. Benefits lists
124. Competitive advantages
125. Gifts
126. Service
127. Public relations
128. Fusion marketing
129. Bartering
130. Word-of-mouth
131. Buzz
132. Community involvement
133. Club and association memberships
134. Free directory listings
135. Trade show booths
136. Special events
137. Name tags at events
138. Luxury box at events
139. Gift certificates
140. Audio-visual aids
141. Flipcharts
142. Reprints and blowups
143. Coupons
144. Free-trial offers
145. Guarantees

THE 200 GUERRILLA MARKETING WEAPONS

146. Contests and sweepstakes
147. Baking or craft abilities
148. Lead buying
149. Follow-up
150. Tracking plans
151. Marketing-on-hold
152. Branded entertainment
153. Product placement
154. Radio talk show guest
155. TV talk show guest
156. Subliminal marketing

Company Attributes

157. Proper view of marketing
158. Brand-name awareness
159. Positioning
160. Name
161. Meme
162. Theme line
163. Writing ability
164. Copywriting ability
165. Headline copy
166. Location
167. Hours of operation
168. Days of operation
169. Credit cards accepted
170. Financing available
171. Credibility
172. Reputation
173. Efficiency

174. Quality
175. Service
176. Selection
177. Price
178. Opportunities to upgrade
179. Referral program
180. Spying
181. Testimonials
182. Extra value
183. Adopt noble cause

Company Attitudes

184. Easy to do business with
185. Honest interest in people
186. Telephone demeanor
187. Passion and enthusiasm
188. Sensitivity
189. Patience
190. Flexibility
191. Generosity
192. Self-confidence
193. Neatness
194. Aggressiveness
195. Competitiveness
196. High energy
197. Speed
198. Ability to focus
199. Attention to details
200. Readiness to take action

chapter 10

Guerrilla Advertising

T HE CORNERSTONE TO PROFITABLE advertising is creativity. Reality helps a whole lot, but creativity is what's going to put you over the top. Some people think they aren't very creative, but that only means they haven't yet learned what guerrillas know about creativity.

10 Things Guerrillas Know about Creativity

1. The best measure of creativity is profitability.
2. Creativity begins with an idea.
3. The idea is to be found within the inner amazement of your product or service.
4. The idea will write its own advertisements.
5. Creativity does not care where it comes from, whether it comes from the president of the company, the creative director of an advertising agency, or the mailroom girl.

6. The best creativity spawns ideas with long lives.
7. Think of advertising as the truth made fascinating. We'll say that again. What is advertising? It's the truth made fascinating.

> *Think of advertising as the truth made fascinating.*

8. The more specific you are, the more creative you can be.
9. Creativity does not come from inspiration.
10. Creativity does come from knowledge. What kind of knowledge? You need knowledge in 10 areas: You need knowledge of your customers, your prospects, your competitors, competitive businesses elsewhere, your own industry, current events, economic trends, your own offering, your own community, and successful advertising.

The purpose of advertising is to sell, right? That's sure one purpose, but there are 49 other solid reasons to advertise. Sometimes your advertising can do several of them for you, but often, one is enough.

Advertising Can Do 50 Different Things for You

1. Produce leads.
2. Educate prospects about your benefits.
3. Help you expand into new markets.
4. Influence the people who influence others.
5. Say your name to those people who don't know you.
6. Set the stage for your other marketing by preselling your product or your service.
7. Expand upon a public relations story.
8. Tell the story of your company.
9. Add authority to your sales presentations. A salesperson standing up in front of a prospect who has never heard of your

company or what your company stands for has a hard row to hoe. The reality is that advertising lends authority to that salesperson's presentation.

10. Build your corporate identity.

11. Build confidence in your product or your services.

12. Dispel an ugly rumor. Perrier had tainted products; Tylenol had poisoned products; Jack in the Box had tainted products. These companies had to use advertising to dispel those ugly stories that appeared about them; now Perrier, Tylenol, and Jack in the Box are selling healthily again. Advertising helped make the ugly rumors go away. Sometimes those rumors were the truth.

13. Keep your name in the forefront of your customers' minds.

14. Head competitors off at the pass.

15. Go after business that your competitors have.

16. Prove your quality with success stories.

17. Make your stockholders happy. When stockholders don't see your advertising, they question their investment in your stock. When they see your advertising, they think you're going about things in the right way. Whether that's true or not, I'm not sure, but I know that advertising does make your stockholders happy.

18. Impress the financial community. You may want to raise funds. You may want to talk to a bank about getting extra money. If bankers see your advertising—and hey, I've seen it happen— they will be impressed when you come and ask for the money you want.

19. Assert your leadership and your prestige.

20. Maintain a constant presence for you and build confidence. You know the importance of confidence. It's the number-one reason people patronize the businesses that they do.

21. Help your direct mail pay off.

22. Assure the success of your telemarketing campaign. It's one thing to call people who have never heard of you. It's something

totally different if they've heard of your company and they have heard of it through your advertising.

23. Make sure that your point-of-purchase signs work. These signs should use the same idea that you express in your advertising.

24. Gain distribution to prove to retailers they should carry your product because you're going to mention their name in your advertising. Or because you are an advertiser yourself, you'll find stores often make their decision as to whether or not they should carry a product based on whether or not that product is advertised.

25. Announce the existence of your product or service.

26. Gain credibility for a new product or service.

27. Make your name become a brand name.

28. Herald a special promotion that you're having elsewhere.

29. Establish your niche in the marketplace.

30. Highlight testimonials from satisfied customers.

31. Test something with a headline or an offer or a price or a specific radio station, TV station, or advertising media that you're using.

32. Create a desire to buy. And that may be one of the best reasons to advertise—the idea not of selling something but creating a desire in the minds of your prospects to buy what you are selling.

33. Establish a presence in your community or your industry.

34. Attract foot traffic into your store.

35. Make sales. Many people think that is the only reason to advertise. They're oblivious to the other 49 reasons and think the only reason to advertise is to make sales. I'm here to say that making sales is one-fiftieth of the reasons that you could be advertising. There are 49 other reasons.

36. Obtain names for your mailing list because you know that the follow-up you will do will make customers for life.

37. Inform people, many people, at once about your benefits.

38. Motivate people to call you on the phone or to visit your website.

39. Persuade people to complete and mail your coupon.

40. Do research by studying the responses to your offer.

41. Emphasize exactly how the competition measures up. Be sure you're telling the truth. You can only knock your competition if you're presenting facts against facts vs. opinions against opinions.

42. Prove your superiority with facts or with graphics or with both.

43. Buy new customers by making an exceptional offer.

44. Demonstrate your own confidence in your offering. If people see that you're advertising, they believe you're confident in your product. If they see you're not advertising, that makes them question whether you have the confidence.

45. Become part of your community or your industry.

46. Put yourself on the level of others.

47. Create reprints for your other marketing. You run the ad once and then you make reprints of it that you use many, many times over many, many years.

48. To be seen with the right crowd. As I say, you're known by the company you keep, and if you're advertising where the right crowd advertises, you become part of that right crowd and you stand above them because of your competitive advantages.

49. Show support for your reps, your distributors, your employees.

50. Earn a profit, which is the underlying reason for the other 49.

10 Things Your Copy Should Always Be

1. Readable
2. Informative
3. Clear

4. Honest
5. Simple
6. Strategic
7. Motivating
8. Competitive
9. Specific
10. Believable

The most well-rounded people who create advertising think of themselves not as writers, not art directors, and not as video producers. Instead they think of themselves as admakers, giving full emphasis to the full spectrum of advertising. The ones who lean the most on dynamite graphics occasionally dynamite themselves in the foot with innocent mistakes.

10 Things Never To Do with Guerrilla Graphics

1. Don't let the art overpower the idea.
2. Don't let the art overpower the headline.
3. Don't let the art overpower the copy.
4. Don't let the art fail to advance the sale.
5. Don't let the art fail to grab casual readers or viewers. Most readers or viewers are casuals. They're not really paying attention to what you have to say.
6. Don't let the art fail to get the ad or the spot noticed.
7. Don't let the art fail to be different.
8. Don't let the art be created in a hurry. Guerrillas are never in a hurry.
9. Don't let the art fight the product identity.
10. Don't let the art dominate the ad. The idea should dominate the ad.

Don't let the art overpower the idea.

10 / Guerrilla Advertising

At this point, it might be helpful to recognize the fatal symptoms of a misguided advertising campaign. We could take a month to write the 2,500 reasons why a heap of advertising is flat out unsuccessful, but all our time being what it is, we can only warn you about the top 25.

25 Reasons Why So Much Advertising Fails

1. *Premature abandonment.* People create the right ad, put it in the right place, say the right things to the right people. But they expect results to happen too fast and so they abandon what could have been a killer campaign.
2. *Silly positioning.* People position their products in the wrong way to begin with. Nothing good will happen if you start out with silly positioning.
3. *Failure to focus.* People are trying to say everything to everybody instead of saying something to somebody.
4. *Starting without a plan.* It's amazing how many advertisements are created by art directors or writers that don't really have a plan for how to proceed.
5. *Picking the wrong media for the right audience.*
6. *Picking the right media for the wrong audience.*
7. *Message is unclear to the real prospect.*
8. *Not understanding the target.* The person who creates the advertising doesn't really understand the customers or the prospects.
9. *Not understanding the source.* The person who creates the advertising doesn't really understand themselves or their businesses.
10. *Exaggeration.* This technique undermines the real truth.
11. *Doesn't keep up with change.*
12. *Unrealistic expectations.* The advertiser should know what to expect.

13. *Overspending on production or underspending on media.*

14. *Trying to save money in the wrong places.* Why save a few hundred dollars in production if you're going to spend thousands of dollars in media and the production will undermine what you have said and done?

15. *Inattention to tiny, but powerful, details.*

16. *Advertisers missing the point about profitability.*

17. *Thinking that it can be done without hard work.*

18. *Unimpressive first impressions.* You only get a chance to make a first impression once, and if it's not impressive you have dug a hole you may never climb out of.

19. *Committees and layers of management.* In my experience, I have never seen a committee or layer of management create a great ad, but I've certainly seen them kill many good ads.

20. *Advertisers not using media to their greatest advantage.* The advantage of newspapers is the news. The advantage of TV is demonstration. The advantage of radio is intimacy. The advantage of magazines is reader involvement. The advantage of the internet is interactivity. The advantage of direct response is urgency. The advantage of telemarketing is customer rapport. If you don't understand the greatest advantage of each of these types of marketing and use the media to their greatest advantages, your advertising will fail.

21. *No support with other marketing.* You know that advertising alone doesn't work.

22. *It starts out in the wrong direction.*

23. *Too much early success.* People allow their first successful ads to instill a sense of lethargy in them, and that lethargy allows them to just rest on their laurels and not improve their advertising.

24. *Judging the future by the past.* You cannot do that.

25. *It's just plain boring.*

Regional Editions

Magazine ads give you more credibility than other marketing media. I'm going to try to talk you into running a full-page in a national magazine such as *Time*. Let's first make you realize that a full-page ad in *Time* magazine costs a national advertiser somewhere in the area of $90,000.

> *Magazine ads give you more credibility than other marketing media.*

However, we don't want you to spend that much money. We also want you to know that real big companies use magazine ads because they know the importance of regularly running ads.

But guerrillas, in this case, run their magazine ad only once and know there are regional editions of magazines. Let's say you live in San Francisco. You don't want to spend $90,000 for a full-page magazine ad in *Time* magazine that's going to appear all over America.

You can appear in a regional edition of *Time* magazine, let's say the San Francisco region. Now that ad costs just a few thousand dollars. The people reading *Time* magazine don't know about regional editions for ads; they just know that in the magazine they see a full-page ad for Rolls Royce. On the next page, they see a full-page ad for Microsoft. On the next page they see a full-page ad for you.

Well, you're known by the company you keep, and so *Time* readers begin thinking new thoughts about your company because of that

> *You can appear in a regional edition of Time magazine.*

magazine ad. You're not going to make much money from that ad running one time, but you are going to make a fortune from the reprints of that ad.

The reprints of that ad cost just pennies. They say at the bottom of them, "As advertised in *Time* magazine." And you can use them for many years. *Time* makes them available to you in the form of self-mailers, in the form of

BREAKING THE BANK 20 YEARS AFTER THE AD RUNS

So we were telling this story to a client in San Francisco in the early 1970s, and he says, "Wait a second, you tell me that if I run a full-page ad in *Time* I'm not going to make any money when the ad runs? I'm going to make a lot of money on the reprints?" And we said, "That's exactly right."

He said, "OK, well, where's the cheapest edition of *Time* magazine in the country?" And we said, "Savannah, Georgia." He said, "How much?" We said, "$700." He said, "Let's run there." So he ran a full-page ad for his San Francisco furniture store in the Savannah, Georgia, edition of *Time* magazine.

The punch line to this story occurs 20 years later when he did mailings to 20,000 people enclosing a copy of his magazine ad that says "as advertised in *Time* magazine." He broke the bank with that mailing because of the enormous credibility that he received from that one magazine ad.

posters, in the form of laminated reprints, so the magazine ads could work for you for many, many years.

When you use a magazine ad like this, one that you plan to run once and then use the reprints of for many years, make it a timeless ad. Don't say silly things like, "Our company is five years old" because next year when your company is six years old, you'll need a new ad. Instead, say the year your company was founded because that will never go out of date.

Never show pictures of your employees in the ad because you don't know, maybe next month one of your employees may get busted for selling crack.

What you want to do is run an ad that will be so timeless you can use it for the next decade. That's what guerrillas do.

Foreground vs. Background

Radio is the most intimate of all the marketing media. Guerrillas divide radio stations into foreground radio and background radio. They know that foreground radio requires active listening. People are listening to it intentionally, and they're paying attention—news shows, talk shows, sports shows, religious shows. These

> *Radio is the most intimate of all the marketing media.*

shows are perfect examples of foreground radio, and people listen even to the commercials on foreground radio. Music radio stations are background radio. Easy to target your audience that way but hard to get them to listen to the commercials; they're listening to those radio stations for the music and don't notice the ads so much. You can listen to all the background radio you want, but you'll probably get the maximum bang for your radio buck with foreground radio.

10 Things that Make a TV Ad Terrible

1. The TV commercial is more entertaining than it is motivating.
2. Not clear with its promise.
3. Not visual. It depends on words, and you know how many people mute those words with their remote control.
4. Too amateurish, homemade, lacking in credibility.
5. It's high pressure or very exaggerative.
6. A fabulous film but a terrible commercial. These days a lot of ads on television are wonderful films but horrible advertising. You've got to strain all your mind to determine who is running this commercial. And that's not what the game should be.
7. So clever, you forget who ran the ad.
8. So wrapped up in special effects it's devoid of an idea.

9. Too complex for an idea to come shining through.
10. Boring, boring, boring.

10 Things that Make a TV Commercial Superb

1. More motivating than entertaining.
2. Very clear about its competitive advantage.
3. Intensely visual.
4. Professional-looking.
5. Believable and compelling.
6. Powerful because it creates a desire to buy the product.
7. Focused on advancing the sale, not on being clever.
8. Wrapped up with the product.
9. Demonstrates the benefits.
10. Fascinating, even the 10th time you see it.

The Dangers of Humor in Marketing

A good joke is very funny the first time that you see it. It's a little bit less funny the second time you see it. The third time you see it, it's not funny at all. The fourth time you see it, it becomes grating. After that, it starts turning you off of the product. Guerrilla advertising is fascinating the 10th time you see it, the 20th time you see it. You never get tired of it. But with humor, you get tired of the joke very fast.

Top 100 Advertising Campaigns

1. Volkswagen, "Think small," Doyle Dane Bernbach, 1959
2. Coca-Cola, "The pause that refreshes," D'Arcy Co., 1940
3. Marlboro, "The Marlboro Man," Leo Burnett Co., 1955
4. Nike, "Just do it," Wieden & Kennedy, 1988
5. McDonald's, "You deserve a break today," Needham, Harper & Steers, 1971

6. DeBeers, "A diamond is forever," N.W. Ayer & Son, 1948

7. Absolut Vodka, "The Absolut Bottle," TBWA, 1981

8. Miller Lite beer, "Tastes great, less filling," McCann-Erickson Worldwide, 1974

9. Clairol, "Does she...or doesn't she?" Foote, Cone & Belding, 1957

10. Avis, "We try harder," Doyle Dane Bernbach, 1963

11. Federal Express, "Fast talker," Ally & Gargano, 1982

12. Apple Computer, "1984," Chiat/Day, 1984

13. Alka-Seltzer, "Various ads," Jack Tinker & Partners; Doyle Dane Bernbach; Wells Rich, Greene, 1960s, 1970s

14. Pepsi-Cola, "Pepsi-Cola hits the spot," Newell-Emmett Co., 1940s

15. Maxwell House, "Good to the last drop," Ogilvy, Benson & Mather, 1959

16. Ivory Soap, "99 and 44/100 percent pure," Procter & Gamble Co., 1982

17. American Express, "Do you know me?" Ogilvy & Mather, 1975

18. U.S. Army, "Be all that you can be," N.W. Ayer & Son, 1981

19. Anacin, "Fast, fast, fast relief," Ted Bates & Co., 1952

20. Rolling Stone, "Perception. Reality," Fallon McElligott Rice, 1985

21. Pepsi-Cola, "The Pepsi generation," Batton, Barton, Durstine & Osborn, 1964

22. Hathaway shirts, "The man in the Hathaway shirt," Hewitt, Ogilvy, Benson & Mather, 1951

23. Burma-Shave, "Roadside signs in verse," Allen Odell, 1925

24. Burger King, "Have it your way," BBDO, 1973

25. Campbell Soup, "Mmm, mmm good," BBDO, 1930s

26. U.S. Forest Service, Smokey the Bear, "Only you can prevent forest fires," Advertising Council/Foote, Cone & Belding

27. Budweiser, "This Bud's for You," D'Arcy Masius Benton & Bowles, 1970s

28. Maidenform, "I dreamed I went shopping in my Maidenform bra," Norman, Craig & Kummel, 1949

29. Victor Talking Machine Co., "His master's voice," Francis Barraud, 1901

30. Jordan Motor Car Co., "Somewhere west of Laramie," Edward S. (Ned) Jordan, 1923

31. Woodbury Soap, "The skin you love to touch," J. Walter Thompson Co., 1911

32. Benson & Hedges 100s, "The disadvantages," Wells, Rich, Greene, 1960s

33. National Biscuit Co., "Uneeda Biscuits' Boy in Boots," N.W. Ayer & Son, 1899

34. Energizer, "The Energizer Bunny," Chiat/Day, 1989

35. Morton Salt, "When it rains it pours," N.W. Ayer & Son, 1912

36. Chanel, "Share the fantasy," Doyle Dane Bernbach, 1979

37. Saturn, "A different kind of company. A different kind of car," Hal Riney & Partners, 1989

38. Crest Toothpaste, "Look, Ma! No cavities!" Benton & Bowles, 1958

39. M&Ms, "Melts in your mouth, not in your hands," Ted Bates & Co., 1954

40. Timex, "Takes a licking and keeps on ticking," W.B. Doner & Co & predecessor agencies, 1950s

41. Chevrolet, "See the USA in your Chevrolet," Campbell-Ewald, 1950s

42. Calvin Klein, "Know what comes between me and my Calvins? Nothing!"

43. Reagan for President, "It's morning again in America," Tuesday Team, 1984

44. Winston cigarettes, "Winston tastes good—like a cigarette should," 1954

45. U.S. School of Music, "They laughed when I sat down at the piano, but when I started to play!" Ruthrauff & Ryan, 1925

46. Camel Cigarettes, "I'd walk a mile for a Camel," N. W. Ayer & Son, 1921

47. Wendy's, "Where's the beef?" Dancer-Fitzgerald-Sample, 1984

48. Listerine, "Always a bridesmaid, but never a bride," Lambert & Feasley, 1923

49. Cadillac, "The penalty of leadership," MacManus, John & Adams, 1915

50. Keep America Beautiful, "Crying Indian," Advertising Council/Marstellar Inc., 1971

51. Charmin, "Please don't squeeze the Charmin," Benton & Bowles, 1964

52. Wheaties, "Breakfast of champions," Blackett-Sample-Hummert, 1930s

53. Coca-Cola, "It's the real thing," McCann-Erickson, 1970

54. Greyhound, "It's such a comfort to take the bus and leave the driving to us," Grey Advertising, 1957

55. Kellogg's Rice Krispies, "Snap! Crackle! and Pop!" Leo Burnett Co., 1940s

56. Polaroid, "It's so simple," Doyle Dane Bernbach, 1977

57. Gillette, "Look sharp, feel sharp," BBDO, 1940s

58. Levy's Rye Bread, "You don't have to be Jewish to love Levy's Rye Bread," Doyle Dane Bernbach, 1949

59. Pepsodent, "You'll wonder where the yellow went," Foote, Cone & Belding, 1956

60. Lucky Strike Cigarettes, "Reach for a Lucky instead of a sweet," Lord & Thomas, 1920s

61. 7 UP, "The Uncola," J. Walter Thompson, 1970s

62. Wisk detergent, "Ring around the collar," BBDO, 1968

63. Sunsweet prunes, "Today the pits, tomorrow the wrinkles," Freberg Ltd., 1970s

64. Life cereal, "Hey, Mikey," Doyle Dane Bernbach, 1972

65. Hertz, "Let Hertz put you in the driver's seat," Norman, Craig & Kummel, 1961

66. Foster Grant, "Who's that behind those Foster Grants?" Geer, Dubois, 1965

67. Perdue Chicken, "It takes a tough man to make tender chicken," Scali, McCabe, Sloves, 1971

68. Hallmark, "When you care enough to send the very best," Foote, Cone & Belding, 1930s

69. Springmaid Sheets, "A buck well spent," In-house, 1948

70. Queensboro Corp., "Jackson Heights Apartment Homes," WEAF, NYC, 1920s

71. Steinway & Sons, "The instrument of the immortals," N.W. Ayer & Sons, 1919

72. Levi's Jeans, "501 Blues," Foote, Cone & Belding, 1984

73. Blackglama-Great Lakes Mink, "What becomes a legend most?" Jane Trahey Associates, 1960s

74. Blue Nun Wine, "Stiller & Meara campaign," Della Famina, Travisano & Partners, 1970s

75. Hamm's Beer, "From the land of sky blue waters," Campbell-Mithun, 1950s

76. Quaker Puffed Wheat, "Shot from guns," Lord & Thomas, 1920s

77. ESPN Sports, "This is SportsCenter," Wieden & Kennedy, 1995

78. Molson Beer, "Laughing couple," Moving & Talking Picture Co., 1980s

79. California Milk Processor Board, "Got Milk?" 1993

80. AT&T, "Reach out and touch someone," N.W. Ayer, 1979

81. Brylcreem, "A little dab'll do ya," Kenyon & Eckhardt, 1950s

82. Carling Black Label Beer, "Hey Mabel, Black Label!" Lang, Fisher & Stashower, 1940s

83. Isuzu, "Lying Joe Isuzu," Della Famina, Travisano & Partners, 1980s

84. BMW, "The ultimate driving machine," Ammirati & Puris, 1975

85. Texaco, "You can trust your car to the men who wear the star," Benton & Bowles, 1940s
86. Coca-Cola, "Always," Creative Artists Agency, 1993
87. Xerox, "It's a miracle," Needham, Harper & Steers, 1975
88. Bartles & Jaymes, "Frank and Ed," Hal Riney & Partners, 1985
89. Dannon Yogurt, "Old People in Russia," Marstellar Inc., 1970s
90. Volvo, "Average life of a car in Sweden," Scali, McCabe, Sloves, 1960s
91. Motel 6, "We'll leave a light on for you," Richards Group, 1988
92. Jell-O, "Bill Cosby with kids," Young & Rubicam, 1975
93. IBM, "Chaplin's Little Tramp character," Lord, Geller, Federico, Einstein, 1982
94. American Tourister, "The Gorilla," Doyle, Dane Bernbach, late 1960s
95. Right Guard, "Medicine Cabinet," BBDO, 1960s
96. Maypo, "I want my Maypo," Fletcher, Calkins & Holden, 1960s
97. Bufferin, "Pounding heartbeat," Young & Rubicam, 1960
98. Arrow Shirts, "My friend, Joe Holmes, is now a horse," Young & Rubicam, 1938
99. Young & Rubicam, "Impact," Young & Rubicam, 1930
100. Lyndon Johnson for President, "Daisy," Doyle Dane Bernbach, 1964

Top 10 Slogans of the Century

1. Diamonds are forever (DeBeers)
2. Just do it (Nike)
3. The pause that refreshes (Coca-Cola)
4. Tastes great, less filling (Miller Lite)

5. We try harder (Avis)
6. Good to the last drop (Maxwell House)
7. Breakfast of champions (Wheaties)
8. Does she . . . or doesn't she? (Clairol)
9. When it rains it pours (Morton Salt)
10. Where's the beef? (Wendy's)

Honorable Mentions

- Look Ma, no cavities! (Crest toothpaste)
- Let your fingers do the walking (Yellow Pages)
- Loose lips sink ships (public service)
- M&Ms melt in your mouth, not in your hand (M&M candies)
- We bring good things to life (General Electric)

Top 10 Jingles of the 20th Century

1. You deserve a break today (McDonald's)
2. Be all that you can be (U.S. Army)
3. Pepsi Cola Hits the Spot (Pepsi-Cola)
4. Mmm, mmm good (Campbell)
5. See the USA in your Chevrolet (GM)
6. I wish I was an Oscar Mayer Wiener (Oscar Mayer)
7. Double your pleasure, double your fun (Wrigley's Doublemint gum)
8. Winston tastes good like a cigarette should (Winston)
9. It's the real thing (Coca-Cola)
10. A little dab'll do ya (Brylcreem)

Top 10 Advertising Icons of the Century

Some of the best-loved ad images of the 20th century have names like Tony, Betty, and Ronald. Others, like the Marlboro Man, may not be as beloved, but grew to have tremendous worldwide impact such as the instant identifier of Philip Morris Co.'s Marlboro cigarettes.

From frozen vegetables to packaged cake mix, from fast food to automobile tires, these carefully drawn characters are the personifications of businesses that began small but grew to become dominant brands in their fields—thanks in large part to their famous icons.

Many of the most famous ad icons were the brainchild of one agency: Chicago-based Leo Burnett Co., under the creative direction of people like Jay Conrad Levinson, who specialized in building brands through the use of enormously popular characters, including the most effective marketing icon of all time, the Marlboro Man.

Advertising Age's list of the Top 10 ad icons of the 20th century recognizes those images that have had the most powerful resonance in the marketplace. The criteria include effectiveness, longevity, recognizability, and cultural impact.

1. The Marlboro Man, Marlboro cigarettes
2. Ronald McDonald, McDonald's restaurants
3. The Green Giant, Green Giant vegetables
4. Betty Crocker, Betty Crocker food products
5. The Energizer Bunny, Eveready Energizer batteries
6. The Pillsbury Doughboy, assorted Pillsbury foods
7. Aunt Jemima, Aunt Jemima pancake mixes and syrup
8. The Michelin Man, Michelin tires
9. Tony the Tiger, Kellogg's Sugar Frosted Flakes
10. Elsie, Borden dairy products

chapter 11

Guerrilla Marketing in the Social Media

A S SHANE GIBSON, WHO CO-AUTHORED *Guerrilla Social Media Marketing* with me, says: Marketing now belongs to everyone, and everyone must be equipped and engaged in the social media space. Your customer with two tweets, a video blog, and a Facebook status update can do more good or harm to your brand than one of your well-planned marketing campaigns.

The guerrilla social media marketing path is one that is blazed with a keen focus on community, innovation, engagement, and, most importantly, profit. The guerrilla path has a beginning, but unless you sell your business or retire, it has no ending. It is a way of doing business and engaging the marketplace that drives real, long-term business results.

Although the path is not easy, if you master and implement what you learn in this book it will be almost impossible for you to

> *Marketing now belongs to everyone, and everyone must be equipped and engaged in the social media space.*

> "The internet is just a world passing around notes in a classroom."
>
> —Jon Stewart

fail. Anyone can become a successful guerrilla social media marketer, but they must commit to the personal transformation and work that is necessary to get there.

Beyond attitudes, marketing weapons, and plans, you must have the right personality traits to become successful. The rewards are huge.

The 10 Personality Traits of a Guerrilla Social Media Marketer

1. Immunity to Hype

There is a lot of hype around social media. The guerrilla searches for truth, verifies information, and executes with dependable tools and strategies. With so many people blasting Twitter updates, sending Facebook messages, and posting blog entries, it's easy to get caught up in the excitement of a new product, tool, or market and dive in headfirst. Here's why guerrillas don't fall into this trap:

Your customer with two tweets, a video blog, and a Facebook status update can do more good or harm to your brand than one of your well-planned marketing campaigns.

- Any new, social media marketing tool or community takes time, energy, and resources to effectively test and evaluate.
- Great technology alone doesn't mean a marketing tool is worth investing in. The tool must be backed by a great company and have the potential for longevity.

- While you chase every trend and new tool, you neglect communities and marketing tools that need focus and commitment to get a long-term return on your investment.
- Hype is a sign that something is broadly used. Guerrillas look for opportunities to have the first-mover advantage instead of following the herd.

Take these steps to protect yourself from the hype:

- Watch other guerrillas and innovators who cater to your target market. What is their feedback in relation to the new technology or tool?
- Look for hard data on the tool, product, or technology. Get your data from multiple sources to confirm accuracy. Forrester Research, MarketingProfs.com (http://www.marketingprofs.com), or your local chapter of the Social Media Club are good places to find accurate information.
- Check the credibility of those who claim to be having success with the technology. Are they profitable? Is what they are doing sustainable and scalable?
- Remember, a good marketing attack takes months or even years to be fully effective. Be careful about jumping from idea to idea without allowing ideas time to mature. The latest thing may not be the most effective thing for your business.

2. Curiosity

Sir Alexander Fleming of Scotland discovered penicillin serendipitously. He was observing staphylococcus and looking for a way to battle this bacteria without harming people's immune system. A not-so-organized Fleming stacked unwashed petri dishes in the sink. He went away on a brief trip, and over this time, several mold cultures grew in and around some of the petri dishes.

Somehow the mold and the staphylococcus were mixed by accident, and Fleming discovered that this fungus was able kill the bacteria. This serendipitous event led to the discovery of penicillin, which has now saved millions of lives. Fleming was constantly trying new things and asking "Why?" and "What if?" Guerrillas aren't afraid to experiment, make mistakes, or try new things to gain a competitive advantage. Like Alexander Fleming, guerrillas need to be willing to combine different elements of marketing and strategy in a creative fashion. They then need to be curious when new and exciting or even unexpected results arise. They also investigate, measure, and document the results so they can replicate the results on a grand scale.

Some "what if?" and "I wonder" questions that a curious guerrilla could ask:

- What if I started giving more reports away for free online?
- What if I blogged five times a week but decreased my length of entry to no more than 200 words?
- I wonder what would happen if I asked Guy Kawasaki to do a guest blog on our site?
- I wonder if it would increase reader retention if I had my podcasts transcribed and posted in my blog?
- What if I asked my readers to contribute content to our blog and rewarded them for doing so?
- I wonder why fewer people blog on the weekends? Is there an opportunity in this?

Ask yourself, "What if I gave 144,000 copies of my book away for free online?" The answer for guerrilla Chris Anderson was a rapid and sustained *New York Times* and Amazon.com best-seller status.

3. The Ability to Sprint

Guerrillas are always ready to exploit small windows of opportunity with all their energy, passion, and resources. The world and the internet move very fast. Sometimes marketing and business opportunities come quickly. Being at the right place at the right time is only one part of the formula. Being prepared and ready to take advantage of these opportunities is the magic ingredient in the formula for success.

Here are ways you can make sure you are ready to sprint:

- Have a plan in place and a team ready in the event that one of your marketing attacks goes viral; make sure your business is scalable for increased demand.
- Be prepared to pull a 24-hour shift or a 14-day work shift when a huge opportunity hits. Once you have momentum, capitalize on it. Things will eventually slow down and you can rest then.
- Things can go south in social media. Sometimes sprinting is about quickly and aggressively dealing with an onslaught of negative feedback or news. Taking 24 hours or even two hours to respond to customer complaints or competitive slander is too long. Be ready to respond immediately and stomp out those brand-burning fires.

4. The Ability to Run Marathons

Many battles are battles of attrition. Guerrillas know how to wear their competition down and build a presence through consistency. One of the biggest costs in marketing is not running bad campaigns or promotions; it's quitting on good campaigns and marketing attacks too soon. The ability to run marathons has many aspects. Guerrillas must:

- Have a long-term plan that goes beyond a monthly or quarterly focus.
- Follow a a marketing calendar daily.
- Focus on business goals and don't get distracted or enamored by the latest technology.
- Understand that a customer may need to be exposed to a message 27 times before brand recognition starts. Frequency and adding value will win hearts and mind-share and therefore wallet-share over time.

- Understand that it's easy to become bored with a social media technology when it becomes familiar. You will be the first person to tire of your blog, Twitter activity, or Google Buzz account. But exciting and effective aren't always synonymous. Focus on what works and what is profitable and don't worry about the cool factor that most early adopters fall victim to.

5. Transparency

Guerrillas know that truth, empathy, and integrity are keys to social media marketing, and they build trust and loyalty through transparency. In the past we could live dual lives as marketers, CEOs, and even citizens. Today we are on stage 24 hours a day. Everyone is armed with a smartphone, video capture devices, and the ability to post information about us and what we are up to.

Guerrilla social media marketers must be transparent, open, and community-focused. Today, trust and credibility are our currencies, especially in regard to those we are connected to in social networks and communities online.

Guerrilla transparency means:

- Thinking before we post content online. Make sure it's true and accurate because people will find any untruths or half-truths, often immediately.
- Being open about business practices and policies and not hiding behind the fine print in our customer agreements. Customers no longer tell 11 friends when they feel like they have been misled; they tell their 10,000 Twitter friends. Secrecy and legal cleverness can become brand killers.
- Be your own true self. Guerrillas know that people buy from people. They want an emotional and personal connection with their suppliers and business connections. They allow their true colors and personality to shine online.

6. Community-Focused

A guerrilla builds, connects, and helps the community. Within that community are other guerrilla allies that will become their assets. Social media marketing is 90 percent community, contribution, and connection. Only 10 percent is about targeted, relevant marketing to people who want and need what you have to offer NOW. By contributing great content and helping customers and members of the community achieve their dreams and goals, you can become successful.

If you're new to social media or have just joined a new social network, take your time. Guerrillas get to know a community; they want to determine what its values and etiquette are, and they also make a concerted effort to identify the key influencers in that community.

After getting in sync with the community, the goal is to become noticed and build your brand through contribution and value. This can come in many forms:

- Finding influencers in the community and helping them promote a project, product or cause they are connected to. Influence those who influence others.
- Providing value-added content such as white papers, studies, tips, free webinars, podcasts, or other business or personal development tools.
- Providing opportunities for other people in the community to connect, collaborate, or do business with each other.
- Introducing more people to the network or community. After we have connected with the community, built rapport, and really developed an understanding of the distinct needs, values, and preferences of the group, we can then plan and launch a relevant, focused, on-target guerrilla marketing attack. Too many marketers skip the community-building stage and jump right into blasting marketing messages off to audiences that are unreceptive.

Guerrillas value and understand community. They take time to really understand and connect with their market.

7. Profit-Driven

Guerrilla marketing measures success by profits, not clicks, visitors, or any cool factor. Many people mistake popularity for profitability. There are a lot of bloggers, Twitter celebrities, and YouTube video moguls who will wow people with their 30,000 followers, 10,000 blog subscribers, or 50,000 video views.

These are important and exciting statistics, but they mean very little to guerrillas unless they create profit or a net positive action. These subscribers, friends, or views have to eventually turn into something. Many companies will boast about their revenues; far fewer boast about profit, and profit is what guerrilla marketing is all about.

There are many self-proclaimed experts in social media who will show you how to get lots of followers, fans, and subscribers. Be wary of these promises. You must value your time and effort and measure your success in terms of profit, not gross sales, or the fact that you are seen as cool or popular.

Guerrillas also use new media technologies to reduce fixed costs and automate business processes. Fancy offices, expensive parking spaces, and nice addresses are hallmarks of things that used to signify success. Successful people also used to boast about how busy they were.

Guerrillas know that today it is about maximizing success while minimizing the impact on your time and overall costs. They are constantly looking for ways to produce a high-quality product or service while automating, outsourcing, or delegating costly activities that impact their most valuable asset—time.

8. Tech-Hungry

Technology is the guerrilla social media marketer's core weapon and competency. They are always learning more about technology. Today's world of business has no place for technophobes. Technophobia will be the demise of many companies and industries over the next decade. It is absolutely necessary to immerse yourself fully into all things tech and study it like your life depends on it. Understanding technology and all of its applications to business better and sooner than your competitors is vital.

9. Self-Developer

Guerrillas know that technology and business move fast. They are constantly learning more to stay ahead of the competition. Because social media makes us highly visible, our actions, business strategy, and innovation will attract a lot of emulators. Our customers and prospects online are also constantly evolving in regard to how they use the social web. You need to constantly be learning and looking for trends and changes in how technology is being used.

You cannot afford to wait for your human resource department to hold a training seminar. We often can't wait for industry experts to compile all the data we needed to make the perfect decision. To maintain a competitive lead, guerrillas must learn, research, experiment, and innovate on the fly.

Einstein was arguably the most accomplished self-developer of the 20th century. He would set a large goal or objective, something that many others wouldn't dare to even hypothesize about. Then he would work diligently toward proving his theory. When he would get stuck or get out of his depth of knowledge he would inventory what specialized knowledge and insight he would need.

Einstein would then totally commit himself to mastering the concept. His ability to completely focus on learning a new competency or field of science quickly and in great depth is what made him a master. Guerrillas often start with a big goal, a plan, and only part of the resources they need to reach that goal. When they get stuck, or come across a challenge, they don't back off or try an easier route. They inventory what they need to learn or discover to take the next step and they intensely focus on that competency until they master it.

Sometimes it means partnering with other guerrillas, but many times when you're breaking new ground in the social media space you will need to innovate and experiment with new approaches and disciplines. Being a self-developer means you can evolve at a rate much faster than the rest of the marketplace.

10. Leadership Mentality

Social media is more of a leadership game than a marketing game.

Guerrillas observe the community and gather intelligence, but they are always thinking about what is next. They create trends and unique solutions and are thought leaders. Think leadership and engagement versus branding and pitching.

The term social media marketing is misleading. It's often seen as a tool or tactic. A lot of people mistakenly see social media and social networks as distribution channels for their clever marketing and branding campaigns. But that is only one layer of the social media.

Tips for Becoming a Guerrilla Geek

- Join www.Meetup.com and look for groups that get together and share information on emerging trends and technology. Many major cities have an abundance of these groups. Some others you may want to join are:
  - *Blogger meetups.* Bloggers share information on the latest blogging tools, applications, automation techniques, traffic-building strategies, and best practices for creating content.
  - *Flickr and photography meetups.* These groups discuss almost everything you need to know about digital photography and image capture devices.
  - *Apple and Mac meetups.* Apple makes some of the top social media tech tools. These are great groups to help you ramp up quickly with all the uses for Apple products in social media.

- *Video meetups*. These groups usually focus on best practices in shooting video, producing video, editing, and even distribution and marketing.
- *Internet search engine and marketing meetups*. These groups discuss and share insights on everything from ranking well on Google to effective shopping cart design.
- *New media marketing meetups*. Most cities will have more than one of these groups. They are great places to meet other guerrillas and share best practices in social media marketing.
- *Local Social Media Club*. The world's largest social media association was founded by Chris Heuer in July of 2006. He started Social Media Club in order to help professionalize the industry and share best practices and ethical issues surrounding social media. One of its other core mandates is to expand media literacy globally.

- Devote time each day to reading selected blogs and listening to podcasts about technology and global business trends. Some great blogs and resources online include:

  - *www.Technorati.com*. This site rates and indexes the top blogs on the internet. The tech category lists the most popular and current tech news from thousands of blogs on the internet.
  - *www.PostRank.com*. This site rates blogs by engagement score, taking into account comments, tweets, links, and social bookmarking to rank how engaged people are with the blog. It lists the top social media and technology blogs and updates their rankings by the day.
  - *www.iTunes.com*. There are literally dozens of high-quality podcasts (audio downloads) on iTunes. You will need to download iTunes software for your PC or Mac. Once loaded, click on the iTunes store button and then click on podcasts. You can search by keyword or browse by category. You will be able to find and subscribe to dozens of free tech podcasts.

- Wired *magazine*. *Wired* has both a network of blogs and a print magazine. It covers everything from mainstream tech trends to the off-the-wall inventions and is a great source for new ideas, trends, and insights.
- *Attend social media and tech gadget conferences.* Attending seminars and rubbing elbows with bona fide social media geeks can help reduce your learning curve. You can often pick up tips, tricks, and insights in a much shorter time than you would by digging for the information online.
- *Start associating with people who have good tech knowledge.* They don't necessarily have to be guerrillas; it would be your job to take the tech insight you learn from them and apply guerrilla principles to the knowledge. Peer mentoring and learning through modeling successful or knowledgeable people is vital. Observe, listen, and watch what these people do.
- *Follow and connect with people who are in the tech space on Twitter, Facebook, LinkedIn, Google Buzz, and any other platform you can find them on.* Often they will tweet or post status updates about new and exciting technology and even provide insight into great blogs, conferences, and resources.

THE 10 PERSONALITY TRAITS OF A GUERRILLA SOCIAL MEDIA MARKETER

1. Immunity to hype
2. Curiosity
3. The ability to sprint
4. The ability to run marathons
5. Transparency
6. Community-focused
7. Profit-driven
8. Tech-hungry
9. Self-developer
10. Leadership mentality

chapter 12

Guerrilla Marketing with Memes

IT WAS ONCE THOUGHT THAT ALL BUSINESSES required a logo because points made to the eye are 78 percent more effective than points made to the ear. Today, guerrillas know that you need much more than a logo. You need a meme. And what exactly is a meme? The answer is found in pre-history.

UBA THE CAVEMAN

The prehistoric man, Uba, spent all day in the drizzling rain trying to catch a fish because his family desperately needed food. But Uba couldn't take hold of a fish from the stream though he occasionally got his hands on one.

Frustrated and weak from hunger, he just couldn't grab any fish firmly enough because it would slither from his hands and return to the stream. Worse yet, the drizzle turned to a downpour, and Uba was forced to seek shelter in a nearby cave.

When his eyes became accustomed to the dark, he noticed a series of paintings in the cave. One depicted a deer. Another showed a godlike figure.

But it was the third that captured his attention. There on the cave wall was a simple drawing of a man holding a long stick. At the end of the stick, a fish was impaled. Suddenly, Uba got the idea!

Within an hour, he returned to his family carrying five fish, all of which he had caught with a sharpened stick. Uba's family was saved by a meme. His culture was saved by a meme. His entire civilization was saved by a meme.

A meme is a self-explanatory symbol that uses words, action, sounds, or (in this case) pictures to communicate an entire idea. Uba may have discovered history's first meme.

Memes can do a lot more than save a family. Memes can save a business as well and propel it into a high-profit mode. Guerrilla creativity means enlisting the wondrous power of memes in your marketing.

What you don't know about creativity subtracts from your potential profits every year. What you are about to learn will add to your profits—now and forever. It's something as foreign to you as the internet was back in the 1970s—but every bit as important as the internet when it comes to your company's profitability.

Creativity in marketing is a lot different than creativity in the arts. Memes in marketing are about profits. And guerrilla creativity has at its core a meme. That's why one of the keys to true guerrilla creativity is a meme.

The wheel is a meme. The Green Giant is a meme. You'll become aware of many more memes as you read on, but mainly, you'll discover the astonishing lack of memes in marketing. Bad as this is, it's a great sign for guerrillas.

Guerrilla creativity tells you it's time for your company to have its own meme. Guerrilla creativity suggests that you get in your prospects'

> *A meme is a self-explanatory symbol that uses words, action, sounds, or pictures to communicate an entire idea.*

Memes travel. Memes spread. Memes are viral. In fact, in scientific circles, they're referred to as "mind viruses."

faces with your meme—and your prospects will make it part of their family.

Memes travel. Memes spread. Memes are viral. In fact, in scientific circles, they're referred to as "mind viruses." Memes are simple to create. And memes can goose your company's profitability, not to mention civilization itself.

Memes save you money because they implant a message that gets repeated until people are clear about what you offer so that you don't have to constantly change your marketing campaign. They break through the sensory overload that increases every day. The bigger that overload, the more you need a meme for your company.

Richard Dawkins, an Oxford biologist who coined the word "meme" in 1976 in his book, *The Selfish Gene*, defines it as a basic unit of cultural transmission or imitation. Guerrilla marketers define it as the essence of an idea, expressed as a symbol or set of words, an action or a sound—or all of these.

Memes make perfect partners for marketing campaigns—where ideas must stand apart in an ocean of other ideas and be communicated instantly, or else.

YOU MUST KNOW THREE THINGS ABOUT THE MEME

1. It's the lowest common denominator of an idea, a basic unit of communication.
2. It can alter human behavior, which to a guerrilla means motivating people to buy whatever the guerrilla offers.
3. It is the essence of simplicity, easily understandable without language in a matter of seconds.

Within two seconds memes convey who you are and why someone should buy from you instead of a competitor. They also trigger an emotional response and generate a desire.

The essence of guerrilla creativity is creating marketing that has meme power. Guerrilla creativity is dreaming up a symbol or words, actions or sounds that convey a concept anybody can understand instantly and easily.

The most commonly used memes in the world today are international traffic symbols. In a matter of seconds they tell you, without words, exactly what you're supposed to do.

Your profits will rise if you create for your business a simple meme—then promote it for years, decades, centuries if possible.

Memes can communicate with words (Lean Cuisine), pictures (the Marlboro cowboy), sounds (the jolly ho ho ho of the Green Giant), actions (Clydesdales pulling the Budweiser wagon), or imagery (flames depicting Burger King's flame-broiled hamburgers). Memes have been the architects of human behavior since the beginning of time.

The wheel was a major improvement in transportation and conveyance but was also a meme because it was a self-explanatory symbol representing a complete idea. Once you see a wheel, you immediately know how to use it and why it's so useful. No instructions are needed. Sure, a wagon with wheels carried goods from place to place, but the important thing was that it carried the idea of wheels from mind to mind.

Memes are born through knowledge and research. They work their wonders by enlisting the unconscious minds of your prospects. Although they've been around since the beginning of humankind, and even since the beginning of life on earth (life forms often leave behind meme-like signals such as half-eaten shrubbery, scat, and shells that trigger other life form behavior), memes are relatively new to marketing.

Don't let them be new to you. Take the most visual benefit that you offer and see how you can transform it into a meme. The longer you use it, the stronger it becomes.

chapter 13

Achieving Guerrilla Marketing Excellence

THE THIRD GUERRILLA MARKETING BOOK Jay wrote was different from the first two. Those were devoted to how-to-do-it-marketing; the third was dedicated to showing guerrillas how to do it with excellence. It steers you clear of painful pitfalls while setting you on a course toward increased profits. It helps you avoid contributing to the enormous sum of money that is wasted each year on misguided marketing by well-meaning business owners.

While it's true the guerrilla knows marketing is like a game that can be fun to play, that same guerrilla knows the game is played for real money. So it's no place for kids, amateurs, or phonies. How you think about marketing has a dramatic effect upon how well it works for you. This book is written so you will think about it in ways that will enhance your bottom line.

The topics in *Guerrilla Marketing Excellence*, that third book, aren't part of standard textbook marketing, yet they're far too important to overlook if you're interested in making significant contributions to the profitability of your business. The guidelines in our previous books have been target-directed. The guidelines set by the "50 golden rules" coming right up fine-tune your aim to the center of the bull's-eye.

The advice rendered here appears in the guise of basic home truths, many of which are already part of your own good common sense. But common sense, as we learn daily, isn't all that common. As a guerrilla, it is crucial that you know all these truths. But that's not enough.

You must possess the guerrilla's attitude. That attitude is characterized by the word knowledge. If you have the right knowledge, you won't be tempted to become a rule-breaker, even when your patience is wearing thin. Obviously, it is not a good idea to break a golden rule.

Knowledge of these rules will be reflected in your profits. Practicing them will put teeth into all your marketing by removing any naiveté or nonsensical notions. Knowledge will elevate your marketing expertise and understanding to the point where competitors hold you in awe, prospects are powerfully attracted to your offerings, and customers reciprocate the respect you feel for them in the form of repeat business and enthusiastic referrals. Can it really be that good? For guerrilla marketers it can.

> Some large corporations get around these rules with bottomless bank accounts. But most small businesses don't have the luxury of ignorance and plenitude.

Some large corporations get around these rules with bottomless bank accounts. But most small businesses don't have the luxury of ignorance and plenitude. They must learn what guerrillas know so that each dollar can do the work of many. And they do learn. Plus—guerrillas have the unfair advantages of speed and flexibility.

If anything that appears in these pages goes against your grain or topples any of your idols, we don't apologize, for that's exactly our intention. It means you're getting the point. It means you're learning the rules.

Guerrillas, like Olympic athletes, go for the gold. These golden rules enable you to do the same. They set you up to succeed by indoctrinating you in the nuances of marketing, the small but omnipotent details untouched by most marketing courses, unpracticed by many marketing departments.

If we may be candid for a moment, and let's see you try to stop us, most marketing in America is generally horrible. When you notice a company grow, gain positive word-of-mouth and word-of-mouse, prosper, and continue to succeed, it is very likely because that company is practicing guerrilla marketing's golden rules, consciously or not, and realizes that the rules lead to higher profits and more focused marketing.

The Gap clothing store chain started small, became large, and practiced these rules all along. Many smaller businesses start with little more than knowledge of these rules, become the dominant store in their areas, and manifest an unswerving devotion to the guerrilla's golden rules.

As a guerrilla yourself, or a guerrilla in training, you should know that you've got to be guided by a simple guerrilla marketing strategy, piloted by a guerrilla marketing calendar, and armed with an arsenal brimming with guerrilla marketing weapons—all while living comfortably in two worlds, online and offline.

Those tools, plus knowledge of the upcoming rules, will enable you to take your fair share—or even more if you'd like—from the land of plenty. That's where your prospects hail from—in both lush and lean times. Businesspeople who approach marketing without a framework take wild risks with their marketing even though they sincerely believe they are following a conservative course. What you don't know will hurt you in this arena, and often hurt your prospects and customers at the same time.

Is it important that you know every one of these golden rules? Absolutely. Is it necessary that you follow each rule in all your marketing forays? It is not. But true guerrilla thinkers know the rules they are intentionally breaking rather than breaking them unintentionally and leaving themselves open to disaster.

Of course, the rules are constantly changing. But golden rules contain some fundamental truths that change much more slowly. And some never change at all. How fast does human nature change? There's nothing to lose by knowing these rules. But there's much to lose by being oblivious to them.

The guerrilla business owner who knows these rules knows how to think about marketing, a talent many competitors never develop. Their actions in business are clinics in marketing, indicating their knowledge and perception of the guerrilla approach.

> *True guerrilla thinkers know the rules they are intentionally breaking rather than breaking them unintentionally and leaving themselves open to disaster.*

Guerrilla marketing's 50 golden rules are yours to follow or ignore. Here, they are presented to you without the need for extensive Google time or an MBA with a concentration on marketing. In the pages that immediately follow, rules are given that will make or break a company. It's that simple and that important. Guerrilla marketing's 50 golden rules are yours to follow or ignore. But your company and your future are dependent upon your decision.

50 Golden Rules

Golden Rules to Guide Your THINKING

1. Blessed with the guerrilla's vision, do not seek instant gratification but find your rewards with farsightedness.
2. The ability to accurately define your precise market or markets dramatically affects your profitability.
3. Gear your marketing to people already in the market and know what they really buy other than instant gratification.

4. It is far easier to sell a solution to a problem than to sell a positive benefit.

5. Your own customer list is the best in the world—but only if it bulges with information about each customer.

6. Consistently display your reverence for your customers by trying to help them with consistent follow-up.

7. Design your business to operate for the convenience of your customers and make it very easy to do business with you.

8. Questions lead to answers; answers lead to customer rapport; customer rapport leads to profits.

9. Marketing is always more effective if it is looked upon as sell-time rather than showtime.

10. When introducing new offerings, enthusiastically announce that they're new, then clearly explain why they're good.

11. The more know-how you have about the overall marketing process, the more profits you will earn.

12. Do everything in your power to employ marketing techniques and tactics that are honest beyond reproach.

13. Everything in your marketing should be designed to increase your profits, not merely your sales, but your profits.

Golden Rules to Guide Your EFFECTIVENESS

14. It is easier to achieve a healthy share of market and share of wallet if you first obtain a healthy share of mind.

15. Emphasize the meat and potatoes of your offering rather than the plate upon which they're served.

16. Your marketing has an obligation to capture the attention and hold the interest of as many prospects as possible.

17. Be sure your timing is on; the right marketing to the right people is only right if the timing is right.

18. People will remember the most clever part of your marketing; be sure it pertains directly to what you are selling.

19. Whatever term you use to describe it, the truth remains that everyone loves a bribe—a gift to encourage a response, not a wad of money under the table.

20. The key to marketing economically is not in saving money but in making every investment pay off handsomely.

21. It is easier to get someone to take the hard step of buying if they first take the softer step of requesting more data.

22. Tiny shares of gigantic markets are abundant and profitable if you serve and market to one person at a time.

23. Don't invest money in originality when the investment should be in generating profits.

24. Profits are maximized when you practice innovative marketing and protect yourself from other guerrillas.

25. Market your services successfully by capitalizing upon the bountiful opportunities to create a unique niche.

26. It is possible to have your product sold in almost any store you choose if you use TV marketing for leverage.

27. Marketing will succeed only if time and energy are regularly devoted to it by you or a person you designate.

28. To assure your marketing success in the future, become more oriented to cooperation than competition.

Golden Rules to Guide Your *MARKETING MATERIALS*

29. Identify or create your competitive advantages, then concentrate your marketing upon them.

30. If you have 10 hours to spend creating an ad, spend nine of them on the headline.

31. The right words will propel a great idea toward success; the wrong words will doom a great idea to failure.

32. Realize that everyone to whom you market is a human being first and a customer next.

33. Avoid the use of humor unless it is pertinent to your offering and does not detract from your offer.

34. The believability and persuasion of your marketing increase in direct proportion to how much specific data you provide.

35. Many marketing weapons attain their maximum effectiveness only when combined with other weapons of marketing.

36. Despite the solidity of the guerrilla's commitment to a plan, sometimes a guerrilla's gotta have a gimmick.

37. Let a pro produce your marketing materials because even a hint of amateurishness can lose sales for you.

Golden Rules to Guide Your ACTIONS

38. The more you spy on your competitors, your industry, and yourself, the more opportunities you'll find to improve.

39. Create a path of least resistance to the sale by paving the path with credibility.

40. Don't fix it unless you're absolutely positive it's broken.

41. It is wise to be first in line when your prospect buys, but it is also profitable to be second in line in case whoever is in first messes up somewhere.

42. More companies will fail than succeed in business, and the ones that succeed will be the ones that prove they care.

43. Companies that think of what they can give to people fare better than those that think of what they can take.

44. To network properly, ask questions, listen to answers, and focus on the problems of the people with whom you network.

45. If you're going to pioneer with a new product or service, you must be prepared for walls of apathy and fear.

46. To succeed at marketing during an economic downturn, focus your efforts on existing customers and larger transactions; stress high value more than low price.

47. If you have an especially important client or customer, market to that person in an especially important way.

48. When planning and producing marketing, then evaluating it, operating from a guerrilla calendar is indispensible.

49. Treat sales transactions not as single events, but as starts or continuations of close and lasting relationships; think the same way about your website.

50. If you don't take control of your marketing, your company's future will be in the hands of your competitors; you eat life or life eats you.

Breaking Golden Rules

Although it's inevitable that rules— even golden rules—are broken, it's crucial to know them inside out so you know what you're breaking and why.

When we told our kids the name of this chapter, they said, "Yep, that's what rules are for." Not true. Not these golden rules.

These rules have been formulated to help you improve your business in the form of more profits, which, hopefully, you can translate into less stress and more free time. Following these rules helps you avoid the pitfalls many business owners have fallen into without knowing there were rules to follow in the first place.

As they broke the golden rules, they were unaware that they were doing so. You don't have that convenient excuse. You know the rules. When you break any of them, you'd better have an extremely good reason because these rules were made to be followed—up a continuously rising sales curve and into an entrepreneurial golden nirvana.

> *Although it's inevitable that rules—even golden rules—are broken, it's crucial to know them inside out so you know what you're breaking and why.*

If you're going to break any rules, drive 56 miles per hour, or tear from your mattress that tag that warns of dire consequences if you do. But follow these golden rules, and bear in mind that even though they are bang on target right now, things do change—and some, but not many, of these rules will have to change, too. That's a shame really, because business is so much easier if you have clear rules to follow.

Guerrilla marketing's golden rules offer you that clarity. There's no shilly-shallying around the basic issues. Market like a guerrilla and follow these rules. We never say it will be simple. We never say it will be a joyride. We never say it will be fast. We only say that if you run your company by these golden rules, you'll enjoy more profits and less heartache.

We all realize that there's a lot more to business than marketing. You've got to have those details down pat, or marketing, even guerrilla marketing practiced by these golden rules, can't work its wonders. These rules provide you with many of those details since so much business can come under the heading of marketing. Don't let a little overlapping get in the way of your success.

Given human nature, I suppose you will be tempted, at times knowingly, to break the rules relating to cleverness, restraint, networking, moving slowly, humor, or originality. That's no surprise to us, because during our careers we've seen that these are the most commonly broken rules. But if you break them, we'll bet you don't do it more than once.

"Ouch! That fire was hot! I sure won't put my hand in the flames anymore!" These rules prevent that painful lesson.

It's more unlikely that you'll try meddling with the rules about profits, honesty, being interesting, economizing, proving you care, or achieving credibility. You're too smart for that. If you've read this far in a book about marketing, you're not too likely to disregard rules of such obvious importance. Try to apply the same steadfastness to the golden rules that might present you with more of a challenge to follow.

Now that you understand the deep-down importance of following the rules, we invite you to go out and discover some rules of your own. The internet is still too new for a body of rules. Same for social media. Make some new rules by experimenting with your marketing. Commitment does not preclude your experimentation if the experiments are conducted in test markets.

In fact, guerrilla marketing encourages experimentation and the risk of failed experiments. Don't let cold feet keep you from potentially hot ideas. If you haven't fallen on your face, you probably weren't trying hard enough, or else you were a guerrilla who knew where the obstacles were. Just realize that experimentation does not necessarily mean breaking the rules.

OK, we've made that clear. Now, let us completely change direction and invite you to think about breaking the rules.

Maybe you can come up with a good reason to do it. Then do it! Maybe you want to make an exception to a rule on purpose, and you've clearly thought things through, including the rule.

Our kids said that rules are made to be broken when in fact rules are made to be followed, but also to be questioned. Many of these rules are the answers to questions posed by guerrillas. Many are the result of following the opposite of the rule and meeting constant frustration. Many have been proven through centuries and throughout the world.

We did not invent these rules any more than Moses invented the Ten Commandments. We merely present them to you, along with our counsel to put your faith in them and trust that they will work for you as they have worked for others.

More to the point: Failure to follow these rules has unraveled the companies of many well-meaning business owners, some quite intelligent in the ways of the world but untutored in the ways of the guerrilla.

To do yourself a favor for which you will offer yourself endless gratitude, ask yourself why you are breaking a rule when you do so. If you don't have a good reason, you've got a great reason to follow a rule. Be sure you know you are breaking a rule when you break it. At least you will be acting with purpose rather than with ignorance.

It's hard to imagine a more unfortunate waste of a company's money than to break a golden rule by accident. Do companies waste billions that way every year? Do Rice Krispies snap, crackle, and pop? At least we can take heart that your company won't be guilty of so wasteful an act as negligent as rule breaking.

As these golden rules combine to give you marketing insight, a good thing for a guerrilla who intends to flourish today and in the rest of this century as well as those that follow, consider yourself blessed. An old Chinese proverb says that if you have foresight, you're blessed, but if you have insight, you're a thousand times blessed. To those insights, we add these golden rules.

chapter 14

Guerrilla Marketing Yourself

WHETHER YOU KNOW IT OR NOT, you're marketing yourself every day. And to lots of people. You're marketing yourself in a quest to make a sale, warm up a relationship, get a job, get connected, get something you deserve. You're always sending messages about yourself.

Guerrillas control the messages that they send about themselves. It's all about intention. Guerrillas live intentionally. Non-guerrillas send unintentional messages, even if those messages sabotage their overall goals in life. They want to close a sale for a consulting contract, but their inability to make eye contact or the mumbled message they leave on an answering machine turns off the prospect.

Whether you know it or not, you're marketing yourself every day. And to lots of people. You're always sending messages about yourself.

> "You only have one chance . . .
> to make a good first impression."

Guerrillas Send No Unintentional Messages

Unintentional messages erect an insurmountable barrier. Your job: Be sure there is no barrier. There are really two people within you—your accidental self and your intentional self. Most people are able to conduct about 95 percent of their lives by intent. But that's not enough.

It's the other 5 percent that can get you in trouble—or in clover. I'm not talking phoniness here. The idea is for you to be who you are and not who you aren't—to be aware of what you're doing, aware of whether or not your actions communicate ideas that will help you get what you deserve.

To Whom Do You Market without Even Realizing It?

- Employees
- Customers
- Prospects
- Teachers
- Parents
- Children
- Bosses
- Prospects
- Employers
- Mates
- Prospective mates

THE THREE BIG QUESTIONS TO ANSWER

To market yourself properly, answer these three questions:

1. Who are you now? If friends described you, what would they say? Be honest rather than complimentary.
2. What do you want out of life? Be specific.
3. How will you know when you've reached your goals?

If you can't answer these questions, you're doomed to accidental marketing, spending your life reacting instead of responding, and the odds are against you reaching your goals.

- Friends
- Sellers
- Landlords
- Neighbors
- Professionals
- Members of the community
- The police
- Service people
- Family
- Bankers

These people can help you or stop you from getting what you deserve. You can influence them with how you market yourself.

How do you send messages and market yourself right now?

With your appearance, to be sure. You also market with your eye contact and body language, your habits, your speech patterns. You market yourself in print with your letters, email, websites, notes, faxes, brochures, and other printed material. You also market yourself with your attitude—big time. You market yourself with your ethics.

How People Judge You

Again, you may not be aware of it, but people are constantly judging and assessing you by noticing many things about you. You must be sure the messages of your marketing don't fight your dreams.

WHAT FEATURES DO PEOPLE USE TO MAKE THEIR DECISIONS ABOUT YOU?

• Clothing	• Hair	• Weight	• Height
• Jewelry	• Facial hair	• Makeup	• Business card
• Laugh	• Glasses	• Title	• Neatness
• Smell	• Teeth	• Smile	• What you carry
• Eye contact	• Gait	• Posture	• Tone of voice
• Handwriting	• Spelling	• Hat	• Thoughtfulness
• Car	• Office	• Home	• Nervous habits
• Handshake	• Sense of humor	• Availability	• Writing ability
• Phone use	• Enthusiasm	• Energy level	• Comfort online

You're fully aware of your intentional marketing and possibly even invest time, energy, and imagination into it, not to mention money. But you may be undermining that investment if you're not paying attention to things that matter to others even more than what you say: keeping promises, punctuality, honesty, demeanor, respect, gratitude, sincerity, feedback, initiative, reliability. They also notice passion—or the absence of it. They notice how well you listen to them.

What to Do Now

Now that you know these things, what should you do? Although Ben Franklin himself said three of the hardest things in the world are diamonds, steel, and knowing yourself, here's a three-step plan to get you started on the road to self-awareness and self-marketing acumen:

1. Write a positioning statement about yourself. Identify just who you are and the positive things that stand out most about you.
2. Identify your goals. Put into writing the three things you'd most like to achieve during the next three months, three years, and then ten years.
3. State your measuring stick. Write the details of how you will know when you've achieved your goals. Be brief and specific.

To guerrilla market yourself, simply be aware of and in control of the messages you send. Do that and your goals will be a lot easier to attain.

10 Requirements for Becoming a Guerrilla

1. You've got to open your mind to the full extent of marketing. It's fuller than you thought.
2. You've got to adapt the personality of other successful guerrilla marketers. Without it, life will be tough.
3. You've got to think about marketing differently. A lot of the old truths have turned into myths. And none of them involved the internet or the social media.
4. You've got to plan your guerrilla marketing attack with an easy-to-understand, easy-to-follow battle strategy.
5. You've got to define what you want your attack to accomplish with precision and realism. If you're not defining, you're not attacking.

The first five requirements are just the fundamentals for winning the battle for healthy, honest, and growing profits. They will serve you well on your way to the battlefield.

6. You've got to attack—do exactly what your plan said you'd do. You must take action.

7. You've got to understand which media can best serve your needs—and whether or not you need the media at all.

8. You've got to orient everything about your business to your customer—that person above all who can help you prosper. Your customer must sense your dedication.

9. You've got to recognize the fast-changing nature of marketing today. It's wilder than ever, but you can master it if you keep up with it. Guerrillas do.

10. You've got to maintain your guerrilla marketing attack. You can fulfill the other nine requirements superbly, but if you don't fulfill this one, you're a goner.

Achieving Guerrilla Marketing Mastery

- Excellence isn't as much a goal as a process.
- "If you have foresight, you're blessed, but if you have insight, you're a thousand times blessed." —Chinese proverb
- A job done 99 percent well is a job done poorly.
- Most marketing these days is being done poorly. It looks a whole lot better than it produces. It is oriented to awards more than sales, so it hits the bull's-eye for laughs, razzle-dazzle, and cleverness while missing entirely the target for profits.
- When people see your TV marketing, they're supposed to say, "Wow! I want that product!" They're not supposed to say, "Wow! What a great film!"
- Guerrillas define creativity in marketing as something that increases profits.
- Guerrillas learn by doing, experimenting, being realistic, keeping track, paying attention, improving, and committing to their successful experiments.

The Guerrilla Marketing Attack

- You are surrounded. All around you are enemies vying for the same bounty. These enemies are disguised as owners of small and medium-sized businesses. They're out for the disposable income currently held by your prospective and past customers. They're out for the attention of every red-blooded consumer.

- Your enemies mean business: your business, your profits. They may be able to outspend you in every arena that money can buy. But they can't outspend you in marketing arenas that money can't buy. And they can't always outthink you. If you put up the time, the energy, and the information, you can gain the same marketing leverage that many of your enemies get by putting up megabucks.

- Good marketing presses certain hot buttons in the minds of prospects. One of the most important words in all of marketing—and football—and relationships is "momentum." When your salespeople capitalize on the momentum of your other marketing, the sale is closer to being consummated.

- "Don't tell people how good you make the goods; tell them how good your goods make them." —Leo Burnett

- Talk to your prospects and customers about themselves and you've got their rapt attention.

- The guerrilla marketing attack is focused on one person at a time, not on demographic groups. Be sure the attack is aimed at individuals, one by one. Prove that you think of them one by one with every word and picture in your marketing.

The 10-Step Guerrilla Marketing Attack

1. Research everything
2. Write benefits list
3. Select weapons and prioritize

4. Create marketing plan
5. Design a marketing calendar
6. Find fusion marketing partners
7. Launch attack in slow motion
8. Maintain the attack
9. Keep track through measurement
10. Improve in every area

THE YARD BOY

There was once a little boy who walked into a store and asked the proprietor if he could use his phone. "Why certainly," the store owner replied.

The little boy dialed a number and said to the person on the other end, "I'm calling you to offer you the services of the best yard boy in town."

"Well, to tell you the truth," the person responded to the boy, "we feel we already have the best yard boy in town."

The little boy then said, "I really called because I want you to have the most beautiful yard on your street, and I want you to feel a sense of pride when you see it." "I must say," was the response, "we do feel a sense of pride whenever we look at our lawn."

"Well, if that's the case," said the little boy, "congratulations, I'm really happy for you." He then hung up the phone and handed it back to the store owner.

"Young man," the owner exclaimed, "I couldn't help but overhear your conversation, and I must say, with an attitude like that, you'll have no trouble getting a job one day as a yard boy."

"Oh, I'm already a yard boy," the little boy proclaimed. "In fact, I'm the yard boy for the people I just called. I was just checking up on myself."

How to Research Your Competitors

1. Order something
2. Visit your competitors
3. Phone your competitors
4. Request something
5. Compare everything
6. Buy something
7. Spy on yourself

chapter 15

The Guerrilla Entrepreneur

GUERRILLA ENTREPRENEURS HAVE LEFT behind many things they had grown to love—or hate. They have embraced new ways of thinking, new ways of working, new ways of living. They well know that they have left behind an age characterized by a worship of profits, a surfeit of working hours, and a neglect of family and self.

Sure, guerrilla entrepreneurs still aim toward profits but not at the expense of draconian working hours or the sacrificing of precious living time. They define success not only by the standard notion of finances, but also by the blessed notion of balance— between work and leisure, work and family, work and humanity, work and self. They seek and find success beyond the profit-and-loss statement, beyond the workplace.

Guerrilla entrepreneurs still aim toward profits but not at the expense of draconian working hours or the sacrificing of precious living time.

Today, there are more entrepreneurs than ever, but few true guerrilla entrepreneurs. The option to be either probably did not exist for your parents or your grandparents because the path had not been blazed by technology and social enlightenment.

The Puritan work ethic of your ancestors has gone by the wayside, along with the Puritans. That work ethic had no place for balance, only for hard work. The guerrilla entrepreneur's work ethic includes both. The hallmarks are the best of the old ways, such as sane working hours, time for family, and humane treatment of employees—with the best of the new ways, such as time-saving technologies, advanced and mobile communication techniques, and enlightened attitudes toward work and social life.

Guerrilla entrepreneurs define success not only by the standard notion of finances, but also by the blessed notion of balance— between work and leisure, work and family, work and humanity, work and self.

Guerrilla entrepreneurs who cuddle up to the new, easy-to-afford, easy-to-use technologies discover opportunities as plentiful and sparkling as raindrops in spring. They have learned that aiming high isn't as important as aiming sensibly. This allows many of them to reach their goals sooner than they expected.

They make profits the third priority, well ahead of sales and leads, but well behind humanity and balance. Their enterprises are flexible, innovative, unconventional, up-to-the-second in technology, low in overhead costs, dependent, interactive, generous, enjoyable, and money-making. One of their objectives is to keep their enterprises that way.

Look at the entrepreneurs around you. If you can't see many, it's because they are not guerrillas; instead they're buried in work, rarely coming up for the fresh air of free time. Guerrilla entrepreneurs seem to be happier with their work and appear to care like crazy about satisfying the needs of their customers. They stay in touch constantly with their customers. They express their passion for working with excellence and transform it into profits.

Their long-term goals are lofty. Those goals exist in the future. Their short-term goals are even loftier. Those goals exist in the present—for that is the domain of guerrilla entrepreneurs. That is where their goals are to be found in abundance.

They thrive on the nontraditional, do the unconventional if the conventional is nonsensical, and know that the real name of the game is the journey—the best of all goals. When the journey is the goal, you can begin with work that satisfies you, spend time enjoying activities other than that work you love, and gain a remarkable freedom from work-related stress. You'll be able to maintain good health and not participate in recessions.

The other goals of the guerrilla entrepreneur: work that is satisfying, enough money to enjoy freedom from worry about it, health good enough to take for granted, a bonding with others where you give and receive love and support, fun that is not pursued but is in the essence of daily living, and longevity to appreciate with wisdom that which you have achieved. To be a guerrilla entrepreneur, you've got to know what one really is.

What Is a Guerrilla Entrepreneur?

Guerrilla entrepreneurs know the journey is the goal. They also realize they are in control of their enterprises, not the other way around, and that if they are dissatisfied with the journey, they are missing the point of the journey itself. Unlike old-fashioned enterprises, which often required gigantic sacrifices for the sake of the goal, guerrilla enterprises place the goal of a pleasant journey ahead of the mere notion of sacrifices.

Guerrilla entrepreneurs achieve balance from the very start. They build free time into work schedules so that balance is part of the enterprise. They respect leisure time as much as work time, never allowing too much of one to interfere with the other. Traditional entrepreneurs always placed work ahead of leisure and showed no respect for their own personal freedom. Guerrillas cherish their freedom as much as their work.

Guerrilla entrepreneurs are not in a hurry. A false need for speed frequently undermines even the best-conceived strategies. Haste makes waste and sacrifices quality. The guerrilla is fully aware that patience is an ally, and plans intelligently to eliminate most emergencies that call for moving fast. The pace is always steady but never rushed.

Guerrilla entrepreneurs use stress as a benchmark. If they feel any stress, they know they must be going about things in the wrong way. Guerrilla entrepreneurs do not accept stress as part of doing business and recognize any stress as a warning sign that something's the matter—in the work plan of the guerrilla or in the business itself. Adjustments are made to eliminate the cause of the stress rather than the stress itself.

Guerrilla entrepreneurs look forward to work. They have a love affair with their work and consider themselves lucky to be paid for doing that work. They are good at their work, energizing passion for it in a quest to learn more about it and improve understanding of it, thereby increasing their skills. Guerrilla entrepreneurs don't think about retirement, for never would they want to stop doing work they love.

Guerrilla entrepreneurs have no weaknesses. They are effective in every aspect of their enterprise because they have filled in the gaps between strengths and talents with people who abound in the prowess they lack. They are very much team players, and they team up with like-minded guerrillas who share the team spirit and possess complementary skills. They value teammates as much as old-fashioned entrepreneurs valued their independence.

Guerrilla entrepreneurs are fusion-oriented. They are always on the alert to fuse their businesses with other enterprises in the community, in America, in the world. They are willing to combine marketing efforts, technologies, production skills, information, leads, mailing lists, and anything else to increase effectiveness and marketing reach while reducing the cost of achieving those goals. Fusion efforts are intentionally short term and rarely permanent. In business relationships, instead of thinking marriage, guerrilla entrepreneurs think fling.

Guerrilla entrepreneurs do not kid themselves. They know that if they overestimate their own abilities, they run the risk of skimping on the quality represented to customers, employees, investors, suppliers, and fusion partners. They face reality on a daily basis and realize that all business practices must always be evaluated in the glaring light of what is really happening, instead of what should be happening.

Guerrilla entrepreneurs realize routine leads to sanity, so they create systems for work activities, rarely going the hit-and-miss route or making things up as they go along. Those systems increase the lifespan of the business while eliminating shoddy work practices, clarifying life and business for employees and associates.

Guerrilla entrepreneurs live in the present. They are well aware of the past and very enticed by the future, but the here and now is where they reside, embracing the technologies of the present and leaving future technologies on the horizon right where they belong until later, when they are ripe and ready. Guerrilla entrepreneurs are alert to the new, wary of the avant-garde, and only wooed from the old by improvement, not by mere change.

Guerrilla entrepreneurs understand the precious nature of time. They don't buy into the old lie that time is money and know in their hearts that time is far more important than money. Instead, time is life. They are aware that customers and prospects feel the same way about time, so they respects their customer's time and wouldn't dare waste it. As practicing guerrillas, they are the epitome of efficiency but never let efficiency interfere with effectiveness.

Guerrilla entrepreneurs always operate according to a plan. They know who they are, where they are going, and how they will get there.

They are prepared, know that anything can and will happen, and can deal with the barriers to entrepreneurial success because their plans have foreseen troubles and shown exactly how to surmount them. The guerrilla reevaluates the plan regularly and does not hesitate to make changes in it, though commitment to the plan is integral.

Guerrilla entrepreneurs are flexible. They are guided by a strategy for success and know the difference between a guide and a master. When it is necessary for change, the guerrilla changes, accepting change as part of the status quo, not ignoring or battling it. They are able to adapt to new situations, realize that service is whatever customers want it to be, and know that inflexible things become brittle and break.

Guerrillas aim for results more than growth. They are focused upon profitability and balance, vitality and improvement, value and quality more than size and growth. Their plans call for steadily increasing profits without a sacrifice of personal time, so actions are oriented to hitting those targets instead of growing for the sake of growth alone. They are wary of becoming large and do not equate hugeness with excellence.

Guerrilla entrepreneurs are dependent upon many people. They know that the age of the lone-wolf entrepreneur, independent and proud of it, has passed. The guerrilla is very dependent upon fusion business partners, employees, customers, suppliers, and mentors. They got where they are with their own wings, determination, smarts, and, as a guerrilla, with a little help from a lot of friends.

Guerrilla entrepreneurs constantly learn. A seagull flies in circles in the sky, looking for food in an endless quest. When it finally finds the food, the seagull lands, and then eats its fill. When it has completed the meal, the seagull returns to the sky, only to fly in circles again, searching for food. Humans have only one instinct that compares: the need for constant learning. Guerrilla entrepreneurs have this need in spades. They know that today, the key is not in learning all there is to know about a topic, but to learn one thing after another.

Guerrilla entrepreneurs are passionate about work. They have an enthusiasm for what they do that is apparent to everyone who sees that work. This enthusiasm spreads to everyone who works with them, even to their customers. In its purest form, this enthusiasm is best expressed as the word passion—an intense feeling that burns within and is manifested in a guerrilla's devotion toward the business.

Guerrilla entrepreneurs are focused on the goal. They know that balance does not come easily and that they must shed the values and expectations of their ancestors. To do this, guerrillas must remain focused upon the journey, seeing the future clearly, while at the same time concentrating upon the present. They are aware that the minutiae of life and business can be distracting and so take steps to make those distractions only momentary.

Guerrilla entrepreneurs are disciplined about the tasks at hand. They are keenly aware that every time a task is added to the daily calendar, it is a self-promise. As guerrillas who do not kid themselves, they keep those promises, knowing that the achievement of their goals will be more than an adequate reward for their discipline. They find it easy to be disciplined because of the payback offered by the leisure that follows.

Guerrilla entrepreneurs are well-organized at home and at work. They do not want to waste valuable time looking for misplaced items, so they organize while working and as new work comes in. This sense of organization is fueled by the efficiency that results. While always organized, the guerrilla never squanders precious time by over-organizing.

Guerrilla entrepreneurs have an upbeat attitude. Because they know life is unfair, problems arise, to err is human, and the cool shall inherit the Earth, guerrillas take obstacles in stride, keeping perspective and a sense of humor. That ever-present optimism is grounded in an ability to perceive the positive side of things, recognizing the negative, but never dwelling there. Such an attitude is positively contagious.

But Wait . . . There's More!

It's not really enough for you just to know the chemistry of the guerrilla entrepreneur. There are other truths out there just dying to

THE GUERRILLA ENTREPRENEUR

- Knows that the journey is the goal
- Achieves balance from the very start
- Is not in a hurry
- Uses stress as a benchmark
- Looks forward to work
- Has no weaknesses
- Is fusion-oriented
- Faces reality
- Realizes routine leads to sanity
- Lives in the present
- Understands the precious nature of time
- Always operates according to a plan
- Sees the destination and how to get there
- Is flexible
- Aims for results more than growth
- Is dependent upon many people
- Learns constantly
- Is passionate about work
- Focuses on the goal
- Is disciplined about tasks at hand
- Is well-organized at home and work
- Has an upbeat attitude

be known by you. Here is a list of "10 Dirty Lies You Have Known and Loved." You need to recognize these statements that have been accepted as truths by many people are lies that will sink a guerrilla entrepreneur.

10 Dirty Lies You Have Known and Loved

1. Time is money.
2. Owning a business means workaholism.
3. Marketing is expensive.
4. Big corporations are like wombs.
5. Youth is better than age.
6. You need a job.
7. Heaven is in the afterlife.
8. The purpose of education is to teach facts.
9. Retirement is a good thing.
10. If you want it done right, do it yourself.

Business Is Now Harder and Easier Than Ever

It's a lot HARDER because of five factors that are well on their way to being the reality of today.

1. Time

Time will become magnified in importance. The luxury of spare time at work is a luxury of the past. Spare time will be revered, but not at work. You will be unable to help but notice the new awareness of time by almost everyone. Customers will demand and expect speed. You will, too.

2. Contact

Less face-to-face contact will remove much of the warmth of working. People now get more than half their messages by nonverbal communication. This means that nonverbal communications will be less accurate and verbal accuracy more valuable. The joy of social interaction will be much abated. Facebook and Twitter plus the other new social media will help in many ways—if you see and keep them in perspective.

3. Change

Change will be thrust upon us, and much that we counted on before will no longer hold forth. Even things we learn will only be true for a short time before being surpassed by new truths. The genius will not be in learning something but in learning one thing after another. If you can't adapt, you aren't cut out to be a guerrilla.

4. Talent

Talent will be diffuse as top people will trade the vitality of a huge corporation for the tranquility of working at home. Well and good for them, but for guerrilla entrepreneurs, this means all the big brains won't be under one roof. You'll have to scout them out.

5. Technology

Technology will be more important in your life, and you'll have to understand it to take full advantage of it. But technical things are becoming easier to use; user manuals are written more clearly, and the nature of training—repetition will be your friend for life—has improved. If you're technophobic, see a techno shrink.

The five ways that business will be EASIER are really 5,000 ways, but for purposes of time let's just go with five right here.

1. Time

You will have more time to do what really must be done rather than busywork because technical advancements will allow for it. Your network of independent contractors will also free up more of your time. Use it to increase your profits, make your business better, or just plain enjoy yourself.

2. Values

Values will change, and they will be more in keeping with your own guerrilla values. In the 20th century, the main value was placed on making money. In the 21st century, that priority will take a back seat to the human values of happiness at work, free time, family, spirituality. As you are discovering, profit-seeking will never be eliminated, only reprioritized.

3. Advancements

New advancements in business, both psychological and technological, will make the workplace more exciting and easier to use, even enjoyable. Flextime and teleconferencing will make for less crowded commuting if you commute at all. The virtual office is the at-home office. And it's here now. We've even expanded that to the RV in which we worked, played, and traveled for six years. We knew it would be fun. We never dreamt it would be that much fun.

4. Procedures

Streamlined procedures and systems will keep your work life efficient, organized, simple, and fast. You won't waste time or effort at work because you'll have learned to become an efficient working machine, and, as a guerrilla entrepreneur, you'll realize that the whole purpose of streamlining is to add effectiveness.

5. People

You will deal with smarter people, but fewer people overall. Your workplace won't be populated with paper-shufflers. Your at-home business will put you into contact with bright, talented entrepreneurs who made the break from the corporate life and are doing very well, just like you. One of your best and most savvy friends will be Google.

The Pitfalls of Being an Entrepreneur

Pitfall #1: The Time Trap

As much as people revere leisure time, they have less of it than ever, averaging less leisure time than they had in the 1980s. Here I am jumping up and glorifying the three-day work week when increasing numbers of Americans are wondering how to get out from under the six-day work week. Habits are much easier to form than they are to break. "I'll just work 60 hours a week for now, and then I'll cut back later." Won't happen.

Pitfall #2: The Large Lure

You'll be offered chances to earn more money, expand, take on more people, move to a larger space, and transform from an entrepreneurial endeavor to a large, corporate-type entity. Hey, it's your life, but you've got to turn in your guerrilla credentials if you opt for large rather than free, for bigness over balance.

Pitfall #3: The Money Morass

Money alters human behavior to the point that it causes well-meaning owners of small businesses, bound for success, to veer in the direction of financial success, steamrolling any chances of emotional, marital, parental, or social success. Money, being easier to attain than balance, is more frequently sought. Those in pursuit of it find that the prices they pay are worth far more than money. Of all the pitfalls, the money morass is the deepest, darkest, and biggest. As lack of money is toxic to human existence, too much money can be equally toxic. That's why entrepreneurs like John D. Rockefeller and Bill Gates spent the first half of their lives accumulating money and the second half giving it away.

Pitfall #4: The Burnout Barrier

You'll search your soul to come up with a method for providing your livelihood, and you'll set up shop with all the right intentions. You'll work hard and smart, and your rewards will be fruitful. But somewhere along the way, you will have lost some of your initial enthusiasm for your work. You'll continue on because you've been successful, but you'll bring less and less joy to your work. The thrill is gone. There is no more enthusiasm. You burned out. What to do now is something else. If the spark is gone, get yourself another dream. Enthusiasm will fuel your fires, and if it is absent, the fire in your soul will go out—the fire that was the key to your success. Guerrillas know that they can relight the fire for a new venture and that studies prove that the more you love what you do the better you'll do it. So if you no longer feel the love, end the relationship and start another.

Pitfall #5: The Humanity Hindrance

We hope like crazy that you never lose your personal warmth, your sense of humor, or your love of other human beings in your quest to become a successful entrepreneur. Sadly, the world has more than enough tales of individuals who left a trail of shattered people on their climb to the top. The guerrilla's priority list places people ahead of business, family ahead of business, love ahead of business, self ahead of business. Keeping your eyes on the bottom line should not make them beady. Putting your heart in your work should not turn it to stone. Attaining everything on your wish list should not put you upon anybody's enemy list. An executive we knew at a Fortune 500 company had a glass eye. When we asked which was the glass eye, we were told, "It's the warm one." There is no rule that says you give up your humanity as the dues for achieving entrepreneurial success.

Pitfall #6: The Focus Foil

It is not difficult to lose your focus, to set it upon a false goal, a tangential journey leading away from your dreams. You become so involved in the details of your operation that you deviate from your prime thrust. Your time becomes gobbled up by details instead of broad strokes. The idea is to grow your mind as you grow your business, but maintain your direction.

Pitfall #7: The Perfection Pit

High atop our own list of time-wasters, life-stealers, and company-ruiners are perfectionists and the pursuit of perfection. We are all for excellence and admire perfection in a bowling game or classroom attendance—two areas where perfection is possible. Guerrillas try to be perfect but don't spend all their time and energy attaining it. They know that the world is teeming with entrepreneurs who spend half their time polishing the unpolishable, steeped in the unnecessary, devoted to the unattainable. May your enterprise be free from imperfections and from perfectionists.

Pitfall #8: The Selling Snare

The selling snare is a trap that forces you to sell the same thing over and over again. The guerrilla's way around it: Make multiple sales with one effort. Instead of selling a single issue of a magazine, sell a subscription. Guerrillas do all in their power to develop products or services that must be purchased on a regular basis. Many offerings are sold with the repeat sales built right in, from our Guerrilla Marketing Association to cable television, from cleaning services to diaper service, from insurance coverage to gardening, from cell phone charges to gasoline costs, from swimming pool maintenance to dental care. The idea is to apply the ultimate in selling skills so that your one-time sale can lead to years and years of profits. If you fall into the trap of selling single shots only, you'll be spending more time selling than enjoying the benefits of your efforts.

Pitfall #9: The Leisure Lure

Don't kid yourself into believing that leisure time is automatically a good thing. Leisure time, when you don't know what to do with it, can lead to a wide variety of problems—from boredom to substance abuse. Truth be told, many people actually enjoy their work time more than their leisure time because at least they know what they'll be doing with their work time, but haven't a clue as to how to spend their leisure hours. Guerrillas do have a clue. And a hobby or avocation and a slew of interests beyond working and earning money. They enjoy their leisure almost as much as their work because they are working at something they love and because they've given a lot of thought to what they'll do with their free time. They know that free time by itself can be a drag.

Pitfall #10: The Retirement Ruse

Horrid but true: More than 75 percent of retirees die within two years of their retirement. When they retire from work, it's as though they also retire from life. Don't make the mistake of planning for retirement. Plan on cutting down, on easing off, but not on quitting altogether. Working keeps you sharp, keeps your brain in shape. Ceasing to work allows your brain to atrophy. What are most retirees concerned with? In one study, 38 percent say they don't have enough money. Another 29 percent say they're fearful of not staying healthy. Eight percent say they have too much time on their hands and they're bored. And eight percent figure they probably won't live long enough to enjoy life. Guerrillas have enough money because they put retirement into the same category as imprisonment. The money continues to flow into their lives long after their cohorts have retired. They stay healthy because continuing to hone the edge caused by work results in the maintenance of health and increased longevity. They do not suffer from the problem of too much time, having just enough for work, just enough for play. And they have been enjoying life all along because they've been engaged in the work they love, a trademark of the guerrilla entrepreneur. Remember that in nature, nothing ever retires, and as we are getting closer to understanding our own relationship with nature, we are understanding that retirement is unhealthy and contraindicated in anyone with brain waves. As an entrepreneur, you are your own boss. No one is going to make you retire. What happens if you are simply no longer interested in the business? Retire from it—then move on to another dream. Just don't retire from life itself. The trap of planning for retirement is like planning your own slow suicide—brought on by inactivity.

Being a Guerrilla Entrepreneur Gives You an Edge

You've got the guerrilla's edge in insight. You've given thought to your priorities. You aren't going to be misled by the entrepreneurial myths involving overwork, overgrowth, and overextending your reach. You realize that your journey is your destination and that your plan is your roadmap. This insight will help you maintain your passion.

You've got the guerrilla's edge in relationships. Every sale you make leads to a lasting relationship. Every customer you get is going to be a customer for life. Your sales and even your profits will probably go up and down, but your number of relationships will constantly go up, and your sales and profits will eventually follow.

You've got the guerrilla's edge in service. You see your service from your customer's point of view, not merely from your own. You realize that your service gives you an enormous competitive advantage over those who may be larger but less devoted to making and keeping customers delighted with your company. You know well the power of word-of-mouth and word-of-mouse marketing and how they equate with excellent service.

You've got the guerrilla's edge in flexibility. You are not enslaved by company policies and by precedent. Instead, you are fast on your feet, sensitive to customer needs, aware of flexibility as a tool for building relationships, profits, and your overall company. You are guided by the situation at hand and not by the way things were done in the past. Your flexibility adds to the passion that others feel about your company.

You've got the guerrilla's edge in follow-up. You don't have to be reminded about the number of relationships that are destroyed by customers being ignored after they made a purchase. Rather than ignoring them, you pay attention to them, remind them of how glad you are that they're your customers, and shower them with special offers, inside information, and care. They never feel ignored by you and reciprocate by never ignoring your company when it comes to repeat purchases or referrals.

You have the guerrilla's edge in cooperation. You see other businesses as potential partners of yours, as firms that can help you as you help them. You don't keep your eye peeled for competitors to annihilate but for businesses to team up with and form networks. Your attitude will help you prosper in an era when people are forming small businesses in droves.

You have the guerrilla's edge in patience. As a guerrilla, you are not in a hurry, never in a rush. You know how important time is, but you also know how speed usually results in diminished quality. Because of your planning, you are able to avoid emergencies and high-pressure situations. Patience is one of your staunchest allies as a guerrilla.

You have the guerrilla's edge in economy. You know how to market without investing a bundle of hard-earned money. You have learned the value of time and energy as substitutes for large budgets. You realize that in most business activities, you have a choice of any

BEING A GUERRILLA ENTREPRENEUR GIVES YOU AN EDGE

1. Insight	6. Cooperation
2. Relationships	7. Patience
3. Service	8. Economy
4. Flexibility	9. Timeliness
5. Follow-up	10. Commitment

two of these three factors: speed, economy, and quality. Guerrilla entrepreneurs get all three. But if you're not one yet, you always opt for economy and quality. Your patience helps you economize.

> *The guerrilla has a lifelong love affair with life.*

You have the guerrilla's edge in timeliness. You run a streamlined operation, devoid of fluff or unnecessary work. Your comfort with technology allows you to operate at maximum effectiveness. Your business is a state-of-the-art enterprise because it operates in the environment of today rather than 10 years ago. Although you maintain your focus upon your plan, you know the magic of proper timing and are able to make adjustments so that you are there just when customers need you.

You have the guerrilla's edge in commitment. This commitment sets you apart from many other businesses. It helps you achieve your aims with certainty. It is so powerful that you feel passion toward the commitment itself—enabling the passion to power your commitment and the commitment to power your passion. Without this inner commitment, even the best plans may go awry. With it, plans turn into a bright reality.

The closer you examine it, the more you see that the way of the guerrilla is a way illuminated by the radiant light of love—love of self, work, family, others, freedom, independence, life. The guerrilla has a lifelong love affair with life. The deeper and more heartfelt the love, the more a guerrilla is capable of generating the fiery and exquisite passion that fuels the fires.

Love Is the Key

1. Love of self
2. Love of work
3. Love of family
4. Love of play
5. Love of freedom

6. Love of independence
7. Love of friends
8. Love of customers and employees
9. Love of a higher power
10. Love of life

The guerrilla entrepreneur's life is a love story, for love illuminates the way of the guerrilla.

part 2

GUERRILLA WISDOM FROM GUERRILLA CO-AUTHORS

One thing that guerrillas excel at is sharing. The first books I wrote about guerrilla marketing apparently spurred others to share their own guerrilla insights. Here, in Part 2 of the *Remix*, are the most valuable insights Jeannie and I could glean from the best guerrilla marketing co-authors. It was very difficult to winnow down to the wisdom imparted here.

Rather than offer up chapters, we offer up snippets, small enough to take a minimum of your reading time and space, but big enough to have a positive impact on your profits. Shall we rave about the credentials and accomplishments of the guerrilla co-authors? Nope, we'll let you discover those for yourself.

Shall we rave about the credentials and accomplishments of the guerrilla co-authors? Nope, we'll let you discover those for yourself. But, it's your accomplishments that mean the most to us.

chapter 16

FROM

The Guerrilla Marketing Handbook

Co-Author Seth Godin

Naming Your Business

Your name should reflect your name and your positioning. Naming a product or a company is a difficult decision. Unlike most challenges you'll face, this one is in a field in which virtually everyone claims expertise. The first thing to remember when naming something is not to rely too heavily on another's advice. Names created by committee are usually losers.

Don't forget about the law. Your name can cause a Jurassic Park-size problem if you don't first conduct a legal name search. The last thing you want is to hit it big, then be forced to change your name because a tiny company has the same name and wants $100 million from you for the rights to it.

> *The first thing to remember when naming something is not to rely too heavily on another's advice. Names created by committee are usually losers.*

First conduct a legal name search.

Start by sitting down and making a list of what you want your name to stand for in the mind of the consumer. Häagen-Dazs is supposed to make you think of cold fjords and rich, creamy milk. It doesn't matter that there's no such person as Häagen or no such place as Dazs—the name serves its purpose.

You must decide what you want your name to imply. It's usually the first thing your prospects learn about you. Here are some of the things your name can tell your prospects about you:

- Quick
- The best
- Convenient
- Highest quality
- Experienced
- Fun
- Outrageous
- Reliable
- Inexpensive
- Guaranteed
- Recommended
- Honest
- Dangerous
- Unique

Once you've got your list of attributes, try it out on peers and focus groups. For example, if you're starting a dry cleaner, ask them if the attributes you've chosen—fast, reliable, and inexpensive—would meet their needs. If not, adjust your list and try again.

Do you want a name that's generic, descriptive, or fanciful?

Now that you've got a list, you've got to make a decision. Do you want a name that's generic, descriptive, or fanciful? Any lawyer will tell you that a fanciful name is the best sort of trademark. It's the easiest to protect from encroachment by competitors, and eventually it makes the strongest name. A fanciful name is one where no picture comes to mind. No one knows what a Nike or a Xerox looks like.

> *A fanciful name is the best sort of trademark.*

The problem with fanciful names is that it takes an awful lot of time and money to persuade the consumer that they stand for something. The name itself doesn't begin by positioning the product or the company. So for most guerrillas, a fanciful name is too expensive to develop into an asset.

The second alternative, which is more difficult to protect, is a descriptive name. These names help position your company or product, and they telegraph information about what you do. Some examples:

- Speedy Muffler
- Ultimate Auto Body
- College Pro Painters

Descriptive names are the guerrilla's favorites. They communicate enough about your product to help the sale, but they're unique and stick in the customer's mind and help stop the competition.

Lastly, you can use a generic name. These names are virtually unprotectable, but they have the ability to immediately telegraph what your business does.

Some generic names include:

- International Business Machines
- U.S. Steel
- Park Avenue Cleaners
- General Foods
- Mister Donut

As you can see, sometimes a generic name takes off and works, but in general, it's an uphill battle—you've positioned your company, but your company has no identity.

Examples of Good Names

- *Fearless Computing*—indicates the positioning of the firm. They will alleviate the fear you feel when you face the prospect of using your computer.
- *Faith Popcorn*—a memorable name that reminds you that she doesn't take things too seriously.
- *National Public Radio*—a simple name that immediately connotes weight, seriousness, and the fact that everyone is involved.
- *Beverly Hills Brownies*—instantly connotes richness and elegance.
- *Staples*—a simple word that brings together a ubiquitous office supply with another word for "essentials." Once learned, the user never forgets what it stands for.
- *Federal Express*—the word "Federal" is great in this instance. It helped them get off the ground when competing with the Postal Service.
- *Head and Shoulders*—the name lets you see the benefit of the product—no dandruff on your shoulders.
- *Apple Computer*—simple, friendly, basic, easy to remember.
- *Tic Tacs*—easy to remember and pronounce but not necessarily reminiscent of the tic tac toe game. Without the toe, connotes clean and crisp.

Product or Company Names to Avoid

- *A name that starts with "International"*—It's not unique, it usually doesn't mean anything, and it's confusing. So many companies use the word "International" to begin their name, it often gets ignored. For example, when you think of International Business

Machines, you rarely focus on the "International" part. Your competitors also do business internationally, so make sure that part of your name separates you from them.

- *Anything with a pun or joke*—you want your business to have a name that attracts potential customers, not one that elicits a long groan and a snide remark. Remember, you have to live with your name for a long time. Hairdressers are notorious for bad names. Consider these examples:
  - Shear Madness
  - Mane Attraction
  - Hair Today, Gone Tomorrow

- *Names that are technology sensitive*—no one wants to buy a car from Consolidated Buggywhips. If you name your business after the technology that you sell, you are wedded to it. For example, if you call your business "Fax-Modems, Inc.," you may be positioning yourself as a dealer in an obsolete technology several years down the line. Don't get yourself trapped like that.

- *Most names that include the name of a person*—such as Wilson, Wilson and Dundas, Davis Consulting Group, or Stew Leonard's. These names are fanciful, just like Nike or Reebok. Unlike a truly fanciful name, though, these businesses are harder to grow (everyone wants to work with a guy whose name is on the door), hard to sell once the founder leaves, and especially vulnerable to scandal. If a scandal involving the owner occurs, it reflects poorly on the business that bears his name. They have one advantage: If the business is very personal, the name tells the customer exactly who stands behind it.

Rules for Choosing a Business Name

- Your name should have a positive ring. Avoid anything negative. Your name should make people enthusiastic and optimistic about working with you.

- Avoid difficult names. If people have trouble pronouncing it or spelling it, they won't remember it. (Embarrassing exceptions: "Häagen-Dazs" and "Guerrilla.")
- Make your name unique. You don't want people confusing you with a business that already exists, especially if it's one with a poor reputation.
- Don't use a name that will limit you down the road. Acme Sleep Shop will limit you to selling sleep products. Acme Interiors is more open to expansion.
- Use a descriptive name, such as Jiffy Lube. Note that this name also conveys a benefit.
- Don't get caught up in trends or fads. While it may be profitable in the short run, you can't ride a fad for the long haul, and guerrillas are more focused on the long haul.
- Your name should reflect your identity: dignity, largeness, local identification, quality, whatever.
- Pick a name that looks and sounds attractive on the phone, on the radio, on your letterhead, and on your website.
- Consider a name that starts with "A" if you plan to advertise in the Yellow Pages. Your name will always come at the beginning.

Magazines are great at names. With only a nanosecond to position themselves, they spend a lot of effort choosing a name that will do the job quickly and well. Here are some favorites.

- *Time*
- *Success*
- *American Demographics*
- *Wired*
- *Mac Week*
- *Vogue*
- *Sassy*

Then there are the magazines that have managed to succeed despite their confusing names, thus rewarding their owners with powerful, fanciful names, such as:

- *Forbes*
- *Vanity Fair*
- *The Utne Reader*

People get very emotional about naming a company or a product. Be careful to limit your naming team—wait until you've narrowed your choices down to two or three before allowing others to vote or comment. One company we know spent more than 250 man-hours (at $50 an hour) arguing about the name for a product line.

Be careful to limit your naming team—wait until you've narrowed your choices down to two or three before allowing others to vote or comment.

chapter 17

FROM

Guerrilla Retailing

Co-Authors Orvel Ray Wilson and Elly Valas

THE BATTLE HAS BEGUN. You are massively out-numbered, outspent, and outgunned, and unless you fight back with everything you've got, you don't stand a chance. You must become a guerrilla, especially during a time that feels like a perma-recession.

There have been creative ways to survive down economies in retailing since the invention of down economies. Guerrillas specialize in using those, considering how few cost any money. It always helps, though, if they have a crystal ball to tell what's ahead. Here's yours, guerrilla.

20 Important Trends in Retailing

1. Experts are forecasting continued success for Walmart and its ilk as shoppers become ever more bargain-conscious.

2. We also see continued growth for the super-center format. Total super-center sales are growing at a record-setting pace.

3. Even so, there are opportunities for conventional retailers to survive in a world dominated by the big boxes.

4. No more one-size-fits-all. Guerrilla retailers will have to take more of a portfolio approach to the market in order to appeal to discriminating shoppers. Even customers who used to shop at superstores like Sports Authority are turning to specialty shops that sell only soccer stuff or only snowmobiles, or the ultimate example: Golf For Her, a retail boutique created by entrepreneur Chris Foy in Broomfield, Colorado.

Customers who used to shop at super-stores are turning to specialty shops.

5. Department stores are in a death spiral. Escalating competition from discounters on one side and specialty stores on the other will continue to squeeze this category, which will face more consolidation and retrenchment.

6. Malls will get mauled. Many will have to change almost beyond recognition in order to survive. The good news for guerrillas is that customers who are tired of hiking through the sameness of mall after mall will be more likely to go to a destination store for just the right product and superior service.

7. Reconcept rather than just remodel. Compressed lifecycles for products, retail concepts, and brands mean the end of large, mass-merchandising chains. There used to be a restaurant on Highland Avenue in Downer's Grove, Illinois, called The Highland Grill. Great food, great service, in the upscale burgers-steaks-and-fries grill-food concept, very successful, always jammed. Then suddenly, BAM, they're closed! Two and a half months later they re-open as Parker's

Ocean Grill with completely new décor, new menu, but the same staff. We asked, "What happened?" The manager explained, "We're part of an eight-restaurant chain, Select Restaurants, Inc., headquarters in Cleveland, Ohio, and we've learned that every four or five years, we have to gut the place and do something completely different before we get stale and our customers get bored with us." Today, they operate 17 restaurants.

Customers who are tired of hiking through the sameness of mall after mall will be more likely to go to a destination store for just the right product and superior service.

8. The experience economy excels. Guerrilla retailing concepts mix content and commerce as never before. The Rainforest Café probably couldn't make it on the quality of their food alone. REI and their two-story climbing walls create an atmosphere of high adventure, even before you get your new gear outdoors.

9. Click and brick. The impact of e-tailing extends well beyond its once-limited share of total retail sales. Forrester Research sees a bright and prosperous future these days, measured in the hundreds of billions of dollars.

10. Smart shopping. Consumers will embrace technologies that give them better information about products and more control over the shopping process. More than half of U.S. consumers already shop on the internet at least occasionally. A larger proportion use the web to research options before going to a brick-and-mortar store to make the purchase. The most successful operators combine information-rich online catalogs with storefront offerings. Guerrilla retailers will set up a terminal with

The impact of e-tailing extends well beyond its once-limited share of total retail sales.

internet access and invite their prospects to check out competing products right there in the store instead of leaving to shop elsewhere.

11. Smart stores. Retailers will adopt technologies that enhance the productivity of store space and associates. Some solutions, including kiosks and self-checkout terminals, will improve staff productivity and make shopping more convenient. Guerrilla retailers will provide floor-walkers with wireless handheld computers that can check inventory, schedule installations, or even write invoices from anywhere on the sales floor. Rental-car agencies and even some restaurants use wireless floor walkers. Soon you'll see a computer display mounted on your grocery cart that beeps an alarm when you pass an item that's on sale, driving multiple-item impulse and companion-item purchases.

> *A computer display mounted on your grocery cart will beep an alarm when you pass an item that's on sale, driving multiple-item impulse and companion-item purchases.*

12. Mobile sales will remain elusive. Starbucks has experimented with micro-marketing. A coupon appears on the screen of your cell phone when you're in the neighborhood. Sales of products and services via cell phones and other mobile devices are on the rise.

13. The global land rush continues. Despite growing world tensions, retailers in other businesses will remain committed to international operations.

14. Retailers will act more and more like suppliers. As retailers grow, they will seek alternative sources of products, leading many suppliers to find that their retail customers are becoming their biggest competitors. Walmart already contracts for apparel directly with factories in China two years in advance.

15. Retailers will become brand managers. Exclusive brands are an important differentiation strategy for guerrilla retailers. You'll see more and more one-brand-only stores like Victoria's Secret, Talbot's, J. Crew, Eddie Bauer, Abercrombie & Fitch, Gap, and Orvis. You'll also see many of them come and go.

16. Suppliers will start to act more like retailers. Retailers will look to key suppliers to become category consultants, setting the strategy for the category, managing inventory, and selling space by location, almost as if they were operating leased departments.

17. Brand sharing. Retailers will plug into each other's shopper database and leverage location by leasing space for a store-within-a-store. Department stores often feature Ralph Lauren, Calphalon, or Nautica stores-in-a-store. Starbucks is setting up shop in your local Barnes & Noble, as well as in Albertson's, right next to the Krispy Kreme.

> *With micro-marketing, a coupon appears on the screen of your cell-phone or GPS when you're in the neighborhood.*

18. Uber retailers. Some giant retailers will leverage their brand identities, customer relationships, and size to fulfill virtually all the needs of certain categories of shoppers. Cabela's has followed the strategy to highly-profitable success specializing in hunting, fishing, and outdoor gear.

19. Suppliers become retailers. Some suppliers will seek to sell directly to the consumer, as in the Nike Store and the Sony Store. BOSE sells its acoustic noise-cancelling headphones directly to consumers in airports as well as in their own stores and by mail order.

20. Customers will call the shots. More and more, customer relationships will be the key competitive aspect for guerrilla retailers.

chapter 18

FROM

Guerrilla Deal-Making

Co-Author Donald Hendon

A S EVEN THE NON-GUERRILLA KNOWS, a good deal requires both giving and taking. Guerrillas are adept at both. Of course, it's pretty easy to take the concessions granted by others, but pretty darned tough to make the concessions that you'll have to grant. These tips will help.

20 Dos of Concession-Making

Acting

1. Make the big dog (or other guerrilla) think your concession is valuable to you when it isn't. Be a good actor.
2. Show physical pain on your face whenever you make a concession. Make them think your concession hurts you.

Agents

3. Use an agent to negotiate for you instead of directly negotiating with the big dog. Agents usually make fewer concessions, and their concessions are smaller.

Attitude

4. Always remember: If you're willing to settle for less, you'll usually get less.

Deadlines

5. Set a deadline only if you want to use it as an ultimatum.

6. Try to find out the other party's deadline. To see if they are serious about their deadline, test them. If it's negotiable, it's not a valid deadline.

Dollar Value

7. Put a dollar value on each concession you make. Say how much this concession is costing you, if it's to your advantage.

8. Try to estimate the dollar value of each concession the other party makes, too.

9. Concede with funny money instead of real money—percentages, price per unit. Percentages sound smaller than dollars: $1 per unit sounds low, but if you're buying a million units, that's a million dollars you're going to spend. Getting the supplier to lower the price by 2 cents per unit will save you $20,000.

10. Break big concessions into several small ones. Give them away over time. The other party will usually think several smaller concessions are larger than one big one, even if the total dollar amount is the same.

11. Give yourself a lot of room. If you're selling, start high. If you're buying, start low.

12. Keep careful records, but don't let anyone know you're doing this. See if the other negotiators have a pattern—escalating,

de-escalating, waiting until the end. This makes it easier to predict what they are going to do.

13. Make the other negotiators work hard for everything they get from you. They will appreciate your concession more and think it's worth more, too. But if they get it too easily, too quickly, they won't think it's that valuable.

14. Always ask yourself, "Is my concession a reasonable one?" If it's not, don't make it.

Limited Authority

15. Use it. Say "I have to check with my boss before I can give you any more concessions."

Listen Well

16. Listen to what your counterpart says is the cheapest concession you can make—and the most important.

17. Listen well, this time with your eyes. Watch the other negotiator's body language when they concede to find out if their concession is important or not.

Timing

18. Make concessions slowly. Space them out.

19. If you concede first, make sure it's only a minor concession.

Trade-Offs

20. Always get something in return when you make a concession.

20 Don'ts of Concession-Making

Assumptions

1. Don't assume reciprocity is always necessary after each concession. There's got to be an end sometime.

2. Don't assume that when you give in on one issue, you'll automatically give in on another issue. You're not necessarily on a slippery slope. When you're on a sticky slope, the ground ahead of you isn't endangered by your concessions. The trick is to create meaningful sticking points with your concessions. Think sticky, not slippery.

Deadlines

3. Don't tell the other parties your deadlines. If you do, you're giving away a lot of your power. That's a silly concession to make. Once they know your deadline, they will probably keep stalling for time and only seriously negotiate when your deadline is almost there. You'll make a lot more concessions then because you're under a lot of time pressure.

4. Don't forget the 80–20 rule: 80 percent of all serious action happens in the last 20 percent of the time before the deadline.

5. Don't set a deadline yourself. Deadlines limit your flexibility. So don't worry about them too much. Always ask yourself, "Whose deadline causes me the most trouble? Theirs or mine?"

6. Don't worry about their deadline. Always remember, their deadline limits their flexibility, not yours. So let them worry about it and defend it. You're a lot more flexible without a deadline.

Dollars

7. Don't make the largest single concession in the deal-making process. The person who does this usually wins a lot less than the other person does.

Ego

8. Don't walk out when you get a ridiculous offer. Control your ego. Be polite. See where this ridiculous offer is going.

9. Don't insult anyone when you get a ridiculous offer.

10. Don't want to be liked so much that you'll give away the store just to see a smile. Like yourself so much that you don't care if the other party likes you personally or not.

Mistakes

11. Don't hide your mistakes. Saying you made a mistake when you take back your concession makes it easier for your action to be accepted.

12. Don't make too many mistakes, though. The other negotiators will think you're pretty ignorant or you're trying to make a fool out of them.

Timing

13. Don't make the first concession. Keep your demands hidden while the other party reveals theirs.

14. Don't be afraid to take a concession back, either. Anything goes until you both sign the final contract.

15. Don't ever be the first one to say, "Let's split the difference." This is probably the biggest don't of all. Why? This tells the other negotiators what your bottom line is before you know their bottom line. The person who says, "Let's split the difference" first has the least to lose.

16. Don't make a single concession without knowing all demands first.

17. Don't reveal too early that you're willing to make concessions. This immediately raises expectations. It's much better to reveal this later on in your deal-making session, as late as possible.

18. Don't accept any concessions too soon. If you accept an offer too quickly without any haggling, the other party will start thinking they gave too much away and will try to get out of the deal.

Words

19. Don't be afraid to say "no." In fact, the more you say it, the easier it gets for you.

20. Don't say, "I'll think about it," too often or too easily. Those four words are actually a concession, because they raise expectations. Once again, don't give away any concession without getting one in return. Say instead, "What will you do for me if I even decide to think about it?" But only if you have more power than the other party does.

Following some of these guidelines will be easy for you because you'll readily agree with them. You may resist following others because what you've done in the past has worked for you. Keep an open mind. Try out new things. I've developed guidelines over a long period of time. My clients all over the world have used them with great success.

If you're an American, these cherry-picked guidelines should make you re-evaluate yourself. Begin with the first reason: thinking we're big dogs—the Santa Claus mentality. If you've got a big ego, get rid of it. Thinking—and acting—like you're number one makes people want more from you, and this puts you at a big disadvantage when you're trying to make a deal. Think small instead. One of the most powerful and underused tactics is, Think small. Guerrillas use it in war, and that's one of the main reasons they're so successful. Business people who think like guerrillas use it, too, with equal success. Here's why:

> *If you've got a big ego, get rid of it. Think small instead.*

Smaller businesses are natural guerrillas—they can do almost anything they want because they've got very little to lose. Large businesses, on the other hand, often feel they have very few choices because they've got too much to lose. And so they're a lot more cautious. It's hard to get executives in large businesses to think like guerrillas, to think small. And so smaller guerrillas can do anything. They can run circles around the big dogs. They take advantage of the big dog's paralysis of caution. Here's what Mao Zedong said in his book, Yu Chi Chan, which means guerrilla warfare:

Attack in the countryside. Withdraw when the enemy starts looking for you. Bleed the enemy dry. Own the countryside. The enemy will retreat to their city fortress, raise their drawbridge, and wait for your attack.

Story About Sam Walton

To think small and be successful at the same time, you need a lot of imagination and creativity. Like Sam Walton, the founder of Walmart. He was a natural guerrilla. He wasn't afraid to fail. But then again, he had a great idea and was small enough to implement it without getting stepped on by the giants of retailing. Like Mao, he started in the countryside, owned it, and eventually moved to the big cities. And he beat the big dogs of the time—Kmart (still around), Woolco (long gone), E. J. Korvette (ditto), and other big discount store chains. Here's the quickie story of the most successful guerrilla businessman of all time:

Sam owned a series of small "five-and-ten-cent-variety" stores in northwestern Arkansas in the 1940s and 1950s. Eventually, he and his brother Ben ran 16 stores in that part of the United States—Arkansas, Missouri, and Kansas. He was losing customers to discount chain stores such as Woolco and Kmart, even though they were located in larger cities more than 100 miles away. People from Bentonville, where he was headquartered, drove over dangerous, curving mountain roads to go to discount stores in Little Rock, Fort Smith, Springfield, Joplin, Tulsa, and Kansas City. He couldn't match the chains' low prices—his stores were too small to buy in bulk. So he decided to outmaneuver them by coming up with an audacious idea that cost him a lot of his assets.

He figured that three stores the size of his original Ben Franklin store in Bentonville would match the buying power of a smaller Woolco or Kmart. So he set up a small warehouse in the center of several small towns in Arkansas. He bought in sufficient bulk so he could match the prices of Woolco and Kmart in those larger cities. He opened his first Walmart in Bentonville in 1962. The big chains ignored him. They didn't want to invade smaller cities anyway. They, like Chiang Kai-shek in China, were too cautious to go after their enemies in the countryside. And they eventually lost the war.

Sam took advantage of the big chains' indifference and kept expanding. He set up more and more warehouses, adding more and more stores. He stuck to small towns. Eventually, like Mao Zedong and Le Duan, the guerrilla architect of North Vietnam's victory over the U.S. and South Vietnam, he decided to attack the large cities in force. He started in Philadelphia, and Walmart there was a big winner. By then, he was too big to be stopped by the big discount chains. He began opening Walmarts in the outer suburbs of large cities, where land was cheaper. His stores were larger than the Woolcos and Kmarts. Economies of scale. Americans were moving away from the cities into the suburbs and outer suburbs, where Sam opened his Walmarts. The older Woolcos and Kmarts weren't as large, clean, and attractive as the newer Walmarts, and they had higher rental and insurance rates. With their higher operating costs, they couldn't match Walmart's efficiencies and had to charge higher prices.

Thinking small is actually thinking big.

Eventually, Walmart became the number-one retailer in the world. Woolco went out of business. Kmart merged with Sears. Other big discounters went out of business, too. Anybody remember E. J. Korvette, a giant discount chain in the northeastern U.S.? Long gone. How about GEM? Treasure Island? Richway? Ditto. The moral of the story: Thinking small is actually thinking big. Think like winners—think small! Even if you're with a big company! You'll win more.

chapter 19

FROM

Guerrilla Publicity

Co-Author Jill Lublin

Media Training for the Digital Age

If you were suddenly called on to perform in a jam-packed stadium on a team of professional athletes, how do you think you would do? Probably not so well. Chances are that you would be over your head, completely out of place; you even might make a fool of yourself. And that's what happens when most people first deal with the media.

When the media contacts you, you must make the most of every opportunity. If you're unprepared or not at your best, you can be in big trouble because that may be the only chance you get. The media has many options, so if you don't perform terrifically, the media will move on to its next story and never give you a second thought. The word will spread, and other media outlets will ignore you. If, however, you're a compelling, entertaining, and attractive subject, the media will feature you again.

When you deal with the media, you enter a different world; a world that you're not prepared to handle. People who work in the media specialize in work that you rarely or never do. They have an intense, single focus: to continually bring their audiences the most gripping and entertaining stories. They know the rules and how to please their audiences—it's their job.

You, on the other hand, are an outsider. You probably have rarely or never been on radio or TV, or been an interview subject. You don't know how the media works or what makes a good story, even though you may think you do. When you deal with the media, you are a visitor in the media's territory. The media is in charge, it asks the questions, directs the action, and determines how your story is told.

Most people, even the brightest and most articulate, are not naturally gifted communicators. You may know your business inside out, but clearly and entertainingly explaining it to mass audiences may not be your forte. Appearing before an audience and articulately answering hard, rapid-fire questions can throw you off.

Many people mistakenly think that they can go before the media, tell their story, and look great. They think that their natural charm, good looks, and intelligence will pull them through. Sorry, but that's seldom how it works. When questioned by the media, many people don't know what to say or how to say it best. They don't know how

GUERRILLA INTELLIGENCE

If you want to promote your goods or services through the media, you need media training, even if you're represented by a publicist. In the digital age, always making a great impression is imperative because every interview and appearance, regardless of how brief or obscure, can quickly be plastered across cyberspace. If you don't look or sound your best, you can find yourself the subject of ridicule—and you can occupy that position forever.

to handle difficult questions, tough interviewers, hecklers, and even unresponsive or hostile audiences. Most don't even know how to dress or conduct themselves.

Media training can be essential in helping you get bookings. Before producers put guests on broadcast programs, they conduct pre-interviews to get a sense of whether an individual would make a good guest. "Pre-interviews are part audition and part pitch and essential in being booked, but most people don't know what to do," explains Jess Todtfeld, president of Media Training Worldwide. Media training can teach you how to talk to producers, understand what they want, why they make key decisions, and how you should act.

Media training will teach you how to attract the media's interest and what to do when it bites. It will show you how to make a great impression with producers and convince them to cover your story and put you on their shows. Then, when you're booked, media training will prepare you to make the best of your opportunity, how to be a great subject, and be invited back.

The message is the information you want to share with humanity, while your hook is what gets you on the air.

Joel Roberts of Joel Roberts and Associates shows students how to distinguish between their message and their hook. "The message is the information you want to share with humanity, while your hook is what gets you on the air," Roberts points out. Hooks are strategies that include the following:

- *Making news.* First and foremost, the media is interested in giving its audiences news, and people in the media love breaking news stories. If your story makes news, the media will want the scoop. If you provide a new solution to a significant problem or create something of interest to a large part of its audience, the media will beat a path to your door.
- *Linking your story to current news.* Connect your story to the news, to items that the media is presently covering. Stories that

are not topical, even those that are fascinating and highly enter-taining, can be replaced by items that the media finds hotter, more current, and more newsworthy.

- *Relating your story to money, sex, and health.* The media believes that the public is obsessed with money, sex, and health, so it is more likely to run stories involving those subjects. If you connect your story to two or even three of these subjects, your chances of getting wide media coverage will soar. To a lesser extent, the media is also interested in relationships and careers.

- *Debunking myths.* After getting scoops and reporting breaking news, the media loves nothing more than to burst bubbles. It delights in taking accepted ideas and disproving them. Debunking serves its audiences by continuing the journalistic tradition of muckraking and is entertaining.

- *Creating new angles and approaches.* The media also likes innovation. It enjoys explaining to its audiences new processes and ways of looking at or dealing with old or existing problems. It likes to teach.

- *Showing problems that exist and explaining how to solve them.* The media wants to serve its audience. So if you convince it that you can solve a significant problem, the media will give you a platform. The media likes to give audiences "take away," concrete items that it can use.

- *Offering tangible benefits to audiences.* If you can offer benefits such as solid information; advice; entertainment; or free, low-cost, or discounted items, the media will pass it on to its audiences.

- *Coming up with catchy words or phrases.* Since people in the media are communicators, many are fascinated with language and especially new and unusual usages. They know that witty and clever language will grab audience attention so will seize upon them and include them in their features.

- *Celebrity connection.* The media knows the public is fascinated by celebrities, so if you can connect your story to someone who is widely known, the media will be interested.

Media trainers also teach you how to broaden your audience and improve your performance. For example, if your product is traditionally aimed at women, they can show you how to pitch it to men or kids. Trainers will teach you how to answer questions: tough questions, easy questions, staying on message, and sliding into your most important points. You will learn how to sit, stand, gesture, speak, buy time, look at the audience, and remain composed.

Trainers can quickly spot your weaknesses and strengths and tell you exactly how to improve them. Many people don't recognize their strengths or know how to build upon them. So they don't fully utilize their biggest assets, the things that the media and audiences like most.

The Process

All media trainers operate differently, so what their training includes depends on the trainer. Most trainers offer several types of training such as group and individual sessions. They are usually available for special consultations as well as brush-ups or refreshers before important appearances. Trainers also give customized sessions for individuals and companies. Since the size of group sessions can vary, check with each specific trainer before you sign on.

Media training is predicated on the fact that interviews and media appearances are not normal conversations that everyone can easily handle. "Interviews and appearances are special situations that require special skills," Jess Todtfeld explains. "People have to learn those skills just like actors have to learn how to act."

Trainers teach students the ground rules for interviews and appearances, for example, that interviewers or hosts are in control because they ask the questions. You are at their mercy because they know where they want to go. "Media training teaches people how to take control of their appearances; how to weave predetermined answers into interviews without hijacking them," Todtfeld notes. "It shows them how to get a clear sense of what they want to get from the interview, to know the points they want to make and how to make them. It gives them a game plan or a road map to follow."

Today, the primary tools for most media trainers is placing students in front of cameras, taping them, and letting them observe themselves. They get students on camera and let them see what they need to change. When people see themselves, they change more willingly and quickly, and their focus improves. After taping sessions, trainers critique and talk to students about their performances. Then adjustments are made, students are again taped, and the process is repeated.

The idea is for students to observe their performances; to see their strong and weak points, which the trainers highlight. "Most of what people learn comes from seeing themselves on camera," Todtfeld states. "We want them to see what they do poorly and what they do well so they can capitalize on it. We tape them frequently, critique each performance, add a piece of information, work on their message, and get them back on camera."

"When preparing for an interview, think energy, energy, energy," Todtfeld emphasizes. "If you're going on television, remember that it's a cooling medium that makes you come across like you have less energy than you thought. Without fail, people display less energy than they think."

Messages

Media trainers teach people how to perfect their outer and inner messages. Outer messages are how they present themselves; how they look and act. It involves everything but the words they speak, which is their inner message.

For their outer messages, trainers show students how to stand, sit, speak, gesture, and respond. They instruct them not to slump down, lean back, grimace, or constantly gesture wildly. Trainers also advise students on what they should wear.

For example, a number of problems occur when TV guests wear white. White is the most dominant color to viewers. So when guests wear white, viewers don't always concentrate on their faces, which can detract from the impact of their presentations. This can create problems because facial expressions convey body language and provide insights into a person's honesty, sincerity, passion, confidence, and more. So media trainers advise their students to avoid wearing white.

Trainers help their students develop and present verbal messages. "The hardest thing for most people is figuring out their message," Todtfeld says. "It's difficult because they aren't used to boiling their message down into one sentence." Since people frequently have multiple points that they want to make, trainers help them whittle them down to the three or four that are most important.

Trainers also teach students how to crystallize their thinking, to add stories and examples that will make their appearances more memorable and entertaining. They also instruct people how to write and give sound bites, to answer questions, and to gracefully include their most important points into their answers.

For tips and videos that will show you how to do a better job with the media, visit http://www.speakingchannel.tv.

Most people are not used to dealing with the media, so before they begin publicity campaigns, they should get media training.

Remember

Most people are not used to dealing with the media, so before they begin publicity campaigns, they should get media training. In today's digital world, media training has become increasingly important because your appearances can be quickly and widely circulated through cyberspace. Media training will teach you how to attract the media's attention, how to answer their questions, and how to be invited back.

chapter 20

FROM

Guerrilla Writing Tips

Co-Author Roger C. Parker

W**RITING PLAYS A MAJOR ROLE** in guerrilla marketing success. The ability to write is a necessity, not a luxury, in today's Web 3.0 and self-publishing world. Your ability to express yourself on paper and on screen is essential if you want to leverage Jay Conrad Levinson's proven *Guerrilla Marketing* ideas into new opportunities and lasting profits.

Although my guerrilla talent is design, as I hope I've proved with my design books and completed projects, it's more as an author, book coach, and marketing consultant that I find myself in this *Remix*. Long before this teaming up, I met Jay when we were members of the Microsoft Small Business Council. Jay and Jeannie asked me to tell you that I've helped guerrilla marketers around the world change their approach to writing. Writing doesn't have to be a source of stress! Writing can become a welcome opportunity to attract a following and build lasting relationships with clients, customers, and prospects.

Universal Ideas

Here are nine ideas that can help you change your approach to writing. The ideas are universal; they work just as well with small projects such as articles and blog posts as they do for larger projects like books, e-books, proposals, reports, and white papers.

1. Identify Your Goals

Clarify your goals before you begin to write. Start by asking yourself the following key questions:

- *Who are my intended readers?* Identify their key characteristics and the reasons you want them to read your book, e-book, blog post, or website landing page.
- *What are my reader's concerns?* Review what you know about your readers. List their obvious frustrations and problems, then go deeper and explore the under-lying causes. Finally, identify their unachieved goals and the reasons they haven't achieved them.
- *What are your goals?* Review the "big idea" you want readers to remember, list the key points you want to share, and end with a conclusion that identifies the next step or action you want your readers to take. Your goal is to find the middle ground between your reader's concerns and your goals. Effective writing creates a bridge between your goals and your reader's concerns, creating a win-win situation for both you and your readers.

> *Your goal is to find the middle ground between your reader's concerns and your goals.*

2. Always Be Selling

You must constantly sell the importance of everything you write! Start to sell in the title and first paragraph. These must engage the attention of your readers and convince them to continue reading.

> *Don't expect readers to read what you've written just because you've written it.*

If you fail to engage the prospective reader's attention with a compelling headline, title, or email subject line, your prospects are unlikely to continue reading. They'll simply move on to one of the thousands of other messages competing for their attention each day. Your writing will have been in vain.

3. Be Specific

Avoid generalities; be as specific as you can in titles and first paragraphs. Identify who you're writing for, the benefits readers will gain from your message, and number of points—or steps—that follow.

It's hard to overestimate the importance of starting with a number! Numbers in titles provide a framework for writing your project. Numbers also help readers track their progress through your project.

> *Never underestimate the power of numbers.*

Your writing process begins when you commit to sharing 3 Steps, 6 Keys, 7 Habits, or 10 Commandments!

Numbers also add credibility to titles when you use numbers to specify the benefits that readers will gain. Which of the following appears more credible?

- *The Inner Guide to Losing Weight*
- *The Inner Guide to Losing 30 Pounds in 3 Months*

The 30 pounds and 3 months focuses attention on the benefits, helping transform a weak "generalization" title into a specific, purposeful program.

Numbers in titles also reinforce the promise of quick results, when used in titles like *Guerrilla Marketing in 30 Days.*

Specificity also involves identifying readers in the title. Notice the difference in the following titles:

- *The Inner Guide to Losing Weight*
- *The Entrepreneur's Inner Guide to Losing Weight*

If you're an entrepreneur, you're more likely to respond to the second title because it has been personalized for you; the information, presumably, has a higher likelihood of helping you lose weight.

4. Create a Content Map

Make the structure of your project as visual as possible. Never start to write without a visual plan for your project. After you commit to a number, as detailed in the step above, jot down the topics that you're going to include in your 3 Steps, 6 Keys, 7 Habits, or 10 Commandments you are going to share with readers.

> *Any plan is better than no plan at all.*

Simply jotting down a list of key ideas on the back of a napkin can help you get started and moving forward!

General George Patton reminded us that a pretty good plan executed today is better than a perfect plan executed tomorrow. Jay, Jeannie, and I agree.

5. Keep It Simple

Avoid writing to impress. Write like you speak—as clearly and simply as possible. Avoid long words and strange words. Use simple, everyday language. Keep words, sentences, and paragraphs as short and to the point as possible. Avoid cluttering your writing with unnecessary ideas and words.

You're not writing for a grade; you're writing to share information that will build and reinforce relationships with clients and prospects. The only "grade" that counts is whether or not you share the right information as concisely as possible.

Avoid an "unending stream of paragraphs." Readers don't want to read page after page, or screen after screen, of paragraphs. You have to break up your message into bite-sized chunks.

You're not going to be graded on the complexity of your writing. Break it up!

Accordingly, use subheads to organize paragraphs and introduce new ideas. Subheads attract attention and "advertise" the paragraphs that follow. Remember that your readers are going to skim your message before they read it, looking for ideas and phrases that compel them to take a closer look.

Likewise, use bullet and numbered lists to present information in easily noticed chunks. Lists add visual interest and white space to your message that enhances readability.

6. Start Early

Avoid the myth that writing is easier at the last minute. It's a popular, but dangerous myth.

Last-minute deadlines are more likely to create stress that can paralyze your thinking and ability to write. You may feel "energized" by the stress, but the stress also undermines your ability to make logical connections and correct choices while writing.

Inevitably, last-minute writing results in embarrassing mistakes, omissions, and a lack of clarity.

Finish a day ahead of time, and review your work the next day. Never post, publish, or submit a project immediately after you finish writing. Instead, put it aside for an hour, or—even better—overnight. Then, carefully review what you've written.

Always read what you've written out loud.

Reading out loud will reveal errors and omissions that you didn't notice the previous day. Reading out loud helps you locate run-on sentences, awkward phrases, and missing or unnecessary ideas.

7. Commit to Consistency

Avoid writing marathons. Cultivate the habit of short, frequent writing sessions. You can make a lot of progress in 15-minute or 30-minute writing sessions spread over several days.

Review what you've written at the end of each day, and think about what you want to write the next day. You'll be surprised how much you can accomplish during short writing sessions.

8. Review Writing from a Search-Engine Point of View

Avoid "writer's myopia." Review your project from a search-engine point of view. Writing myopia occurs when you focus exclusively on the ideas of your project and overlook the keywords and search-engine optimization needed for prospective clients to locate your writing.

After editing your project for correct spelling and grammar, review the keywords and keyword phrases that you know are important to attracting qualified prospects. Make sure you have included them in your titles, headings, and key opening and closing paragraphs.

> *It's not enough to write a great piece; you have to make sure prospects will find it when searching for information.*

9. Strive for Efficiency

Avoid the tendency to reinvent the wheel each time you begin a new project. Create a system for tracking your ideas and recycling, reformatting, and reusing them in different ways for future projects. For example, look for ways to convert blog posts into articles, chapters in future books, podcasts, speeches, or tutorials.

In addition, look for opportunities where you can syndicate your content as articles or rewrite them as guest posts for other blogs in your area.

Track the results of your writing. Note which blog posts and topics attract the most comments and social media referrals. Pay attention to the keywords that attract the most visitors to specific blog posts and website pages.

Save and back up your work in a way that allows you to easily locate and access previously written files. If you write blog posts in WordPress, for example, copy, paste, and save each post as a separate file in a word-processing program.

Conclusion

Writing is a process, not an event. There are few landmarks along the road. Writing is more a frame of mind than a silver bullet or skill you can master during a weekend conference.

The only thing that successful writers agree on is that the more you write, the better you'll become and the more comfortable you'll be with your ability to create and organize the projects needed to implement the timeless wisdom shared by successful guerrilla marketers around the world.

chapter 21

FROM

Guerrilla Copywriting Tips

Co-Author David Garfinkel

G UERRILLA COPYWRITING ISN'T ABOUT YOU, your product, your service, or your company—it's about your customer! That is, it is about how what you offer makes your customer's life better.

Once your customers know that, some of them will—at the very least—want to find out more about you, your product, your service, and/or your company. At the very most, they will want to buy something from you right away! And in either case (and everywhere in between), writing compellingly about how you will make your customer's life better creates the kind of relationship between you and your market that money itself cannot buy.

> *Guerrilla copywriting is about how what you offer makes your customer's life better.*

The Benefit of Benefits Lists

To discover how what you sell makes your customer's life better, you need to start with a benefits list. Actually, all guerrilla copy both starts and ends with a benefits list.

Here's how to write your list:

- Have a meeting. Invite your key personnel and at least one customer—because customers are tuned in to benefits that you may not even consider to be benefits.
- Listen—and write. Again, keep your eyes and ears open to benefits you have may have never thought of before.

> *All guerrilla copy both starts and ends with a benefits list.*

- Once you have a list of your benefits, select your competitive advantage because that's where you'll hang your marketing hat.

If you haven't got a competitive advantage, you'll have to create one because you'll need it. After all, anyone can come up with a benefits list. Figure out why people should patronize your business instead of your competitor's business.

With your benefits list and your competitive advantage, you now have the bricks and mortar of all your copy, whether it is to be used on

FOR COPY IDEAS, SEEK KNOWLEDGE IN 10 AREAS

1. Customers
2. Current events
3. Prospects
4. Economic trends
5. Competition
6. Your own offerings
7. Equivalent businesses elsewhere
8. Your community
9. Your own industry
10. Successful advertising

With your benefits list and your competitive advantage, you now have the bricks and mortar of all your copy.

a website, in a tweet, on a blog post, in a radio ad, in a national magazine, or in a flier at a local flea market.

With your benefits list ready, now you're ready to begin writing your copy.

The Power of Powerful Headlines

Every message must begin with a headline or its equivalent. Your headline must either convey an idea or intrigue the reader into wanting to learn more.

Focus like a laser as you direct your headline to members of your target audience, one person at a time. Even if 50 million people read it, they will read it one person at a time. So don't think target audience; think person. Experiment with headlines that use a news style.

Experiment with headlines using all of these words—one at a time: new, announcing, presenting, and now. If possible, put a date in your headline. In radio ads or tweets on Twitter, the rules about headlines apply to your first sentence.

Start your headline with a question to which the answer is yes. That begins the momentum. And it's all about momentum. Keep the momentum going. The more you can get people nodding, even silently, the more likely it is that they will say "Yes!" when you ask them to take action.

Never forget the single most powerful word in the language of advertising—it's "FREE," followed fairly closely by "YOU."

Never forget the single most powerful word in the language of advertising—it's "free," followed fairly closely by "you." Why? Because everyone likes something for free. Including rich people! And after their own name, the sweetest sound to everyone alive is the word "you."

21 / From Guerrilla Copywriting Tips

Selling by Storytelling

Take gentle hold of the reader's or listener's attention by telling a story. The more personal your story the better. A secret (apparently little-known in many sectors of the advertising world) is that even the biggest corporations are made up of people! With names. And faces. And fascinating stories that others would like to hear.

Remember that headlines and opening lines and subject lines are the initial bonds with your prospects. The more connected they feel to you, the more likely they are to buy—and keep buying. If they feel connected, they are also much more likely to refer you enthusiastically to others.

Of course, what you have to say is important, but how you say it is equally important; and if you say it right, it's even more important. Use testimonials in your copy, as your headlines, as your subject lines. (But be careful with testimonials. Don't promise results that you can't document as "typical.")

A healthy mindset for copywriters is that the reader or viewer is definitely going to move on to something else—anything else—unless you stop them cold. Not easy. So keep the reader's attention and make what they read from you the most important event of their day.

COPY MUST ALWAYS BE

1. Readable
2. Strategic
3. Motivating
4. Informative
5. Clear

6. Honest
7. Simple
8. Competitive
9. Specific
10. Believable

Words to See, Words to Hear

Some words are ear words, ideal for broadcast, while others are eye words that look best when being read. "Guerrilla" means one thing to the eyes, another to the ears.

Traditional copywriting was about grammar, vocabulary, and spelling. Guerrilla copywriting is about motivation, persuasiveness, and passion. Don't hide your passion, excitement, and intensity from your readers. They're human, too. And once they're reminded that you are too, your copy will go a lot further with them.

Verbs activate the mind in very cool ways. "Do it now." "Pay close attention." "Write better copy." "Run, don't walk." "Click here."

Mark Twain was tough on copywriters. He said, "Eliminate every third word. It gives writing remarkable vigor." Thomas Jefferson was even tougher. He said you should eliminate half the words. After trying both, Ernest Hemingway said he was convinced that copywriting was much tougher than novel writing.

To be a good copywriter, think in terms of creating original clichés.

Make every sentence you write lead to the next sentence. This lets your copy flow all the way to the last word. "Like the black plague." "Like a swarm of locusts." Avoid rhymes, puns, and clever writing. They definitely are fun to write and even to read, but most of the time they are beside the point and disrupt the flow.

And here's the worst news of all: Clever, catchy copy smothers sales. Dead before arrival. Don't let this happen to you. The opposite of clever and catchy is compelling and conversational. Strive for that!

Embrace the magic words of

- Free
- New
- You
- Sale

- Introducing
- Save
- Money
- Discover

- Results
- Easy
- Proven
- Guaranteed
- Love
- Benefits
- Alternative
- Now
- Win
- Gain
- Happy
- Trustworthy
- Good-looking
- Comfortable
- Proud
- Healthy
- Sexy
- Safe
- Right
- Security
- Winnings
- Fun
- Value
- Advice
- Wanted
- Announcing
- Your
- People
- Why
- How to

Avoid the tragic words that can undo otherwise fine copy:

- Buy
- Obligation
- Failure
- Bad
- Sell
- Loss
- Difficult
- Wrong
- Decision
- Deal
- Liability
- Hard
- Pay
- Death
- Order
- Fail
- Cost
- Worry
- Contract
- Stress
- Must

Never forget, even for an instant, that the primary purpose of your copy is to earn a profit.

Never use a long word when a short word will do. Never use a long sentence when you can use a short sentence. Never use a long paragraph unless you want your readers to struggle through your copy.

Try to write as you speak—using contractions, sentence fragments, and informal language, especially in the area of your vocabulary. The best words are usually those in shirtsleeve English.

Never forget, even for an instant, that the primary purpose of your copy is to earn a profit.

Guerrilla copy is much easier to write if the starting point is an idea. If it is, trust the copy to write itself.

The purpose of guerrilla copywriting is to get people to act, using only the brute force of your ideas and words. Once you have mastered this skill, you have the ultimate leverage in business. You can attract and keep customers at lower and lower costs. With social media and web video, you can often advertise effectively at no cost whatsoever. And with good copywriting skills, your words will create business and enviable relationships—with people you have never even met!

chapter 22

FROM

Guerrilla Marketing for Job Hunters 2.0

Co-Author David Perry

Why You Need to Become a Guerrilla Job-Hunter

Under siege from layoffs, outsourcing, off-shoring, right-sizing, downsizing, and bankruptcies, America is in the midst of a profound business transformation. It is the result of developments in information and communications, technologies, changing human values, and the rise of the global, knowledge-based economy. The sheer complexity and technical sophistication of business has transformed the job market. Business is becoming knowledge-based and technology intensive.

> "It's not the strongest of the species, nor the more intelligent, that survives: It's the one most responsive to change."
>
> —Charles Darwin

YOU NEED A CLEAR, DETAILED PLAN

Every year, 20 to 40 million Americans change jobs. Already reeling from the struggling economy, workers looking for the remaining jobs face tougher competition than ever. The rules for getting jobs have changed, and global competition ensures that the rules will change again tomorrow. Many people needlessly drift in and out of dead-end jobs because they don't know which industries have a future or how to present their value in the right terms to the people who have the authority to hire them.

To succeed in this new job market, you must have a plan that is clear and detailed in every way. It must be

- Clever
- Results-driven
- Marketing-oriented
- Inexpensive to execute
- Achievable

No government agency, educational institution, or think tank has a genuine crystal ball to make a call on the future; there are simply too many unknown factors when it comes to industry and job creation. One thing is certain, whether you are employed but unhappy or unemployed and in need of a new opportunity: As a job-hunter you're at a strategic fork in the road.

Knowledge workers are the backbone of the United States. They are employed in all sectors of the economy, most prominently in the information technology and communications sector, but also to a growing extent in health care, manufacturing, education, finance, natural resources, defense, and government—in any field that requires innovation to sustain competitiveness. Competitive advantage is rooted in the new ideas of these skilled workers.

The New Global Theater

The United States is again at a crossroads in history. The current "jobless recovery" is a consequence of the economy's rapid evolution from a natural resources and manufacturing-based economy to a knowledge-based one.

We are witnessing the first economic recovery in what has become a full information economy.

For most of the 20th century, a recession was a cyclical decline in demand—the result of excess inventory that needed to be sold off. People were temporarily laid off, inventory backlogs were reduced, and demand would snap back. As product demand increased, workers returned to their pre-existing positions in factories, or they found an equivalent job with another company.

Over the past few years, dramatic advances in information technology have allowed companies to establish tightly integrated demand and supply chains and to outsource manufacturing and low-end service jobs to save money. Rightly or wrongly, many of the jobs that have entirely disappeared from North America have reappeared in India, China, and Latin America. Rather than furloughs, many people were let go, forcing them to switch industries, sectors, locations, or learn new skills to find a new job.

Instead of resources or land, capital today means human capital . . . . The real capital is intangible: a person's knowledge level, combined with an aptitude for applications.

If job growth now depends on the creation of new positions, you should expect a long lag before employment rebounds. Employers incur risks in creating new jobs and require additional time to establish and fill positions. Investment in new capital equipment is no longer a pendulum swinging from recession to recovery and back again.

Instead of resources or land, capital today means human capital. It doesn't take a shoe factory to go into the shoe business these days.

Nor do you need raw materials or fleets of trucks. Nike became a shoe industry leader by concentrating on the value-producing capacity of its employees for design, marketing, and distribution know-how. The real capital is intangible: a person's knowledge level, combined with an aptitude for applications.

Why You Need to Be a Guerrilla

With a radically smaller pool of skilled workers and the increased demand for profits, the original "war for talent" of the late 1990s has

LISTEN UP!

A man applied for a job at an office. When he arrived at the busy, noisy office he was told by the receptionist to fill out a form and wait until he was called.

He completed the form and waited with four other candidates who had arrived earlier.

After a few minutes he got up and went into the inner office—and was subsequently given the job.

The other candidates who arrived earlier were angry. The manager explained why the man had been given the job.

What was the reason?

This happened in the 1800s. The man had applied for a job as a telegraph operator. Among the background noise was a Morse code message: "If you understand this, walk into the office."

It was a test of the candidates' skill and alertness. He was the only candidate who passed.

morphed from a quantitative to a qualitative one, best described as "war for the best talent" by author Peter Weddle in his 2004 *Generalship: HR Leadership in a Time of War.* The old "bums-on-the-seats" mentality of many employers is quickly being replaced by "brains-on-the-seats."

> *The people who market their talent the best will win.*

Faced with stiffer competition and tougher hiring requirements, companies of every sort are becoming single-minded about productivity and bottom-line performance. Consequently, competition for jobs is increasing as management seeks and hires only those individuals who appear to have the most potential for helping to boost the company's profits. For many companies, employees are now viewed as a variable cost—hence the term "human capital"—to remain on the books only as long as they continue to produce. Looking for an old-fashioned job like the one Dad used to have is a waste of your time—jobs are temporary in the new economy—henceforth you always need to be looking for the next opportunity.

The people who market their talent the best will win.

chapter 23

FROM

Guerrilla Research

Co-Author Robert Kaden

N OTHING WILL EVER REPLACE entrepreneurial inspiration—those heady days when you just know your product or service will make you millions. The energy, joy, and exhausted delight that come from knowing with certainty that one day your vision will become a profitable reality.

Legions of companies have sprung up from the fertile minds of entrepreneurs. Leonard Lavin and Alberto-Culver. Harland Sanders and KFC. Bill Gates and Microsoft. Andrew Groove and Intel. Walt Disney and Mickey Mouse. George Halas and the Chicago Bears. And on and on. Did those geniuses listen to the customer? Probably not—at first anyway.

What Does Listening to Customers Really Mean?

Market research is not intended to be a substitute for inspiration, although it can often foster breakthrough thinking. It is intended as a connection with your customers or prospects that, if used fully, will get you where you want to go faster and more profitably.

At the very heart of market research is the keen belief that listening to the opinions of the consumers is important. That, when asked the right questions, consumers will tell you what to do to make your business more profitable. That, by listening to consumers, you will do the smart thing far more often than if you just decide to go it alone.

An entrepreneur once asked, "Where would I ever get money for research? I don't even have enough money for all the boxes I should order to pack my products." He walked off and left me thinking that his new shampoo was no different from dozens of competitors and that a little research would probably have rightly convinced him to look for something else to sell.

LOST IN TRANSLATION

Be sure to be sensitive to cultural diversity when advertising globally. One of the most successful advertising agencies in the U.S. acquired a Middle Eastern account. Their first ad made them a laughing stock.

Why?

The agency forgot that people in the Middle East read from right to left. People saw a series of pictures showing "Before" and "After" for the use of a certain washing powder. It indicated to them that the powder made clean clothes dirty!

NEW COKE DEAFNESS

Remember when Coca-Cola introduced New Coke—and failed miserably? Here is what Sergio Zyman, who was Coke's chief marketing officer at the time, had to say about listening to the consumer:

> We orchestrated a huge launch (of New Coke), received abundant media coverage . . . were delighted with ourselves . . . until the sales figures started rolling in. Within weeks, we realized that we had blundered. Sales tanked, and the media turned against us. Seventy-seven days after New Coke was born, we made the second-hardest decision in company history. We pulled the plug. What went wrong? The answer was embarrassingly simple. We did not know enough about our consumers. We did not even know what motivated them to buy Coke in the first place. We fell into the trap of imagining that innovation—abandoning our existing product for a new one—would cure our ills.
>
> After the debacle, we reached out to consumers and found that they wanted more than taste when they made their purchase. Drinking Coke enabled them to tap into the Coca-Cola experience, to be part of Coke's history and to feel the continuity and stability of the brand. Instead of innovating, we should have renovated. Instead of making a product and hoping people would buy it, we should have asked customers what they wanted and given it to them. As soon as we started listening to them, consumers responded, increasing our sales from 9 billion to 15 billion cases a year.

In the case of New Coke, listening to the consumer might have prevented an expensive disaster. Yet like with so many businesses large or small, there is often too much entrepreneurial ego or downright stubbornness to listen to the consumer. Particularly for small businesses, consideration is rarely given to the importance of research and listening to the consumer. And if it is even considered, it is likely to be written off as being unaffordable.

Well, perhaps that is what they'd say. I don't really know because he was too stubborn to look at the situation objectively. Maybe they would have said that the restaurant décor was too old-fashioned or that the lighting was dim and depressing. They might have said that they remembered the food wasn't very good when they visited the restaurant umpteen years ago. Maybe they would have said something simple, like they wished the menu would offer less than the featured elaborate six-course dinners because they always left the restaurant feeling uncomfortably stuffed.

> *Listening to the customer starts with listening to yourself. It means suspending your ego and setting your stubbornness aside.*

Whatever they might have said, I assure you that the restaurant owner would have been more informed and certainly clearer about his problem.

Listening to the customer starts with listening to yourself. It means suspending your ego and setting your stubbornness aside.

Ask Yourself These Questions the Next Time You're Likely to Go It Alone

- If I'm wrong, how much will it cost me?
- How long can I afford to be wrong before I run out of money?
- Would input from customers or prospects that have no stake in whether I succeed or fail help me make better decisions?
- Do I know with certainty why prospects go to a competitor rather than me?
- Have I asked customers and prospects what they need and want from me and my business?
- Do I know if my customers think I'm giving them what they need and want?
- Do I know what else I can provide customers so that they'll pay me more . . . and be happier about it?

- Do customers and prospects know the benefits of buying from me?
- Do I feel that I can't afford market research?
- Can I accept the possibility that my customers might be smarter than I am in helping my business grow?

Do Customers Really Tell You the Truth?

It never really made sense to me, but I have encountered many business types who don't use research because they think customers will lie to them. Or that customers and prospects will be unjustly critical. In my 35 years in market research conducting more than 4,000 focus groups and 3,000 surveys, I have never run into a respondent in a focus group or analyzed data from a survey where it was evident that customers or prospects were lying or were overly critical just out of spite.

No, customers don't lie. They don't really know how to lie about your business because they haven't a clue what you want to hear. Mostly, they don't care enough about your business to tell you anything other than the truth about what comes to their minds at the moment you ask them a question.

A bigger problem is that you often get customers or prospects who don't think very deeply about the issues that you are researching.

> *Customers don't lie. They don't really know how to lie about your business because they haven't a clue what you want to hear.*

Therefore, the real challenge in talking with customers is getting them to give you enough depth of thought so their answers tell you something that will allow you to take actions that result in greater sales. It is never an issue of lying. It is always the issue of getting to the real truth!

It is your job as the researcher to dig below the surface, to probe customers again and again to uncover the below-the-surface factors that will motivate them to buy more. Think of an onion with its many layers. It's the same with

GIVE-AND-TAKE FROM ACTUAL FOCUS GROUP FOR HOME IMPROVEMENT RETAILER

Moderator question: What is the most important thing that will cause you to come into our stores more often?

Consumer answer: Lower your prices.

MQ: Besides lowering prices, what would be important?

CA: Probably faster checkout. There are usually long lines when I go to any of your stores.

MQ: Anything else?

CA: Well, it would be nice if the employees knew more about the products. Usually, they can't answer my questions. I think I know more about the products than the people working at your stores.

Look back at the line of questioning. The moderator asked the initial question in a totally objective manner. Stopping there, without further moderator probing, the indicated action would have been to lower prices. I will also tell you that there is not a marketing problem in the world where customers won't first respond, "I'll buy more from you if you cut the prices." And it's always a red herring. It's not a lie. It's a knee-jerk customer response—and while it's a legitimate response, it can't be taken at face value.

customers. They don't lie. They give you what's top of mind, and you have to be smart enough to know what to accept and act upon and what to discard.

In the focus-group example (see above sidebar), chances are that the customers would be likely to buy more from the home improvement retailer if they knew they could get in and out of the store faster. Or they might be inclined to visit the store more often if employees were more knowledgeable.

Customers don't tell us what we do or don't want to hear. They simply respond to our questions. The tale of an insightful research study, then, is in asking the right questions in the right manner.

Certainly there are times when lowering prices is, in fact, the right answer, or perhaps the only answer. But the street is lined with failed marketing programs and obscure products where marketers took customers and prospects literally and simply lowered prices to compete. Usually providing better value is a bigger factor in satisfying customers than providing better prices.

As you use research, you will begin to understand those factors that will make a big difference. Sometimes, when you've tried all the rest, when you've probed deeply and there is nothing left to make you competitive, price becomes your only point of leverage. But following a price strategy can be perilous, as has become evident in the airline industry.

The inability of American, United, Delta, and USAir to differentiate themselves on aspects of value has brought them to the brink. Not a single carrier has been able to convince fliers that paying a little more to fly with that carrier is worth it. As a result, the airlines continue to compete on price alone and seem to be in a never-ending financial spiral—downward. Someday one of them may figure out how to add enough value to justify raising prices.

Will I Really Learn Anything I Don't Already Know?

In countless research presentations, I've heard clients say, "You aren't telling me anything I don't already know." I always found this a defensive and self-defeating attitude. It smacks of someone who is unsure or lacks discipline to follow his or her own convictions. If it's something you already know, I've reasoned, why aren't you doing it?

If research tells you what you think you know—but haven't acted upon—great! Act upon it. If it confirms what you've already been doing, great. Continue doing it, and learn how to do it better.

USEFUL OUTCOMES FOR RESEARCH

Gerry Linda of Gerald Linda and Associates Marketing says:

Sometimes research will confirm your pet theory about customers, the market, the competition, your product's advantages and disadvantages. If this is the case, have you wasted your money? Absolutely not! Turning a theory into a fact is a highly useful outcome. It allows you to move forward with confidence. And you're likely to spot a nuance in the data that will help you move ahead better.

The point is simple. Customers and prospects are the ultimate judge of your success. If you listen to them closely, you'll hear many ideas for growing your business. While you can always decide not to follow their advice, failure to listen is a much bigger mistake.

Does Research Work for All Types of Businesses?

Research works as long you have customers, prospects, or both. Research works everywhere, for any business, and for any product or service where people can give you opinions. It may even mean doing research among your own employees.

Research will help any business determine the potential for making more money, whether that business happens to be selling gaskets to other manufacturers or cereal to children.

Some of my more interesting clients include:

- A manufacturer selling switching equipment to phone companies
- A cemetery selling grave sites
- A company selling wallpaper over the internet
- A catalog selling office furniture

- A company selling pantyhose to women who weigh more than 250 pounds
- A company trying to convince smokers to quit
- A tobacco company trying to convince tobacco chewers to change brands
- A mail-order music club trying to convince members to buy DVDs
- A technology company trying to convince web developers to use its software
- A popcorn company interested in creating new popcorn flavors
- A museum generating donations
- A charity needing to increase donations
- A publisher of encyclopedias selling its yearly updates
- A publisher of art selling its limited-edition prints
- A health insurance carrier trying to get policy holders to participate in wellness programs

At the very heart of market research is the keen belief that listening to the opinions of the consumers is important.

In conclusion, remember that at the very heart of market research is the keen belief that listening to the opinions of the consumers is important.

chapter 24

FROM

Guerrilla Marketing on the Internet

Co-Authors Mitch Meyerson and Mary Eule Scarborough

FROM *GUERRILLA MARKETING* on the Internet, by Mitch Meyerson, Mary Eule Scarborough, and me (Jay), we learn that today's marketplace is jammed with competition, and that is even more true on the internet. If your goal is to tower above your competitors and grow a profitable business, you're going to have to arm yourself with the right insights, knowledge, and tools.

But before delving into the "how-tos," we want to debunk the most common internet marketing misapprehensions and blunders so you're not operating under false illusions as you proceed online.

We'll begin by reiterating that internet marketing must be part of your overall marketing efforts, regardless of your business size, industry, location, or type. If it isn't, you're severely handicapping your chances of success.

Following are five basic rules. Read them, understand them, write them down on Post-It® notes, and tape one to your forehead and the other on your computer screen because they are the underlying principles for everything we're going to cover in this chapter.

Five Basic Rules of Internet Marketing

Rule 1

Every business, government agency, and nonprofit organization must have some type of website or internet presence. There are no exceptions to this rule.

> *Every business, government agency, and nonprofit organization must have some type of website or internet presence. There are no exceptions to this rule.*

Rule 2

Guerrilla websites have one main purpose: Generate direct or indirect income.

Rule 3

Being online or having a website is not internet marketing. Anyone who wants to earn money using the internet must learn and use effective online marketing strategies and tactics. You just must know marketing to succeed with internet marketing.

Exactly what do you need to know? What is the right way to do this thing called internet marketing? Finding the answers to these questions is similar to holding smoke in your hands. The minute you grab it, it disappears.

Online marketing's fundamental nature is fluid and unstructured, and it will continue to be that way for years to come, as innovative technologies improve and evolve, and ordinary people try to figure out to how to make it fit into their lives and businesses comfortably. For most of us, online technology is both exhilarating and confusing.

We love hearing about the latest gee-whiz gadgets and software and can't wait to get our hands on them, only to find that we're frustrated and often cursing the very things that were supposed to make our lives easier. Sound familiar? If so, you're not alone. This is but one example of the many times we've all felt that "progress" isn't always what it's cracked up to be and we may even be better off avoiding it altogether. That's why there are two more rules to add to your list.

Rule 4

If you're going to compete in today's marketplace, you must be open to learning about and using new technologies because, when used correctly, they will have a dramatically positive effect on every aspect of your life.

> *If you're going to compete in today's marketplace, you must be open to learning about and using new technologies.*

Rule 5

Sometimes technology exists because it can. If a little is good, more is not necessarily better. Bigger, brighter, faster, new and improved software, buttons, and features are worthless if you can't, don't, or won't use them. Although this chapter is devoted to talking about how to use internet equipment and technology to improve your lifestyle and your business, keep in mind that there are many other innovative technologies out there and we couldn't possibly cover them all. And we wouldn't even if we could, because it would be overwhelming, and more importantly, unnecessary. There are literally hundreds of ways you can use the internet to grow your business, so one of your biggest challenges will be narrowing your selections, choosing the ones that best fit, developing a prioritized plan, and implementing it. If there's one thing for certain, it's that nothing is for certain about the internet. Guerrillas are always paying close attention.

Take some time now to learn how to avoid the 12 most common mindset, strategy, and action mistakes that business owners make when marketing on the internet.

Mistake #1: Not Starting with a Plan

Businesspeople who choose to engage in internet marketing begin for many very good reasons, all having to do with their desire to achieve their loftiest dreams. So they begin their journey down a path armed with good intentions and enthusiasm—but no plan. Their passion and energy carry them for a while, but over time their shortsightedness weakens their ability to respond properly to unforeseen challenges and opportunities. In fact, many internet marketers plan their vacations in more detail than their businesses.

For example, let's assume that our friend, David, who lives in Baltimore, Maryland, has a clear objective. He wants to arrive in Boise, Idaho, in four days. He decides to drive, even though he's never done so before. Given this, David would be foolish to hop in his car and leave. If so, he would greatly increase his chances of encountering problems along the way that could have a devastating effect on his ability to arrive in Boise in good shape and on time.

Most of us would agree that it would be much wiser and safer for David to carefully plan his trip and make sure that he had the resources and wherewithal to accomplish his goal before jumping into action.

For instance, he might replace the bald tires on his car with new ones; have his car checked out by a mechanic; pack his clothes and toiletries; make sure he's got enough money to buy gas and food; map his route; determine how far he'll travel each day; and double-check that he's got a spare tire, jumper cables, driver's license, vehicle registration, credit cards, emergency numbers, and hotel reservations.

If he does those things, David is thinking ahead. He understands what it will take to arrive at his final destination and is improving his chances for succeeding. Even better, he'll get there cheaper, quicker, and less stressfully.

This straightforward analogy illustrates how vitally important it is to plan backwards.

Begin with the destination. Small-business owners squander billions of dollars every year because they misunderstand the reality of marketing and rush into it headlong—particularly on the internet.

A huge amount of this wasted money is being spent on websites that are developed, posted, and ignored. If you don't know what we're talking about, just hop online and check around. There are gobs of disjointed websites that look like they haven't been updated since 1999—replete with outdated or missing information, broken links, ear-jarring music, and annoying animation. Visitors may have no idea what to do when they arrive or what type of business is represented. They are confused, frustrated, and annoyed, so they leave quickly and never come back.

As guerrillas know, it's hard to get prospects interested enough to visit your website, so the last thing you want to do is disappoint them once they find you.

Remember that it's critically important to carefully plan every aspect of your website's development—and all your other internet marketing efforts—before it goes live, as well as how it will be maintained and updated moving forward.

The moment you know where you're going and how you're going to get there, you'll feel a tremendous weight lifted off of your shoulders. No matter where you are on the path, you can always move further along as long as you have the foresight to plan for the unexpected.

Mistake #2: Falling in Love for the Wrong Reasons

Even though beginners are far more likely to commit this blunder, seasoned businesspeople also fall in love with a cool product or creative idea and rush headlong into a venture without conducting objective research in advance. Sure, it's a great idea to take a look at the things you love to do most and see if there's a way to turn those passions into viable products or services, but it's not enough. If not enough people share your enthusiasm or have a desire to purchase your products, you're sunk. Additionally, it's important to make sure the marketplace isn't oversaturated with competitors so that you can create a unique niche that you can call your own.

The good news is that the internet is full of resources—way too many to list here—for obtaining free information quickly and easily. Use keywords to find out how many people have used specific words or phrases to search for products and services in the recent past. Once there, type in the words or phrases you figure your targeted prospects would use to find them—think wedding toasts, 20-inch 14K gold chains, marriage counseling, flea shampoo for dogs, shrimp, and grits recipes.

You'll get back a list of keywords and phrases—the ones you entered and similar ones—and the approximate number of times they've been used to conduct a search. To drill down even further, double-click on any word or phrase in the list. If you use more general terms, your numbers will likely be higher. For instance, a word such as "tennis" would result in much higher search numbers than "pink tennis socks," "titanium tennis racquets," or "tennis tutorials for beginners." It's a balancing act.

There needs to be enough people in your target pool, but quantity is not as important as quality. If you sell "tennis bracelets" it does you no good to bring people to your website who are looking for tennis lessons. You get the idea. And it always helps to check out your competitors. Find out what they're selling and how their websites, services, and prices compare with yours. Go to Google and type in the same keywords you used in step one, see what you get, and visit several. As you're looking over the websites, jot down your answers to questions like:

- How do their products and services compare with mine?
- Are they priced similarly?
- Do they have a wider or narrower selection?
- What types of packages do they offer?

Then look for ways to make your site stand out by continuing to bore down into your niche for products that appeal to the same target market. Your target audience size will be smaller, but you'll attract more qualified prospects or uncover unfulfilled needs. Alternatively, drill down even further and become the expert in a specific service area. Although your recycling consultation services might be beneficial to the entire planet, you might be better off specializing in recycling solutions in dry climates or for dry cleaners.

Guerrillas take the time to find out what others are selling or talking about, particularly on the internet. Use websites such as ClickBank.com, Amazon.com, and eBay.com to find out what people are buying; news sites such as CNN.com, NYTimes.com, and online magazines to find out what people are doing; and chat rooms, forums, and blogs to find out what people are talking about.

Once again, an easy way to keep your finger on your target audience's pulse is to go to any search engine and type in phrases like "French bulldog blogs" or "small business marketing forums" and follow the links.

Mistake #3: Not Understanding the Power of Design

Online consumer research studies confirm that when visitors land on a website, they experience "stay" or "go" moments within the first 10 seconds. If it looks unprofessional or hard to use, they leave and usually won't be back. In other words, your target audience will judge you, your products and services, and your company in a snap—and you're likely to get only one chance to impress them.

Given this, all website owners should be doing everything they can to ensure that their online visitors are blown away by their website's look, feel, and navigability. Unfortunately, this is often not the case. Quite a few shortsighted entrepreneurs underestimate the negative impact of poorly written copy, amateurish design, and convoluted navigation. Remember that this is one of those areas where it doesn't pay to be penny wise and pound foolish—it's just too important. Don't annoy or—worse yet—alienate prospective customers because your cousin's friend's aunt's next-door neighbor's brother volunteered to design your website on the cheap.

Mistake #4: Not Understanding Direct Response Marketing

Direct response marketing has one main goal: Get the intended audience to take action. Guerrillas create direct-response copy almost exclusively because it's an extremely effective form of promotional communication that can easily be adapted for all delivery vehicles.

We mention it now because, in spite of all the available help, most small-business owners fail to use extremely effective direct-response copy elements in their website's written, audio, or video communication.

In our opinion, most websites do not contain such things as attention-grabbing headlines, risk-free guarantee policies, and compelling customer testimonials. Instead you'll usually find something like "Welcome to Our Website" or the company's name splashed across the top of the page, exactly where a benefit-driven headline belongs.

We understand how cautious many consumers are about handing over money in exchange for products or services, so why not make it as easy as possible for them to do so by shifting the risk from them to you with an ironclad guarantee?

Additionally, third-party feedback is one of the fastest and most effective ways to establish credibility, yet few entrepreneurs take advantage of its immense power and showcase customer testimonials throughout their websites and other locations.

Direct response explains the direction in which marketing and business is heading. Rather than shouting fuzzy messages to the masses, marketers are crafting specific messages for particular people and encouraging them to act as directed. These guerrillas understand that interactivity is at the heart of direct response and that the internet is the best direct-response technique in the history of the world.

Mistake #5: Not Understanding the Power of Your Email List

Ask any successful internet guerrilla marketer this question: "What is the holy grail of online marketing?" They'll tell you it's their email list. Regardless of whether they're selling packaged products, giving away free information, or anything in between, they will all be focused on obtaining their website's visitors' names and email addresses. Why? Because people who opt in have essentially given them permission to send promotional emails and/or other information.

But many entrepreneurs fail to collect this invaluable information— and it's a huge mistake. One of the reasons for this mistake is the erroneous idea that marketing is a one-shot transaction. Too many entrepreneurs focus their efforts on making immediate sales instead of using a sound relationship-building model of marketing. Internet marketing is like building a personal relationship: It takes time, effort, and commitment to develop lasting bonds. To accomplish this, create a system that leads your prospects down a comfortable and natural path to the first sale and to many more after that.

So unless you sell impulse-buy products or your target audience is pre-sold before they land on your site—the two exceptions to this rule of thumb—we strongly encourage you to use a marketing funnel approach.

This solid strategy works because it addresses two fundamental consumer psyche laws: People are more apt to purchase products and services from people and companies they know, like, and trust; and it is more effective and less expensive to get more from existing customers than to attract new ones.

Mistake #6: Not Having a Traffic-Generation Strategy

Not having a traffic-generation strategy is a boo-boo supreme.

Many entrepreneurs erroneously believe that the famous phrase "build it and they will come" applies to their websites. They're wrong. If you want to get people to your site, you need to understand and apply the basic laws and contributory principles that govern internet traffic.

Guerrillas understand that great marketing is a methodical and accountable process. There are no secret tricks that will effectively drive tons of qualified visitors to your website. Even though there are many things you can do to jump start your progress, you'll need to carefully plan each one if you want your site to be a not-to-be-missed feature on the internet. For now, keep in mind two things:

1. Your goal should be to entice the right people to your website, not just warm bodies.
2. The right people don't visit your website by happenstance. They'll get there because you developed a comprehensive plan and executed it using well-thought-out strategies and tactics.

> *Your goal should be to entice the right people to your website, not just warm bodies.*

Mistake #7: Not Using Web 2.0 Social Media and Technology

During the early days of the internet, individuals were busy learning how to use their new computers and software, so they were less concerned with connecting to the World Wide Web.

Today, however, most folks have moved beyond the basics and are more focused on finding new ways to connect with people by using the internet. And we're seeing evidence of the effects more and more each day. For instance, a major TV network used the internet's powerful technology to obtain real-time feedback and questions from viewers during a televised debate in January 2008. The show's producers set up an interactive forum on Facebook, which allowed viewers to submit and answer questions. Even better, the results were aired immediately, and the show's hosts could add new questions and receive answers on the spot. Talk about a great marketing weapon! Unfortunately, however, far too many entrepreneurs miss out on incredible opportunities like this because they fail to take advantage of inexpensive and easy-to-use web-based, social media tools.

Marketing is not about reinventing the wheel. It's about working less and gaining more. It's about knowing what's out there and choosing the tools and weapons that will provide the greatest impact for the best cost. And if you're not using the internet's new culture and technology to your advantage, you're making a big mistake.

Mistake #8: Not Using Online and Offline Marketing Combinations

Guerrillas know that having a website is not an option nowadays. They also realize that most consumers still purchase the majority of their goods and services and obtain most of their information in the offline world—for now—so they work hard to achieve top-of-mind awareness there. Unfortunately, many small-business owners focus their efforts on one or the other—a big mistake. For example, they fail to put their website addresses on their business cards and signs, or provide directions to their brick-and-mortar locations on their websites.

Don't let this happen to you. Plug your website in your ads, on invoices, business cards, brochures, fliers, newspaper ads, specialty gifts, catalogs, gift certificates, newsletters, and more. Refer to it in seminars, radio and TV ads, direct-mail letters, faxes, and anywhere your company's name appears. In other words, actively promote it; it should not be an afterthought. Talk enthusiastically about your website, and you'll get more people there. You'll know you're doing a great job when people start asking you if your last name is "dot.com."

But don't stop there; feel free to get creative. For instance, place a small, inexpensive ad in your local paper's classified section that reads something like this:

"The 7 Things Local Real Estate Agents Don't Want Homeowners to Know. Selling your house? Don't even think of it until you read this. Go to yourwebsite.com to obtain your FREE report."

Then, when interested prospects go to your website, they'll be asked to provide their names and email addresses in order to download the report. Once you have this information, you can send promotional emails about your mini e-course on real estate sales. You get the idea.

Mistake #9: Failing to Track Marketing Campaigns

Every type of advertising costs something—time, energy, people power, or money. That's why you must track everything you do. It's the only way you'll ever know what's working and what's not. This is the only way to build a successful business. Unfortunately, lots of business owners don't take the time to track and measure their activities and end up wasting thousands of dollars and precious time.

If you've been around marketing for a while you've probably heard the phrase, "You can't improve what you don't track." But it can also be said like this: "If you track it you will improve it." Tracking your results allows you to amend or stop whatever is not working.

Let's say you sent out five promotional email messages; two of them worked well and three didn't. You'd simply get rid of the three that didn't do well and keep the two that did. Then you'd continually test new ideas until you beat the winner.

You need to know key metrics such as the number of unique visitors to your website, opt-in conversion rate, how many people get to the order page, and then how many of those buy.

Mistake #10: Thinking You Can Do It All Yourself

Too many small-business owners think they can do it all. So they fail to develop time-saving systems and neglect to look for ways to put routine tasks on autopilot. What happens? They answer phones, write emails, purchase inventory, deal with suppliers, write sales letters, design logos, and more. Consequently, they are burned out and have to live with below-average results. There's absolutely no good reason to continue doing this when there are so many affordable resources on the internet. These days you can outsource one-time tasks or hire virtual assistants for your ongoing duties, even if your operating budget is very limited.

Additionally, many entrepreneurs end up going it alone another way by failing to develop beneficial fusion marketing relationships or to expand their social and business networks.

Teaming up with other people via strategic alliances, joint ventures, and affiliate partnerships is the key to online marketing because it's one of the best ways to increase traffic, build subscriber lists, grow product lines, and more. The future of internet marketing will be based on people working together, so if you've got a Lone Ranger mindset, it's time to get rid of it.

Mistake #11: Failing to Create a System

Most entrepreneurs have not created a system for following up with their prospects and customers. This is a huge mistake for the following two reasons:

1. It can take up to 27 reminders before an interested prospect turns into a customer.
2. Customers who are ignored after a sale will take their business elsewhere.

Guerrillas know that excellent marketing requires patience and commitment and that one of the best ways to get and keep lifelong customers is to communicate with them often and consistently. In the old days, guerrillas wrote and mailed letters; today they use affordable, web-based, automation technology and stay in touch without breaking a sweat.

Let's assume that 40 percent of your website's visitors opt in—that is, they give you their names and email addresses, even if they didn't purchase anything. By providing this information, your prospects are granting you permission to market to them. This is called permission-based marketing.

Your goal is to develop a detailed plan for utilizing automation software to send out both informational and educational emails to prospects that remind them of your products' benefits and features.

Mistake #12: Not Understanding How Technology Can Help

We decided to add this one final caution even though it doesn't really fit under the internet marketing umbrella. We felt it was still important to cover here because it's often difficult for entrepreneurs to keep up with today's fast-paced technology while they're doing a myriad of other things. If you ignore this critical aspect of your business, it's going to greatly hinder your ability to attain your goals.

Additionally, today's technology affords us the opportunity to do many things ourselves, tasks we hired specialists for in the not-too-distant past. This is a wonderful thing for small-business owners because it allows them more freedom of choice. It allows them to save money on some things and put it to work for them elsewhere. As a result, most companies have computers and a lot of software to go with them. Some business owners only use their computers from time to time, but they're the exception. Nowadays, most entrepreneurs rely on their computers. They expect them to perform a multitude of vital tasks on demand such as tracking marketing efforts, communicating with customers and prospects, designing marketing collateral, housing their clients' private information, and much more.

When they get to their desks each morning, business owners expect their computers to work. They have confidence that the documents they saved on Tuesday will be on their hard drives on Wednesday. They assume their software will work today if it worked yesterday. They don't see the need to back up important customer information because they don't anticipate problems. They think that a $400 laptop can easily handle their workload. They're usually wrong.

Do your research and make sure your computer equipment is robust enough to handle your business needs. There are lots of people who earn their livings because computers crash. It's not a question of if—it's a question of when.

> *Computers are a lot like cars. They're machines. They have a definitive useful life and require regular maintenance and care.*

And that's another thing: Inexpensive computers rarely come with free troubleshooting assistance, so even though you may be saving money on one end, you're surely paying for it on the other. Many small-business owners who are trying to save money purchase inexpensive computer equipment. This is often a mistake that comes back to haunt them. Computers are a lot like cars. They're machines. They have a definitive useful life and require regular maintenance and care. If you use them a lot and load them up, the wear and tear will show. You can't expect computers to outperform engineered specifications, but many entrepreneurs do just that.

This is not one of those times when cheaper is necessarily better. Yes, you can get sturdy computers for less than $500 these days. But if you rely on your computer to generate any part of your income, it's a big mistake. We're not implying that they won't work—they're perfectly fine for light use—but don't shortchange yourself with a cheap computer that's not designed as a business machine. Do your research—there are many online resources—and evaluate your computer as you would the foundation of your house. Ask yourself: Can this computer withstand the weight of my business or will it crack? A good rule of thumb is to buy twice the power and ability you think you need.

Laptops, tablets, and desktop computers are only as good as what they carry. The type of software you use can make your job easier or more difficult, so it's up to you to research what's available and choose wisely. There are two general types of software available: commercially licensed, which you must purchase, and open source, which is free. Each type has its distinct advantages and disadvantages, so do your homework.

> *Unfortunately, the phrase "set it and forget it" does not apply when it comes to information systems.*

Choose software programs that fit your needs and are highly rated among current users. With all the headlines about data theft and identity theft it's no wonder computer security has become a priority for every small-business owner. Make sure your computer and business systems are equipped with the latest spam blockers and anti-virus protection.

It's astonishing how many business owners never back up their critical information, or if they do, never test the recovery of their data. Millions of dollars are lost and hundreds of businesses in the U.S. are shut down because they don't have a reliable and secure backup system for the information that they process.

Unfortunately, the phrase "set it and forget it" does not apply when it comes to information systems. Much like a car, your computer needs to be tuned up and maintained. Get an information technology pro to check yours every six months at a minimum. Information is power, and powerful businesses are the ones that allow customers, suppliers, employees, and others to have 24/7

20 QUESTIONS TO CONSIDER ABOUT YOUR WEBSITE

1. What is the immediate, short-term goal of your website? Be specific.
2. What specific action do you want visitors to take? Be specific.
3. What are your objectives for the long term? Be specific.
4. Who do you want to visit your site?
5. What solutions or benefits can you offer to these visitors?
6. What data should your site provide to achieve your primary goal?
7. What information can you provide to encourage them to act right now?
8. What questions do you get asked most often on the telephone?
9. What questions and comments do you hear most often at trade shows?
10. What data should your site provide to achieve your long-term objectives?
11. Where does your target audience go for information?
12. How often do you want visitors to return to your website?
13. What may be the reasons you don't sell as much as you'd like to?
14. Who is your most astute competitor?
15. Does your competitor have a website?
16. What are some ways you can distinguish yourself from competitors?
17. How important is price to your target audience?
18. Who is your market?
19. What information does your market need in order to want to take the action you desire?
20. What are you doing to make sure your market visits—and revisits—your website?

access to them. Given today's smartphones, portable USB devices, and other mobile equipment, there's no reason to lose touch. Try to lend big-business credibility to your small business.

Remember, the internet is exploding with new ideas, new friendships, and new opportunities, so take advantage of it.

Does your website

- Load quickly?
- Communicate your area of expertise?
- Describe the products or services offered?
- Offer information that will benefit visitors?
- Describe your unique competitive advantage?
- Invite visitor participation?
- Create a sense of professionalism?
- Establish credibility?
- Include contact information on every page?
- State the length and terms of your guarantee or warranty?
- Provide a pleasant visiting experience?

chapter 25

FRO M

Guerrilla Social Media Marketing

Co-Author Shane Gibson

ONVENTIONAL BUSINESS WISDOM spawned the saying, "It's not personal . . . it's just business." Guerrillas know customers take the way you treat them very personally. At the end of a marketing campaign, most people count the number of tweets, website visits, Facebook friends, and YouTube video views that they amassed during the campaign. At the end of your marketing campaign, you need to focus on how many new relationships you started and how many existing relationships you deepened to greater levels of consent. Although profit is how we need to measure the success of our marketing over time, strong customer relationships are what lead to those profits.

Relationships lead to a point where the customer will give you consent to market specific things of interest to them. As Jay Levinson says, "Never fail to distinguish between your B-List customers who

> "Never fail to distinguish between your B-List customers who should
> be treated like royalty, and your A-List customers who
> should be treated like family."
>
> —Jay Conrad Levinson

should be treated like royalty, and your A-list customers who should be treated like family."

There are several levels of relationship development in social media. In fact, after the initial purchase by the customer, most marketers and salespeople feel their job is done. The initial purchase is actually just the beginning of a long-term, profitable relationship based upon genuinely contributing and connecting at all stages. Before the purchase, there are several stages of relationship development that you will move through with customers: the five stages of consent.

THE FIVE STAGES OF CONSENT

1. Discovery
2. Consumption
3. Interaction
4. Connection
5. Consent

Discovery

Discovery is exactly what it sounds like. For the marketer, you will discover new clients and new community members through the use of guerrilla intelligence tools and, of course, referrals from the community.

For consumers, discovery can happen in many ways. They may hear your name tweeted several times by their community; their friend may email them a link to an interesting blog article you've written; or Google can deliver them right to your website through a keyword search. This step is about finding the right connections and being found by the right connections. One of the reasons why guerrillas always have to be on and ready to engage is that we usually have less than 15 seconds to make that good first impression to move consumers to the next step. This can be done by building your guerrilla headquarters, which is your blog or social site. It is, however, vital that your website or blog is designed in a way that immediately establishes credibility with the audience you are targeting.

Consumption

Now that you've qualified your visitors and they have not abandoned your site or clicked away from your Twitter profile, they will begin to consume the content you create. Too many people at this point immediately spring into action, blasting their visitors or new connections with marketing messages, special offers, and various other types of "me" marketing.

In order to engage, establish trust, and make people want to invest more time, energy, and effort into learning about us and what we can do for them, guerrillas need to exceed prospective customers' expectations with high-value content. This is where the quality of your blog writing, the helpfulness of your studies and white papers, and the entertainment value of your YouTube videos all become very important. You gain consent by being trustworthy, and trust is based upon credibility.

You gain consent by being trustworthy, and trust is based upon credibility.

Credibility is challenging because it is contextual. Every human being has a slightly

> *Credibility is challenging because it is contextual.*

different set of values that drives what he or she feels is valuable. Some people who read two blog posts they like about you may sign up for your email newsletter and send you a quick tweet. Other people may read your blog for six months, follow your Twitter stream, and lurk about on Facebook observing you before you ever know they're there. Consistently produced, high-value content using multiple social media weapons ensures that your visitors can consume the information they want in the format they want at a time that is right for them. All of this leads to interaction, where the customer you don't know hits your radar.

Interaction

Interaction can happen in several ways. Sometimes you can jump right into the interaction stage if the timing is right. If you own an automotive garage and notice that someone on Twitter asked a question about winter tires, this person will most likely be open to your interacting with him and giving him answers. Interaction can also occur by your being proactive and visiting the blogs, Twitter profiles, and Facebook pages of your target market and making value-added comments and initiating conversation.

The other form of interaction is, of course, the customer-driven version where, after reading your blog for a time, prospects begin making comments. They may even ask a question or contribute their own content to your Facebook page or Flickr group, or share a tweet of yours with their followers. All of these are door openers to the next stage of relationship development.

Connection

Connection is a soft step in the stages of consent, but is often mistaken for consent to market. Connection is when someone adds you as a friend on Facebook, a connection on LinkedIn, or mutually follows you on Twitter. In the world of dating, it would be the equivalent of a connection on Match.com; it doesn't mean you're going to agree to go on a date, but it does say, "I'd like to learn more about you." It also says, "I would like you to learn a little more about me."

Resist the temptation to push marketing messages, special offers, and all those other types of "Me Marketing" at your connections. At this point, the person wants to learn more about you, not buy from you. This step is very important in credibility building. When someone connects with you on Facebook or LinkedIn, in particular, that person is allowing you to see more of his world, his business, and his personality, enabling you to adjust your marketing and communications to match his credibility model and values.

Consent

If relationships were currency, consent would be the gold standard. A lot of companies spend a lot of time gaining customers but neglect to truly build relationships, and so they miss long-term opportunities. On the other hand, there are a lot of social media marketers who have friendly chats and feel very liked and popular but lack consent to market. Consent is where you move from feel-good, fuzzy marketing to monetization. You have consent when someone has agreed to subscribe to your newsletter and given you an email address for that purpose. Consent can also be in the form of a question or inquiry over Twitter, when someone asks you a specific question about a service you offer or a product you sell.

If relationships were currency, consent would be the gold standard.

Other forms of consent are when someone attends a free webinar by your company. It is usually assumed that you will give real educational value, but at the end of your webinar people expect a certain level of marketing for information on your product or services. After your webinar, a follow-up email thanking people for attending and providing some information on your business and offerings is also acceptable.

Offline connections where someone bumps into you at an event and lets you know he wants to learn more about your business is, of course, one of the oldest forms of consent. Guerrillas value this level of permission so much that they are very careful to respect boundaries and still keep a good ratio of high-value, content interaction relative to marketing-speak or offers.

A proper guerrilla marketing attack has a beginning, a middle, and, in most cases, no end. The same holds true for relationships. Once consent is gained, you'll automatically broaden that consent more through your natural sales or marketing process with that prospect. During this period, customers will still be consuming your great content on your blogs, Twitter, GoogleBuzz, or any other platform they're connected to you on. The difference is these tools now are used to expand a customer's knowledge of what you can do for them and expand your knowledge of their core needs, challenges, and goals.

> *It costs a lot of money to gain a good, loyal customer, and guerrillas use relationships as insurance on that investment.*

After the initial sale, your goal is to continue to develop greater levels of intimacy, insight, and relationship with your customers. It costs a lot of money to gain a good, loyal customer, and guerrillas use relationships as insurance on that investment. If nurtured properly, those relationships can pay year after year in the form of direct purchases as well as referrals.

Guerrilla social media marketing is both a strategy and a way of thinking and living virtual lives. It's about applying time-tested principles of community-building, relationship development, innovation, and imagination to the lightning-fast world of digital social networks. As we have said earlier, a guerrilla social media marketing attack has a beginning, a middle, but no end. You need to sustain that attack one year or even longer before you reap the full benefits. Guerrillas know that in order to sustain a vibrant and powerful marketing campaign, they must have a home base from which to launch, and they learn how to build and protect their guerrilla social media marketing headquarters.

> *Guerrilla social media marketing is both a strategy and a way of thinking and living virtual lives in the lightning-fast world of digital social networks.*

Guerrilla Social Media Marketing Weapons

Hardware

- Smartphone with a data plan
- Notebook computer
- Video camera
- Digital camera
- Good microphone
- Boingo Wi-Fi membership
- Webcam

Software

- Graphic and photo editing software
- Audio editing software
- Video editing software
- Software to manage contacts and customer relations
- Browser with social media and Google plug-ins

Social Networking

Facebook
- Facebook profile
- Facebook pages
- Facebook groups

- Facebook events
- Facebook applications

LinkedIn
- LinkedIn profile
- LinkedIn slideshare
- LinkedIn Google pre-sentations
- LinkedIn Twitter
- LinkedIn blog import
- LinkedIn groups
- LinkedIn answers
- LinkedIn events

Other Sites
- Orkut
- Hi5
- Xing
- Ecademy
- Brazen Careerist

Self-Branded Networks
- Ning
- BuddyPress
- Jive Software
- Pluck
- Awareness, Inc.
- Acquia
- Drupal

Nanoblogging Weapons
- Twitter
- Complete Twitter profile
- Public Twitter lists

- Private Twitter lists
- Status updates
- FriendFeed
- URL shorteners, such as Bit.ly and Ow.ly

Third-Party Social Networking Applications
- TweetDeck
- HootSuite
- SocialToo
- Seesmic
- Ping.fm

Photo Sharing
- Flickr
- Picasa

Document Sharing
- SlideShare
- Scribd

Audio and Video
- Podcasts
- YouTube
- Viddler
- Niche and specialty networks
  - Vimeo
  - FameCast:
  - blip.tv
  - Facebook video
  - Vbox7
  - Nico Nico Douga
  - Tudo

– Strutta

Real-Time Social Media
- Ustream
- Justin.tv
- Skype
- CoveritLive
- Tinychat

Webcasts and Web Conferencing
- GoToMeeting
- WebEx
- Screencast.com
- Your website
- Forums
- Microsites
- Your blog

WordPress, Self-Hosted Blog Sites and Weapons
- WordPress.com
- WordPress.org
- WordPress themes

Plug-Ins
- All in One SEO
- ShareThis
- Tweet This
- Google Sitemap Generator
- PowerPress
- Google Analytics
- WPtouch
- WP-o-Matic
- Akismet

- WP to Twitter
- WordPress.com Stats
- Commenting system
- Disqus
- IntenseDebate

Content Management Systems (CMS)
- Joomla!
- Drupal
- Mambo
- Ubertor (real estate)
- RSS feeds
- Feedblitz
- Yahoo Pipes
- Wikis

Light Blogging Tools
- Tumblr
- Posterous

Social Bookmarking
- Digg
- StumbleUpon
- Reddit
- Delicious

Mobile and Location-Based Tools
- foursquare
- Brightkite
- Facebook Mobile
- Qik

Guerrilla Intelligence Tools
- search.twitter.com

By words
By language
People
Within a specific distance
Dates
By attitudes
Containing links
Including re-tweets
- Twitter Grader
- BackType
- BackTweets
- Twellow (Tweetup)
- PostRank
- Radian 6

Guerrilla Management
- Biz360 community
- Twazzup
- PostRank Analytics
- Payment systems

Directories
- Blog directories
- Podcast directories
- iTunes
- Twitter directories

The Major Directories
- Klout
- Twellow
- Twibes
- WeFollow
- Twitterholic

Google Weapons
- Google apps
- Gmail for business
- Google calendar
- Google docs
- Google groups
- Google sites secure
- Google video
- Google profiles
- Google friend connect
- Google wave
- Google alerts
- Google feed reader
- Google feed bundles
- Google buzz

Email
- Your email signature
- Email newsletter

List Management Software
- AWeber
- Constant Contact

Event Marketing Tools
- Meetup
- Eventbrite
- Tweetup organizing sites

Cutting-Edge Weapons
- Augmented reality applications
- Social CRM
- Smartphone payment systems

chapter 26

FROM

Guerrilla Marketing Goes Green

Co-Author Shel Horowitz

CUSTOMERS WANT TO DO BUSINESS with companies that share their values—and these days, those values include strong awareness of climate change and other environmental issues.

We live at a powerful moment: For the first time, the environment has penetrated our collective consciousness deeply enough to move a whole lot of people toward "green" lifestyle changes. At the same time, technology (especially the internet) has made it possible to run a global business with little or no staff or resources, and without a big infrastructure.

This opens all sorts of opportunities for the green guerrilla who honestly fits into this market.

For the first time, the environment has penetrated our collective consciousness deeply enough to move a whole lot of people toward green lifestyle changes.

HOW YOU BENEFIT BY MARKETING GREEN

When you look at all the advantages of running a green company, it's hard to understand why every company in the world hasn't shifted.

- Green goods and services are much easier to market.
- They often command a premium price, and thus are more profitable.
- Of course, they're better for the environment: They use fewer resources, less energy, and more organic and natural materials. They create less pollution, have a smaller carbon footprint (which means they add less to the global warming problem), and are easier to dispose of.
- Contrary to conventional wisdom, green products can actually be cheaper to produce—if properly designed.

Worldwide, consumer consciousness on these issues is growing by orders of magnitude. As recently as 2004, discussions of climate change and sustainability were rarely heard in mainstream discussions; now, those discussions are everywhere. One example: *Plenty* magazine named "10 ideas that will change our world," and six of those 10 (turning waste into new inputs, green affordable housing, green media, green jobs, carbon labeling, and pay-as-you-go energy retrofits) are directly and explicitly rooted in green thinking. The other four all have a green component.

Areas of living that we used to take for granted are now being re-examined under a green microscope. Suddenly, green is an issue in every single industry.

Another example: The very successful e-zine *Healthy, Wealthy, and Wise* recently ran an article on choosing a green pediatrician. The doctor-author writes, "As you did when choosing an ob/gyn, you want to find a pediatrician who is top-notch medically. How much better if he or she is also on the journey to an environmentally sustainable perspective on pediatrics!"

The more effectively a company can demonstrate commitment to environmental values, the easier it will be to convince those consumers to channel their business to that company. Here are some examples of moves that have worked.

> *Areas of living that we used to take for granted are now being re-examined under a green micro-scope. Suddenly, green is an issue in every single industry.*

- The hotel industry's change in towel washing policies met essentially no consumer resistance because this cost-cutting move was successfully marketed as a green initiative.
- Publishers move to slash print inventories and eliminate the practice of allowing bookstores to return unsold books, citing both environmental and economic reasons.

Green May Save You Some Green

Conveniently enough, many green initiatives not only make the company more attractive to consumers, but they actually cut existing costs. And those are the ones that can survive corporate restructuring.

> *Conveniently enough, many green initiatives not only make the company more attractive to consumers, but they actually cut existing costs.*

If green moves actually both save money and make money, they won't be on the chopping block when the company faces hard times or a new management team.

Companies that don't leverage their environmental achievements and commitment in a way that produces business value often find that green is the first thing to go when times get tough—when there's a change in leadership, when shareholders raise questions, or when your company otherwise finds that being seen as an environmental leader is no longer convenient. On the other hand, if you can say, "Our sustainability initiatives have reduced costs and boosted revenue by creating new markets, adding new products, and deepening loyalty with customers," you can create a long-term justification for a sustainability strategy and for environmental issues broadly.

Reframing this discussion in line with an abundance mindset, which makes you more comfortable with material gains, Melissa Chungfat advises companies to "move away from the language of sacrifice. Find ways to talk about how your product or service is easier, healthier, more convenient or lower maintenance. Be positive and solutions-focused." She also suggests pointing out actual achievements, rather than sometimes-vague commitments.

How to Get Attention for Going Green

A printing company ran an ad in a local business publication noting that 60 percent of its electricity came from renewable hydropower and asking prospects to choose this company if commitment to sustainability was "as important to you as it is to us." The main text of the ad uses light and dark type (all capitals) to form the shape of an electrical plug. Outside of the main text is the logo and brief explanation of the Forest Stewardship Council and the printer's name and contact information. The headline simply named the printing company followed by an ellipsis (. . .) and the word "Unplugged."

This ad combines a happy accident—that the company's local utility happens to provide clean hydroelectric power—with a true environmental commitment: Forest Stewardship Council certification, a very big deal in the paper and printing industries.

As we see it, it's a step in the right direction but also a lot of wasted opportunity.

First off, the headline doesn't tell the story. It's focused on the company and has no benefit other than to arouse just a slight bit of curiosity about why a printing company might do acoustic music.

Then the mix of light and dark type, all of it dense and all in capitals, and with words broken across lines in mid-syllable without even hyphens is just too hard to read; and it takes at least two glances before the image forms itself into an electrical plug.

Nobility of purpose must be matched by reality in design or the nobility is wasted.

Not clearly communicating a great idea understood is decidedly ungreen.

chapter 27

FROM

Guerrilla Marketing for Nonprofits

Co-Authors Frank Adkins and Chris Forbes

YOUR ORGANIZATION'S CAUSE can be the most important one in the world, but people won't be interested in
joining you in what you are doing unless you can make a
meaningful connection with them. You need to find a compelling
and inspiring way to describe why you exist,
what you do, and why it makes a difference in
the world. Most nonprofit organizations have
formally stated mission objectives, but they
usually don't use these statements to inform
how they do their marketing. The stakeholders
in your cause will judge your every move when
you present your organization as a solution
to needs in the community. So guerrillas pay

> "There are two great days
> in a person's life—the
> day we were born and the
> day we discover why."
>
> —William Barclay

WHAT A MISSION STATEMENT DOES FOR YOUR ORGANIZATION

- Strengthens strategic planning and capacity building
- Helps develop stronger brand messages
- Keeps everyone working toward the same objectives
- Affects how you approach people and treat them
- Permeates all your messages and media

very close attention to how they submit themselves for community consideration. Nothing is left to chance because they know having a clear vision about where they are taking their organization can inform the purpose and enhance the impact of their marketing.

Your mission statement also determines how you will measure success. The metrics for how you track your progress are not really how much money you raise, how many volunteers you recruit, what kind of campaigns you stage, what your org chart looks like, how you keep records, or even how you relate to your board. These are very important things, but they are not the most important thing. The most important thing is how well your organization effects sustainable change that fulfills your mission. All the other important aspects of your nonprofit are necessary, but, if you are not careful, they can become a drain on your ability to accomplish your mission. You could work your way into failure without realizing it. We have never encountered a nonprofit that couldn't use a little more cash on hand. But in nonprofit guerrilla marketing, money is not the motive, impact is. Your "profit" is to make the most impact for your mission with the resources you have. Do you have what guerrillas have, the ability to know what profits your mission, or what hurts your organization's desired outcomes?

Turn Your Mission Statement into a Marketing Weapon

Be honest; if you're like many organizations, you have a mission statement that sounds academic or institutional. Is reading your organization's mission statement also a good cure for insomnia? To mobilize people you have to capture their imaginations. You have to stir their hearts. You have to make them believe you can deliver on your promises. Normal mission statements don't do that well. A guerrilla mission statement helps you turn it into a marketing tool. It can help you clearly focus your current purpose statement in ways that also serve to get the attention of the people you want to reach.

Guerrillas know that every point of contact your organization has with people is marketing. Your mission statement touches everything you do and is seen by everyone you connect with. With something that important, it makes sense to look at it with an eye for marketing. Why are mission statements often written academically or by committees? Shouldn't they be written with the intent of using them as persuasive communication?

Even the Declaration of Independence, though drafted by a committee, was written by a single person with a knack for words— Thomas Jefferson. Your mission statement should be written with no less thought than the most expensive advertising campaign receives. You wouldn't expect a Super Bowl advertisement to be written by lawyers, would you? Restating your purpose with a marketing mindset can help you connect better with people. Ask yourself, if your mission statement came up in an internet search (a very likely scenario), would you want to click it? What would be the keywords people could use to find you anyway?

Here's how you write your guerrilla marketing mission statement. Remember, the three things that will make your organization the most successful are:

1. Your passion
2. What you are best at

3. A clear sense of what is the bottom-line impact you are trying to make

Is reading your organization's mission statement also a good cure for insomnia? To mobilize people you have to capture their imaginations.

Sit down and struggle with all the data you have; pare down everything you know about what your organization is and does into just three sentences.

Your three sentences need to be short sentences. Put too much information in your phrases, and your audience's attention starts to wander. Imagine you are going to use this as your "elevator speech." Suppose you have just gotten on an elevator and as soon as the doors close, another person in the elevator asks you to tell them about your organization. You get to tell them in the time it takes to go from the first floor to the second floor what they need to know about your nonprofit. If you can't say who you are, what you do, and why it is important in 30 seconds, you may be too complicated to become the subject of people's conversations. If that is the case, you may have bigger problems than marketing.

We wish we could write your statement for you, but you're a guerrilla—you have to do it yourself, and the sentences need to come out of your passion. After you've written them, you can enlist help in

WRITE THREE SENTENCES THAT DESCRIBE YOUR ORGANIZATION

1. Why do you exist? (Make sure you talk about your passions.)

2. What does your organization do? (Talk about what you are best at.)

3. What difference does it make? (Tell what impact your organization is making.)

MARCH OF DIMES

Why do you exist? Our mission is to improve the health of babies by preventing birth defects, premature birth, and infant mortality.

What do you do? We carry out this mission through research, community services, education, and advocacy to save babies' lives.

What difference does it make? March of Dimes researchers, volunteers, educators, outreach workers, and advocates work together to give all babies a fighting chance against the threats to their health: prematurity, birth defects, low birth weight.

To raise funds for these noble and necessary causes, the skill of a guerrilla must be applied, especially in fundraising.

polishing them. But getting the statements first from your heart will change you forever. These statements become the tools you can use in your progression toward unimagined success for your nonprofit. Never, ever underestimate the absolutely awesome power of written words—especially your words.

Seven Golden Rules for Fundraising Success

For non-guerrillas, fundraising is a mystery that is about as unpredictable as the weather. One minute they are flooded with donations, the next they are in the midst of a serious drought. Guerrillas are not taken by surprise with the winds of financial change; they know they can become a fundraising force of nature because they understand and apply the rules of fundraising success. Just as there are rules in nature that can be used to predict the weather, there are rules in marketing that can take the guesswork out of fundraising.

Fundraising success is not only about what you do to get people to give. It's what you do to make your nonprofit an organization worthy of receiving support. You want donors to do more than write checks; you want them to take ownership of the mission themselves. This won't happen until you are thinking from their perspective.

The golden rules that follow will play an important part in guiding you as you develop your marketing materials. Success will require your time and effort, but as you practice to become familiar with these rules, it will become second nature.

> *Fundraising success is not only about what you do to get people to give. It's what you do to make your nonprofit an organization worthy of receiving support.*

Rule 1: Know Your Donors

The basis of good fundraising is the treatment and cultivation of donors and the ability to ask them to support your organization in proportion to their ability to give. The urgent need for your nonprofit is to know your donors as well as you possibly can. The foundation for having this kind of relationship is quality research and good information. When times get tough, it may be easier for them to donate only their time, but it is up to you to keep them supporting your organization financially. This challenge is one you must overcome.

Ninety percent of most nonprofit funding comes from individuals. Grants, endowments, corporate gifts, and special fundraising events can never replace the support that comes from individuals. Create a donor list with much more information than names, addresses, and phone numbers. If you're thinking like a guerrilla, your list will have details about your donors' lifestyles, such as their hobbies and achievements and where they eat, vacation, and play, and other small but important details. Can you imagine the time it takes to gather all that information? You should, because it's part of paying the dues for being a guerrilla.

When you calculate the value of that donor over a lifetime, you will be more inclined to go out of your way to keep that person donating. Knowledge of this rule is golden.

Rule 2: Educate Your Donors

Guerrillas know the meaning of the adage, "What people are not up on, they are down on." Guerrillas reassure their supporters that giving to their organization is a smart move and that their contribution will be spent wisely. Education calms fears and improves communication.

You can't offer a money-back guarantee for donations, but you can offer peace of mind, by showing your deep commitment to service. Guerrillas reassure with testimonies on their websites or in newsletters. Your reputation is credibility, and credibility is free, so leverage it as much as you can.

Rule 3: Help Donors Find Personal Fulfillment

Donors are more likely to contribute if they feel involved. With involvement comes momentum, and that is the catalyst that propels your marketing.

When your organization can find a way to help people find fulfillment though charity work, they will be more willing to jump on board to help your cause. Donors are more likely to contribute if they feel involved. With involvement comes momentum, and that is the catalyst that propels your marketing. Develop a radar and offer solutions to problems donors do not even realize they have. This rule is so important to your organization that it's golden.

Rule 4: Build Trusting Donor Relationships

Can there be honesty in marketing? Guerrillas know the answer to that question is YES. But do your supporters believe it? A reputation that took years to build could come crashing down in a matter of seconds if you're not careful. There is a very fine line between exaggeration and dishonesty, and once you cross it, it's very difficult, if not impossible to regain the trust of your donors.

Be careful not to set off the disbelief alarms. Pretend the world's biggest cynic is sitting on your shoulder. Every time you create a marketing piece listen to the cynic. He is there to make sure you stay on the straight and narrow path, and to make sure you are following this golden rule.

Rule 5: Respect Your Donors

Most nonprofits say they care about their donors, but guerrilla marketers prove it. Your marketing can say all the right words and tell donors how important they are, but unless you take concrete steps beyond those words, they won't believe you. Many companies lavish attention upon their donors, but only guerrillas excel at caring.

Prove you care by paying attention to the details. When things go wrong see to it that the donor comes out on top. Do all you can to eliminate complaints, and you will prove once again that you care about your donors. This golden rule tells you never to leave things up to fate.

Rule 6: Focus on Current Supporters

Why do you think that it costs five times as much to raise a donation from a new donor than from an existing one? The answer is easy—because the price is high to find a new donor while the price is free to find an existing one. Keep communicating with donors so when it's time to give, it will be easy for you to ask.

One other way to focus on current supporters is to have them focus on themselves. Simply ask them, "Why do you donate to our cause?" Be prepared for the answer that you didn't know. This tactic embodies the spirit of guerrilla marketing because it relies upon imagination and energy instead of your bank account. When you do these things, repeat and referral giving are your just and generous rewards for sticking to this golden rule.

Rule 7: Make Giving Fun

Your guerrilla marketing is outlined by a serious and specific marketing strategy, but that doesn't mean you can't have a little fun while raising money. Some fun ideas that have worked with various organizations to increase their donations are shown in this chapter. Try adding some ideas of your own, then include them in your marketing plan and calendar.

You don't want the cornerstone of your donations to hinge on fun events, but it certainly adds flavor and spice. Later on, analyze and evaluate them for their effectiveness. Follow this golden rule to engage in marketing that will amaze the public and motivate your donors.

THE ABC'S OF FUN-RAISING

- *Auctions.* Gather people to bid on art, jewelry, cars, antiques, baskets of food—almost anything. Companies love giving away merchandise and services to sell at auctions because of the added benefit of fusion marketing with your organization.

- *Boss for the Day.* Let people bid on being boss for the day. Highest bidder wins. This is great at schools and can be used for principals, teachers, coaches, etc.

- *Car Wash.* This works well for students as well as adults. Ask a gas station or office to let you use their facility. Ask for donations instead of setting a price.

chapter 28

FROM

Guerrilla Marketing Meets Karate Master

Co-Author Chet Holmes

HERE ARE FOUR WAYS to double your sales in the next 12 months. Each of these concepts separately can double sales, but put them all together and you could be in for a banner year. Let's get right into it.

The number of ideal buyers is always smaller than the total number of buyers, so you can market to ideal buyers more cheaply and yet earn greater rewards.

1. The Best Buyer Concept

Completely grasp the power of this: The number of ideal buyers is always smaller than the total number of buyers, so you can market to ideal buyers more cheaply and yet earn greater rewards.

I took over the advertising sales of a magazine owned by billionaire Charlie Munger.

The magazine sent 2,200 potential advertisers monthly promopieces. Of those 2,200 advertisers, 167 of them bought 95 percent of the advertising in a competitor's magazine. We started what I call "The Dream 100 Sell," a concept where you go after your "Dream" prospects with a vengeance. When I say "I," I mean me, Chet Holmes, Jay's one-time neighbor, frequent collaborator, and forever friend.

We sent the 167 "best buyers" a letter every two weeks and called them four times per month. Imagine that you are one of these prospects and you suddenly start hearing from us SIX times per month. It doesn't matter if it's the biggest CEO in the world, if he starts hearing from you six times per month, he will get to know exactly who you are in a very short period of time.

Since these were the biggest buyers, the first four months of intensive marketing and selling brought no actual reward. In the fifth month, only ONE of these dream clients bought advertising in the magazine. The top management of the magazine became nervous thinking that maybe this guy Chet Holmes wasn't the man his reputation said he was.

> *Even the most hard-bitten and cynical executive or prospect begins to respect you when you just will not give up.*

In the sixth month, 28 of the 167 largest advertisers in the country came into the magazine all at once. And since these were the biggest advertisers, they don't take out small ads; they take full pages and full-color spreads. These 29 advertisers alone were enough to double the ad sales over the previous year. The magazine went from number 15 in the industry to number one within 15 months.

As I always say, there's no one that you can't get to as long as you constantly market to them, especially after they say they're not interested. People will not only begin to respect your perseverance, they will actually begin to feel obligated. This doesn't happen right away, but even the most hard-bitten and cynical executive or prospect begins to respect you when you just will not give up. The publication I ran for Charlie Munger doubled sales two more years in a row because we constantly marketed to the best buyers much more aggressively than we did to all buyers.

That's B2B (Business to Business), What About B2C (Business to Consumer)?

If you sell B2C, chances are your best buyers live in the best neighborhoods. If you are a dentist, accountant, chiropractor, real estate broker, financial advisor, restaurant owner, or even a multilevel marketer, consistently go after the folks who live in the best neighborhoods. They are the wealthiest buyers who have the money and the greatest sphere of influence. If you send them an offer every single month without fail, within a year you'll have a great reputation among the very wealthy.

Affiliate Growth Strategy

Who is already reaching your ideal buyer? And what if they endorsed you to this buyer? Could you grow 10 times faster in no time? It took me two years to get my first meeting with Jay Abraham. That meeting has been worth more than $15 million to me. It took me 17 years (off and on) to get an in-depth meeting with Tony Robbins, and this relationship is reshaping my entire future.

> *Who is already reaching your ideal buyer? And what if they endorsed you to this buyer? Could you grow 10 times faster in no time?*

It took six months of my best work to get Morgan Stanley as a client. Nine intensive days of telemarketing techniques to get George Zimmer of the Men's Wearhouse on the phone to talk my way into a meeting. Got them as a client too.

I have 100 stories like this. And even better ones from folks like you who learned this technique, applied it, and watched it double their sales a few years in a row.

Who are your DREAM prospects? And how committed are you to getting them as clients?

To hear my talk about this for free, go to http://www. howtodoublesales.com.

2. Educational-Based Marketing

You can attract far more prospects to take a look at you by offering to teach them something of value than you'll ever get by offering your product or service.

TELESELLING

I had a client that sold telephone systems. His employees would call hundreds of companies per day and ask if they were interested in talking about a new telephone system (product offer.) No dice.

But when they started calling and asking folks if they wanted to learn "The nine ways you're wasting money on your voice and data spending," they were able to increase their appointment setting tenfold, from three appointments per week to 30 appointments per week. This tripled their pipeline in the first three months alone.

What kind of a free education could YOU offer that would make your prospects want to meet with you?

Bad offer (using real estate as an example): "Let me teach you why you should list your house with me." Much better offer: "Let me teach you the five mistakes everyone makes when they go to sell their house. No matter who you list with, you'll need to know these things." This offer will get you a lot more appointments.

I've helped many a company double and even triple sales using just this one concept. I've even helped clients who were in deep trouble experience a total turnaround on their falling profits.

I had a client who owned newspapers that had fallen 40 percent in gross revenues and all of their profits. Newspaper employees used to call up clients and say: "Hi, we'd love to come and talk to you about advertising in our newspaper." They were quickly shut down and shut out.

I convinced them to provide a "community educational service to help our local businesses succeed," which resulted in a significant increase not just getting in to see prospects but in sales as well. This client went up $100 million in sales in a single year.

You can attract far more prospects to take a look at you by offering to teach them something of value than you'll ever get by offering your product or service.

If your local newspaper called you up and offered to teach you the seven things that make all businesses succeed, you'd probably find that pretty hard to turn down. They'd still have to talk you into the meeting, but it would be an easier sell than talking you into a meeting to pitch advertising.

Naturally, there's more to this concept, and the subtleties are where you succeed, but fear not, I'll give you a way to learn this idea so thoroughly that you will out-market your competitors at every turn.

To see me talk about this, go to http://www.howtodoublesales.com.

3. Superstar Strategy

This concept that has brought great success to many a client or student of my material teaches companies how to put star sales talent into their organization. No matter how small you are, you would be surprised to learn that you can get others to grow your company for you—all you have to do is be willing to share the wealth.

> *No matter how small you are, you would be surprised to learn that you can get others to grow your company for you—all you have to do is be willing to share the wealth.*

I was 19 years old when I got my first real sales position, selling furniture. They had a quota (this is 1980) where you had to sell $20,000 worth of furniture per month to get your bonus. I thought to myself that I'd never be able to sell $20,000 worth of furniture in a month. So I took a week of vacation from my job as a movie theater manager and took that week to see how I would do. I sold $18,000 worth of furniture in a single week. Within three months, I was outselling everyone in a chain of six furniture stores, including guys who had been selling furniture their entire lives. In fact, I tripled my quota regularly, whereas most struggled just to meet theirs.

Obviously, it wasn't training. Everyone had the same training. It was psychological profile. I loved working with people. I bonded quickly, was extremely outgoing, and expected folks to buy. I remember the sales manager teaching me: "You're doing folks a big favor by helping them buy so they can stop looking. And believe me, son, when folks buy, they're happy. Watch how they can't wait to get the items in their home." He was so right. And though he gave every sales rep that speech, why was I the one that closed so many more deals than everyone else?

Psychological profile. Something you really can't teach. I went on to become the top producer in every job I ever had. Never number two. I also broke every sales record in every position I ever held; i.e., most sold in a week, most sold in a month, most new clients sold, biggest sale ever made, etc. You name it, I broke it.

My organization has an entire seminar on how to hire top producers. Even for one-person armies, this can be one of the best fast-growth strategies you can deploy.

There are 19-year-old future sales stars out there who have not yet discovered they can make millions per year. They are very inexpensive to retain when they are young, some even free. I've perfected the art of finding these eager beavers while they are young and inexpensive. One of the keys is how you advertise the position.

Here's a sample ad that has attracted some of these types. Put the ad under "sales" in your local paper or online help wanted advertising vehicle.

Sales Superstar Wanted

Must be fantastic at selling, presenting, bonding with clients and closing. Earn up to $XXXX (put biggest number possible here—what a TOP producer would earn) per year if you're a real star. Young or old, if you have the stuff, we'll know. Email resume or letter to:

Obviously, you cannot advertise for young folks. That's illegal. But you can say what we've said here: "Young or old, if you have the stuff, we'll know." But the reality is that if the person is a REAL star, you probably can't afford them if they are well accomplished and middle-aged. But that statement tells the younger folks that you'll recognize their greatness. And make no mistake; the type I'm talking about has a deep feeling that they can do anything. That "psychological profile" is in fact why they do things others don't.

They BELIEVE, so they ACHIEVE. An ad like the one above CALLS to the type of person I'm talking about. They believe in themselves when all else doubt them, and they are looking for someone who will see their greatness when they may not yet have proof.

The next trick to attracting these future superstars is to create a compensation plan that rewards them for great performance. And make sure you put the range in the ad.

Superstar Stories

I had a client that paid $9 per hour, plus commissions. So he would put "$9 per hour plus commission," in his ads. He had one sales rep that was so good at his job that he actually earned close to $100,000 per year counting his commissions.

So I asked this client: "Do you want more $9-per-hour folks or would you like someone who can even outsell your top producer?" The answer is obvious. So we put "earn up to $100K per year for real star performance." That changed the entire quality of candidates he attracted.

I had another client who had invented something that needed to be sold to very large companies, but he personally had no chance of making those sales. He didn't have the skills or the psychological profile. The average sale would be $1 million, and he could easily afford to pay 10 percent ($100,000 per sale) to the sales rep. Estimating that the sales rep might be able to sell just 10 deals per year, we put the following in the ad: "Earn up to $1 million per year."

What kind of candidates do you think an ad like that would draw? He ended up getting a retired millionaire (a 50-year-old superstar deciding to go back to work) who didn't even need a salary. So for nothing—nada, zip, zero—money down (except the cost of the ad), this client got himself a serious player with fantastic skills and resources who has already added $6 million in income to his business in just eight months. Both are very happy.

I had another client who worked out a generous commission plan for new sales reps. His product was something that sold right away. New reps could start on Monday, and if they were good, by the end of the week, they could actually have earned some commission.

So he hired five salespeople on straight commission, following my advice. Not only did they create all kinds of innovations he never thought of, but he grew his business 500 percent over a two-year period. He used to do all the selling himself. Now he plays a lot and reaps the rewards of five superstars driving revenue every day.

To see me talk about this live, for free, go to http://www.howto doublesales.com.

4. Zero to $100 Million Learning Curve

Ninety-five percent of companies will never reach $1 million in annual sales. If you've done that, you are in the top 5 percent of entrepreneurs, and you are rare and to be congratulated. But of those that get that far, 95 percent won't ever make it to $5 million. And of those that get that far, 98 percent won't get to $10 million. And think of the tiny, tiny percentage of companies that make it to $100 million in annual revenue. We only have 500 companies in the USA's Fortune 500. Not 5,000. Only 500.

So what makes the difference between Joe's corner bank and Wells Fargo Bank? Or the difference between Arnold's corner coffee shop and Starbucks?

Answer: It's not the product or service; it's the SKILLS of the entrepreneur. What kind of PERSON builds a company? That's the key question.

Set aside one hour per week, every week without fail, to work on the skills of yourself and your staff.

In my 30 years in the world of business, some 20 of which have been at the top of the game, working for billionaires, personally selling my services to more than 60 of the largest companies in the world and having helped three companies grow to $100 million, I've learned what it takes to be a great builder of businesses.

It's all about the skills. And it's about YOU making a commitment to build those skills. Most companies have little to no ONGOING skill development. Imagine if you have two salespeople going after the same market. One has been highly trained and constantly polished on cold calling, gatekeeper concepts, establishing rapport, qualifying the buyer, asking great questions, overcoming objections, closing techniques, follow-up procedures and so on. The other may have received some initial training but from that point everything else was just up to the individual. Which salesperson do you think is going to win in the battle of business? The one who is highly and consistently trained or the one who is not? Set aside one hour per week, every week without fail, to work on the skills of yourself and your staff. Even a one-hour week beats 99.99 percent of all companies.

What a guerrilla would do now to double his sales in the next 12 months is go to http://www.howtodoublesales.com.

chapter 29

FROM

Guerrilla Marketing in 30 Days

Co-Author Al Lautenslager

THERE'S POWER IN POSITIONING, both in tough times and good times. Your marketing requires positioning for success. Positioning is considered one of the core elements of a marketing strategy.

The Foundation of Positioning

Positioning is more than a catchy tagline or a heavily promoted feature or brand. It is more than being in the right place at the right time, and it is more than having a crackerjack sales team (although any of these can cause one-time windfall profits). Positioning is actually a base upon which to develop all

Your marketing requires positioning for success. Positioning is considered one of the core elements of a marketing strategy.

POSITIONING FOR SUCCESS

During a recent World Series game, there were 12 pop flies and six singles. Batters hit to fielders in position to catch the pop flies for easy outs those 12 times. The six times the balls were struck for singles, the batter hit where fielders weren't positioned to make a play. As Wee Willie Keeler said in 1897 in response to how a man of his size could hit so well, "It's simple. I keep my eyes clear and I hit 'em where they ain't." In Willie's case, he positioned his hits for success. In the fielders' case, they weren't in position for success.

other marketing focused on the goal of building relationships with a target market.

David Ogilvy, one of the best-known names in British and American advertising circles, stated that marketing results depend less on how advertising is written than on how the product or service is positioned.

Positioning is more than clever manipulation of a market's perception. It truly is a statement of your company or organization's true identity and true value to a target market. It is truly what your business will stand for in the minds of your prospects and customers.

Positioning truly is a statement of your company or organization's true identity and true value to a target market.

Positioning involves planting these "seeds of perception" in the minds of prospective customers. When and if a prospect or customer wants what you're offering, you want them to think of you first and eventually buy from you. This will happen if you have planted enough of these seeds of perception. That's positioning. That's guerrilla marketing.

All of these define a company much more strategically than a catchy tagline or a repeat commercial during the Super Bowl. These form the foundation of the relationship that a company has with the market it serves. And you know how important relationships are in the world of guerrilla marketing!

While the baseball example given in this chapter describes a physical positioning, your marketing world requires a mental positioning. That mental positioning has to happen in an already crowded mind. With the daily communication barrage, being first, unique, and memorable becomes the underlying challenge of the best positioning. It requires targeting your message to a very narrow segment within your target market, directly to the minds of your potential customers.

> *With the daily communication barrage, being first, unique, and memorable becomes the underlying challenge of the best positioning.*

Positioning Your Product in Your Prospect's Mind

Harry Beckwith, in his book *Selling the Invisible*, says, "A position is a cold-hearted, no-nonsense statement of how you are perceived in the minds of your prospects." He goes on further to explain, "It is the positioning statement that describes how you wish to be perceived. It is the core message you want to deliver every time you market."

According to Al Ries and Jack Trout in their marketing classic, *Positioning: The Battle for Your Mind* (McGraw-Hill), "Positioning is not something you do with a product. Positioning is what you do in the mind of a prospect. That is, you put the product in the mind of the prospect." The same goes for services.

Positioning strategies must have amazing clarity. When stating positioning to clients or prospects either in writing or verbally, you want them to remember what you are positioning and motivate them to want more information about what you have. In most cases, you only have a very short time to do this. This positioning isn't always just rattling off a fancy tagline or revealing feature after feature. The positioning states what your prospects want so they will bust down your door trying to get it.

In *The 22 Immutable Laws of Marketing* (HarperBusiness), Ries and Trout state, "All that exists in the world of marketing are perceptions in the minds of the customer or the prospect. The perception is reality."

> "All that exists in the world of marketing are perceptions in the minds of the customer or the prospect. The perception is reality."
>
> —Al Ries and Jack Trout

Stating Your Position

It takes a visionary outlook to decide how you want the target marketplace to perceive you. Your positioning statement must also be visionary. You must have vision related to the value of your product or service and why it is unique and different from what the competitor is offering. This vision, coupled with all your benefits, is the primary component of a positioning statement.

Answering the questions, "Who is my target market?" and "What am I really selling?" will provide the basis for your positioning. These two questions should be asked more often than just at the start of a new business. Markets change, customer demands change, and competition changes. The answers to these questions may direct you to more than one target, too. Once you identify all of your target markets, you are ready to take aim for their profit bull's-eyes with your positioning arrows.

Guerrilla marketing says that when you have clearly focused on your markets, you can clarify a market position. This focus should measure the position against the following four criteria:

1. Does my position offer a benefit that my target market audience really wants?

2. Is it an honest-to-goodness benefit?
3. Does it truly separate me from my competition?
4. It is unique or difficult to copy?

WELL-POSITIONED ORGANIZATIONS

Although positioning is more than a catchy tagline, there are associations that sound like taglines that describe companies in terms of the perceptions in their customers' and prospects' minds. Consider these examples.

- *Southwest Airlines* is the no-frills, fun airline—definitely a perception and positioning.

- *7-Up is the Uncola.* We've all heard it, and we all know exactly what its position is in the soft drink market.

- *United Airlines.* Friendly skies and friendly service globally.

- *Federal Express.* Trust us to get it there overnight. This is a good example of a positioning with two components—overnight and trust, again putting a particular perception in the mind of the consumer.

- *Crest Toothpaste.* Fewer cavities.

In your guerrilla marketing mindset, you are probably thinking, "These are nice and these are brands I recognize. But I thought guerrilla marketing was geared toward small businesses like mine." You are correctamundo!

Consider these examples of some small businesses you have probably never heard of but will recognize as niche-oriented and well-positioned.

- *Expert Plumbing.* We never close—positioned as open for your emergencies 24/7.

- *Inline Chiropractic.* Chiropractic services for figure skaters, definitely a niche. Would you go there if you were a baseball player?

- *The Diabetic Chef.* Take-out meals for diabetics—again, niched and positioned in the minds of diabetics wanting take-out meals.

Unless the answers to these questions make you the positioning king or queen, keep refining. Customer input will help you refine further.

When you are satisfied with your answers, you will have a sensible position—a position that will lead to your marketing and company goals. No guerrilla marketer would think of doing any marketing without a proper marketing plan that includes strategic thinking and a statement related to positioning. Guerrillas must carve out a position where their company or organization stands tall for something. The ensuing marketing must reflect that carved-out position and that tall stance. This carved-out position is stated in the marketing plan and is apparent in every marketing weapon used. If it isn't, repeat this chapter.

Some Potential Positioning Opportunities

- An appliance business that can provide the most affordable kitchen appliances to cost-conscious buyers.
- An education-oriented company that has the largest selection of tapes and books for parents of teenagers.
- The most cost-effective place for sports aficionados to purchase sporting goods online.
- The most complete source of health and fitness tips for people over the age of 50.
- The only company that combines online purchasing of French wine with in-home sampling.

Notice how crystal-clear and narrowly targeted each of these are. Once you have a crystal-clear positioning statement, communication to your target market becomes easier.

Positioning Yourself

When creating your own positioning statement, consider these factors:

- *Be unique.* What one thing can you say that positions you as the only company in the world that can do it? Think extremes—the fastest, best, largest, most convenient, and so forth.

- *Make it profit-oriented.* You know your target audience. You know what they want and need. You know what will satisfy them the most and what will keep them coming back to you. What will always keep you at the top of their mind? What will always keep you at the top of their wallet from a purchasing point of view?

Capitalize on Your Strengths and the Competition's Weaknesses

Your strength must be promoted, communicated, and remembered the most. Your weaknesses—yes, we all have them—should be minimized in your communication and marketing. Aiming your strength right at the weakness of a competitor is a rifle shot to your target with your positioning ammo.

Position Benefits as Value-Oriented

Price is not always the number-one value that a consumer is seeking. Your analysis of your target market's wants and needs will determine what value is required. Unless you are the lowest-cost producer or deliverer, don't let price lead your positioning. Added value is an overused term from the 1990s, but it does apply here if value is truly offered and is a part of the customer experience.

A final point of positioning involves implanting that perception seed that you are an expert. Many reading this will immediately proclaim, "I don't think I'm an expert, or, can I really tell people I'm an expert?"

Everyone reading this chapter right now is an expert in something. I am a guerrilla marketing expert and proclaim myself so. That is a part of my positioning. Your positioning can be a similar proclamation of your expertise. What are you an expert at? I recently ran across a "transportation expert." This came from a taxi-cab driver in New York City.

EXPERT ADVICE

I recently followed up with a contact that I made at a networking event. During the course of the follow-up discussion, I very pointedly asked the person what her job was. She indicated to me that she was a consultant. When I pursued this description, I found out she was a consultant who works with companies to put leadership programs and training in place. I immediately notified her that she was no longer to position herself as a consultant but as a "leadership expert."

She called me the day after our lunch meeting and exclaimed that she had just been successful signing a contract with a prospect that she had been working on for many months. She positioned herself as an expert and got the business. People like to buy from experts, people trust experts, buyers have confidence in the work of experts. Use the title. It's OK to do so.

Positioning is no-cost marketing and is very powerful. Many parts of guerrilla marketing can be highly leveraged marketing. That leverage is good when revenues skyrocket and marketing costs are low or nonexistent. That leverage happens with positioning.

> *Whereas positioning is the battle for your mind, your marketing is the battle for your prospect's wallet.*

Whereas positioning is the battle for your mind, your marketing is the battle for your prospect's wallet. If you don't position and battle for it, your competition will.

Market positioning can be viewed as a promise from you to your target market. Delivering on that promise is done with all of the tactics you choose to employ. Positioning is a true guerrilla marketing component. Keeping your promise is a true guerrilla value.

chapter 30

FROM

Guerrilla Profits

Co-Author Stuart Burkow

YOUR BUSINESS HAS UNIQUE profit potential and untapped resources you may not even be aware of. The simple, startling fact is that most businesses miss profit opportunities on almost every transaction or customer/client relationship. They have unique profit potential that goes completely untapped, and they are limiting their incomes without even knowing it.

The purpose of this chapter on guerrilla profits is to help you capture that extra money from your business—by using highly ethical, underutilized, lesser known, or unconventional methods. In this chapter, we want to focus on the additional profit sources that come from applying new methods to the activities within your business.

> *Most businesses miss profit opportunities on almost every transaction or customer/client relationship.*

Getting the Most Out of Your Business Activities

Your business also has its own unique profit leverage points that offer you the greatest amount of return for your investment of time, energy, and resources. You may instantly recognize your profit leverage points as you read the list of the top seven below.

You may find it useful to read through this section with a notepad and pen close by so you can get some work done on the spot . . . and jot down ideas as they come to you. With that in mind, let's jump right in to the Top 7 Profit Leverage Points.

Profit Leverage Point #1: Know What's Really True About Your Business

In all business undertakings, the first and primary starting point is to know the truth about your business environment—and your specific business numbers—so you can adequately prepare, respond, and operate. You need to know what your primary goals are—and your ultimate outcome—so you'll be able to gauge whether or not the actual numbers (results) of your business are taking you in the right direction and if they'll get you where you want to go in a reasonable amount of time.

Of course, this is standard practice for most larger businesses. But too often, smaller business owners "wing it"—and have no idea of what their target is. Frankly, if you don't know what you're aiming for, how can you know if you'll hit your target? There's a line from Lewis Carroll's *Alice in Wonderland* that says, "If you don't know where you

> "If you don't know where you are going, any road will get you there."
>
> —Lewis Carroll

are going, any road will get you there." Unfortunately, that sums up the truth about many businesses.

Profit Leverage Point #2: See Profit Opportunities That Others Don't

One of your highest-value leverage points, which has the ability to provide you with breakthrough profit opportunities and cash windfalls, is your ability to see things differently than most people. And it's often one of the more difficult things to achieve when you're in the daily thick of things in your business. But let's just imagine for a moment that you had the ability to try out Superman's X-ray vision for a day on your business.

Becoming very good at looking at things differently—and finding hidden opportunities that most people miss—is the skill you want to grow.

What would it be like to apply that completely altered-state ability to profit seeking? Maybe it would mean that you would be looking at each transaction or deal for alternative profit opportunities. Or maybe it would mean that you could look at something others would consider a "distressed situation" or "negative news" with the ability to see the positive spin. Whatever trigger needed to train your mind to be constantly looking for opportunities in each business situation that presents—that's what you're after. Becoming very good at looking at things differently— and finding hidden opportunities that most people miss—is the skill you want to grow.

Profit Leverage Point #3: Dramatically Boost Your Marketing Results

Here's where things can get very interesting in your business—very fast. If you aren't already steeped in the marketing of and for your

> *When it comes to profits, your marketing is more important than the product or service you provide.*

business, let me state clearly: When it comes to profits, your marketing is more important than the product or service you provide.

Simply put, you can have the best products and/or services, the best business operationally to deliver them, the best quality items or work done, but, if you can't market it properly, no one will know about it!

That's why you've got to get very good at targeting the right prospects—and selling more to your existing clientele. Marketing is the total process, from your messages (more on that in Leverage Point #4) to your advertising channels to the steps you use to follow up to your sales process to the overall presentation, customer processes, and CRM systems (customer relationship management). All of these combined go into the mix of what it takes to attract and sell to the right people—but you've got to be targeting the right people in the first place.

Profit Leverage Point #4: Create Exciting Promotions and Campaigns

The next step in the marketing jigsaw puzzle is to get very good at creating powerful messages and promotions to help boost your response rates and conversions (sales). When you get this step right—and combine it with your targeting discussed in Leverage Point #3—you can create a powerful and unbeatable marketing engine that can drive an abundance of new business to you.

Most businesses are very passive about their messaging. They occasionally send out an email, distribute a flier, or perhaps even mail out a postcard—but the "active" approach to promotions and events may be seen as too time-consuming or difficult. But actually, it can be quite enjoyable—and very profitable. So, make a game out of thinking about how you can make your business more fun and interesting for people.

These might include contests, surveys, limited-time offers, or specials and exclusives for your best customers. Doing things that help break through the clutter is the key—along with giving people ample incentives and good self-interest reasons to respond. That combined with a sense of urgency in your promotions and campaigns—and you'll be on the right track.

> *Doing things that help break through the clutter is the key—along with giving people ample incentives and good self-interest reasons to respond.*

Profit Leverage Point #5: Capture More from Your Current Business

When you are already in the middle of a transaction, there are always additional opportunities to capture more business. In the book, *Guerrilla Profits*, Chapter 3, Strategy #3: "Capture More From Your Transactions," we discuss in depth the "7 Common Transaction Methods" that include the more common ways to add to a transaction, such as up-sells, cross-sells, and add-ons. In addition, in that same chapter, methods are discussed for transforming a one-shot sale into recurring business and ways to increase the value of the transaction.

All of these are just the starting point for how to capture more money from the business already coming to you in the course of your current transactions.

Profit Leverage Point #6: Connect with Others Who Can Help You

An underlying, recurring theme in guerrilla profits is that opportunities are just waiting to be tapped through others who are "gatekeepers" and who already have access to your ideal target prospects. And then, it's simply a matter of contacting these people with a compelling

> *Opportunities are just waiting to be tapped through others who are "gatekeepers" and who already have access to your ideal target prospects.*

reason why your proposal would be a good idea and a good match for both parties. In essence, you are marketing through these businesses, organizations, or groups. You are also marketing to these people (the gatekeepers) differently than how you'd be marketing to the individuals that usually come in to your business. And you'll want to systematically cultivate and develop these relationships so that you stay "top of mind" with them—and so that they do feel special—and are participating with you at a different level than being merely another customer or client.

Most businesses act as if they're an "island in a sea of marketing." They generally act and promote independently from what other businesses are doing around them (or in their industry). But let me suggest that other compatible businesses could be an untapped reservoir of new profits for both of you.

Profit Leverage Point #7:
Harness Your Secret Ingredient for Success

The real "gold" in any business are the relationships you have with your customers and clients. These are the people who are loyal to you—and who keep coming back again and again—and will usually continue to come back unless something gets screwed up, they move, they die, or a competitor steals them away from you with a better offer.

> *The real "gold" in any business are the relationships you have with your customers and clients. These relationships are the true essence of your business.*

These relationships are the true essence of your business. They are what feed you and make it possible for you to be in business. And they are the measure of the true wealth that can be monetized—should you ever decide to sell your business. But don't let the fact that it's listed last out of the Top 7 Profit Leverage Points diminish its importance. That's actually done on purpose because the last item covered is often the thing that is remembered best.

THE TOP 7 PROFIT LEVERAGE POINTS

1. Know what's really true about your business
2. See profit opportunities that others don't
3. Dramatically boost your marketing results
4. Create exciting promotions and campaigns
5. Capture more from your current business
6. Connect with others who can help you
7. Harness your secret ingredient for success

chapter 31

FROM

Guerrilla Marketing to Women

Co-Author Wendy Stevens

I LEARNED EARLY THAT ONE should never assume anything. When I was eight-and-a-half months pregnant, I visited a store called Pea in the Pod. After I strolled around a bit, I ran into another woman with that familiar round, distinctive belly. I asked her, "When are you due?" She scoffed, "I'm not." I wanted to crawl under the store carpet and disappear. I learned the number-one rule of guerrilla marketing from a personal encounter: Never assume anything. Had this woman been a customer of mine, my comment could have destroyed my relationship with her, or at best, made it a brutal uphill climb to establish a connection.

What we assume to be true about marketing, and particularly marketing to women, and what is actually true, are often two different things. Assumptions in marketing are the source of huge mistakes that waste millions of dollars of hard cost and hundreds of millions of dollars in lost opportunity. Guerrilla marketers never assume; they ask questions, search, and gather data that result in discoveries that allow them to zoom in and target their niche market. Making assumptions about a target audience is a surefire way to destroy a marketing career. Getting past this issue can bring marketing success.

Blind assumptions about how to market to women pose the biggest hurdle that today's marketers must overcome. Eighty percent of women feel advertisers do not understand them, and they generally don't trust ads. Many marketers continue to spend huge amounts of time and money on advertisements that end up repelling women. This chapter presents solutions to marketers that will help them understand how to advertise to women.

> *Many marketers continue to spend huge amounts of time and money on advertisements that end up repelling women.*

Women Wield Market Power

Today's women play a large role as earners and spenders, certainly wielding more power in these fields than ever before. As we crawl out of the biggest economic downturn since the Great Depression, one thing stands out about the economy: Women control large amounts of money. In fact, women comprise 80 percent of all consumers, and they spend $100 billion on luxury goods and services each year. Women's incomes have increased by 63 percent in the last four decades, and men's by just .06 percent. Between 1985 and 1995, almost 68 percent of the gains in the financial management and accounting sectors were by women. Seventy percent of women who earn above $100,000 per year earn more than their husbands. Women control 48 percent of estates worth more than $5 million, while only 35 percent are under the control of men. Women own 47 percent of assets valued over $500,000.

Women comprise 80 percent of all consumers, and they spend $100 billion on luxury goods and services each year.

The Hispanic female market is growing at a rate of 1.7 million consumers every year, with a combined purchasing power of more than $700 billion. As the buying power of Hispanics rises, culturally focused marketing has become more critical. The Hispanic woman is of particular interest for marketers who want to cultivate a relationship with a woman who exhibits strong brand loyalty, price consciousness, and quality assurance, since buying the best for her family is paramount, rendering price points a non-issue.

A picture emerges of the woman as the dominant consumer in most families, making household spending decisions on behalf of her family. Women want to buy things; they want to spend money on what they need, but they do not trust advertisements to help them make decisions. In fact, 91 percent of women interviewed in a single survey indicated that advertisers misunderstand them (66 percent felt misunderstood by health-care marketers, 59 percent by food marketers, 74 percent by automotive marketers, and 84 percent by investment marketers). Why? Most women see advertisements as worthless and even demeaning; they feel insulted that advertisers assume they're stupid enough to believe the nonsense that appears in advertisements. For example, a recent TV commercial shows Sarah Jessica Parker using a boxed hair dye that costs $10 at the grocery store. Do advertisers really expect women to believe that Sarah Jessica Parker uses boxed hair dye? This ad, in trying to capture women, only disgusts them and pushes them away from the product.

Women want to buy things; they want to spend money on what they need, but they do not trust advertisements to help them make decisions.

Another recent ad campaign aggravates customers the company has already won over. Skechers Shape-ups, a type of shoe, have become very popular among women, especially boomer women; my relations and friends all have them and wear them constantly. The shape of the shoe allows a woman to tone her posterior simply by walking. Although this is a nice idea, most boomer women are health-conscious and realistic about what it takes to stay thin. They understand the need to exercise and watch what they eat, and they don't expect the shoe to do all the work. That's why women find the commercials for these shoes ridiculous. Skechers' 2011 Super Bowl commercial, for example, pictured Kim Kardashian showing off her beautiful figure in a skimpy workout outfit with Skechers Shape-ups on her feet. She fires her very attractive male physical trainer, saying he is obsolete now that she has these shoes. A follow-up ad features actress Brooke Burke in a similar scenario. Are advertisers claiming that this product, already loved by women, can make them look as good as Kim Kardashian or Brooke Burke? In Burke's commercial, she puts the shoes on as the camera focuses on her toned legs; then she struts around, stating that this is her workout. Women watching this think, "I know that's not all she does to keep that body." Kim Kardashian's own reality show often shows her working out at the gym with a trainer, so we know there is much more to her workout than just wearing a particular shoe.

These examples show how many marketers completely misinterpret their current female customers, not to mention the ones they are trying to attract. Skechers Shape-ups are the number-two selling shoe brand on the market, and they're very popular among women. However, Skechers risks losing its market with commercials women find insulting.

What Do Women Really Want?

So, let's not insult women; let's understand them. What, exactly, is going on with women and the cultural shift? Boomer women have successful careers, massive investments, and inheritances from husbands or parents, making them the most financially empowered

> *Boomer women have successful careers, massive investments, and inheritances from husbands or parents, making them the most financially empowered generation of women in history.*

generation of women in history. According to MassMutual Financial Group, women above age 50 control more than $19 trillion and own more than three-quarters of the financial wealth in the nation. This category represents the wealthiest, healthiest, and most active female generation in history.

This more mature, luxury consumer is extremely discerning and places a high priority on experiences and memories. Women want the experience that goes with an item, and they expect superior quality in all their products. Their quest for more information can be seen in their increased engagement in online social media. Baby boomer women comprise the fastest-growing demographic on Facebook. Figures indicate that women who earn more than $74,000 annually are increasing, with 94.3 percent accessing the internet every month. Half of these women are considered heavy internet users, with TV, radio, direct mail, and newspaper use declining within the segment. Yet many marketers continue using these old media to reach out to women. Why?

Boomer women and their younger counterparts love social networking. They also love to save time by buying online. Most advertisers still do not seem to understand these concepts. According to one study, women represent a majority of the online market: 22 percent shop at least once daily online and 92 percent convey information on finds/deals to others. In addition, women have an average of 171 contacts in their mobile or email contact lists. Recent research indicates that a majority of women and mothers (79 percent of mothers with children younger than 18) look to recommendations made by friends on message boards, blogs, and social media websites before buying. In fact, 40 percent of mothers polled in a study on social media moms said an item they bought was based on a recommendation on Facebook, with 55 percent saying they based the decision on a personal review blog. To create a connection with women, marketers must use blogs, social media sites, and message boards. Another study shows that peer group recommendations generated by social media ensure that businesses become highly visible to women and mothers.

> *Peer group recommendations generated by social media ensure that businesses become highly visible to women and mothers.*

Not many companies do this actively. Guerrilla marketers need to get with the program; using this technology and capitalizing on it is the best way to target women shoppers. This is a surefire way to promote products and earn the trust of female customers, who tend not only to be loyal, but also to recommend things to friends and thus bring more customers along with them. This technology is the key to achieving success in guerrilla marketing.

Reaching Women Through Social Connections

The popularity of social networking and the internet as a purchasing sphere for women makes sense when we look at how women make their purchasing decisions. While men are active and response-oriented when viewing advertisements, women hate ads and opt to focus on awareness and the thoughts of other women in their social fold. The internet generally gives them quick, easy access to their friends and the opinions of their social groups. This makes women's purchasing decisions increasingly more grounded in reality and in the connections they make within their social circles.

Women prefer to understand the experience of someone they trust before they buy a particular product or service. They sort through recommendations from friends that they consider credible. A company will obtain a woman as a customer if their product or service makes

MINING FOR GOLD

Let's have a look at Pam, a successful baby boomer executive. She comes home and finds her TV is broken. She decides to get a new one, but she wants to ensure she gets the "right one." She goes online that night and researches TV sets, focusing on reading customer reviews. Before she goes to bed, she has narrowed her choices down to four.

She knows her best friends have recently bought TVs, so she calls them and gets their feedback. She then goes on Facebook and posts her four choices to her friends. They respond by the next morning with their opinions. She mixes all this together in her "thinking pot," and, by the following evening, she orders a TV online. It arrives the next day.

Pam had a great purchasing experience and is impressed by how quickly the TV arrived, so she goes on Facebook and tells all her friends about it. This is gold for the winning company; they also have a Facebook page, which Pam adds, shows her friends, and comments on. Now the business can cash in on double the gold. Most companies do not have Facebook pages, and therefore do not cash in on this gold.

Up to 75 percent of companies that women would like to access on Facebook have not signed up for the free service. So, the question for marketers is: Why not use this popular form of free advertising?

sense to her, and if their claims match the recommendations from her investigations.

Men are rash; they hunt and buy. Women take their time to ensure the decision-making process is comprehensive.

So, what's the bottom line? As marketers, we need to stop assuming that our advertising works in today's society—it doesn't. Marketers are failing to reach the female who holds the purse strings in the family. Research shows that not only is advertising not working—it's insulting, and it repels women. To promote our products successfully, we need to revise our strategy. We need to target women, especially boomer women, and we need to stop assuming we know what they need.

> *Men are rash; they hunt and buy. Women take their time to ensure the decision-making process is comprehensive.*

Instead, we need to ask questions, analyze women's needs, pay attention to the research, and revise our approach. Start integrating social networking into the mix. Make your website accessible on a cell phone or iPod: A mother can research while she watches her kids' soccer games. Make sure it's easy. Marketers must respect the modern woman and use technology to simplify her buying experience. If they succeed, they will gain a loyal customer willing to provide them with more loyal customers, who will provide them with more loyal customers—and the cycle will continue.

chapter 32

FROM

Guerrilla Rainmaking

Co-Author David T. Fagan

I N 1984, JAY CONRAD LEVINSON created a revolution in the marketing world with his book *Guerrilla Marketing*, which has become one of the perennial bestsellers and one of the best-read books ever published on marketing. This led to an entire series of *Guerrilla Marketing* books by Levinson, often co-written with other marketing experts.

Many if not all of the lessons in the *Guerrilla Marketing* series are just as pertinent today as they were in 1984, but what Jay couldn't have known or anticipated way back then was the birth and rise of the internet to become the dominant force in communication on the planet. And it really has had a dramatic

> *The internet has become the dominant force in communication on the planet.*

effect on the way the world does business as it reaches into the most remote places on earth. Go into a village in Ethiopia and ask a 12-year-old what Google is. Without missing a beat, he will tell you that's where he goes online to find what he is looking for.

> *Online sales will be the dominant way goods and services are purchased.*

Here in the good 'ol USA, the dollars spent buying products and services online are rising every year in geometric proportions. Some are predicting that online sales during the Christmas season of 2011 will equal and surpass that of brick-and-mortar retail stores. What is certain is that the day is coming—much sooner than may make you comfortable—when online sales will be the dominant way goods and services are purchased.

Guerrilla Marketing Automation—The Next Revolution

A guerrilla marketer (like you) is going to have to master the techniques of sales and business automation if you intend to be profitable and grow, particularly for small- to medium-sized businesses.

So if anything from this chapter gets burned into the hard drive between your ears, let it be this:

The people who will rapidly grow their businesses now and in the future and drive sales and profit to record levels will be expert at automating their sales and marketing processes, without adding any new staff.

A bold statement, we admit. The extent to which you embrace this new business truth will determine your ability to run with the big dogs and create the life of your dreams. Reject it, and you will soon be losing sales right and left, and businesses that you didn't even consider in your league will steal your customers and drive you out of business.

So why is it so important to automate the way we market and get sales? After all, you may have been in business for years doing it the old

Your Yellow Pages ad is going to drive less and less business to you as time goes on.

way and you aren't doing too badly. Well, there are three answers to this question.

First, as I mentioned earlier, in the very near future almost all your business may be coming to you online. Even if you sell a product in a brick-and-mortar building, without an internet presence you are leaving a lot of dollars on the table.

Your Yellow Pages ad is going to drive less and less business to you as time goes on. Ask anyone under 21 where they go to find a business phone number or to look up a place to get a new skateboard, and they will always tell you the internet. Many adults do too. I know that at my house, as soon as the never-ending delivery of the new phone books arrives, they hit the recycle barrel in my garage.

The second big reason is that by automating your sales and marketing on the internet you can make a whole lot more money, and you can do it without adding any additional staff.

But for me, and many business owners I know, the biggest reason to automate is lifestyle. What do I mean by that?

I doubt anyone ever opened up a business because they wanted to work 100 hours a week, miss all family events, and never take a vacation. But that is the reality many business owners face. They believe money is being made only when they are working.

When you automate as much of your business as possible, you are making money even when you are not in the office.

But when you automate as much of your business as possible, you are making money even when you are not in the office. You can be making money when you are sleeping.

Owning a business should be about making a great living and having time to enjoy the fruits of business ownership. It should give you the ability to lead a self-directed life and to do the things that matter to you—whether that is playing nine holes of golf a day, traveling, or volunteering at your church.

So now that we know some of the many reasons why guerrilla marketers want to automate everything they can, let's look at how this is all done. It is not hard to do, but it is complicated to the person new at this. Don't let that discourage you.

I am no technical genius, and neither are most of my friends that own businesses. Some of them hate technology and rarely use computers at all, but when they see the benefits and how they can actually double their sales in a short period of time, they learn and they learn fast!

Leads and List Building

When business owners are asked to identify their most important business asset, they often say it's a piece of machinery, some process they specialize in, or maybe their employees. But they're missing the boat and giving the wrong answer.

Their most important asset is the list of their customers and prospects. You can survive the loss of a machine, a process, and even an employee, but it's a lot harder to survive the loss of the list of the source of your revenue and profit: your customers.

> *You can survive the loss of a machine, a process, and even an employee, but it's a lot harder to survive the loss of your customer list—the source of your revenue and profit.*

Why is it this way? People get into businesses because the work attracts them; a guy who loves cars and engines opens up a car repair shop; another gets a degree in accounting and opens up an accounting business. No one—or very few people—opens up a business because they like to market things. So what you have is skilled people getting into businesses where they can leverage their skills and make a living. That's OK.

But as these people open up businesses, they suddenly understand that they have to find a way to attract customers. The old way would have been to buy the biggest Yellow Pages ad they could afford, create some brochures, maybe offer a coupon deal or two. And for some, their methods were successful, at least for a time. Bottom line, they were highly skilled in their trade, but they were dreadful marketers.

Don't blame them. That's how it was for most people. I think it goes back to a time when we all lived in small villages, and there was one of everything. There was one butcher, one baker, one candlestick maker—because the village only needed one of each. There was no need to advertise and market your offering. If you were skilled at what you did, you had all the business of the whole village.

But as modern transportation was developed and people spread out into what became cities, they couldn't get by with just one baker anymore. Lot's of bakeries opened up, and suddenly people had a choice about where to buy their bread and pies. This led to advertising and marketing. Even back in the early days of our country, businesses that marketed better got a bigger share of the sales and became bigger and more profitable, driving smaller businesses out of the game.

> *Today, with the billions of dollars being spent online, you can compete with the huge companies.*

This goes on today much like it did in the past. We've all read the stories that when that big box retailer moves into town, all the small businesses complain they can't compete and end up going out of business. Many people think it's because they can't compete on price. That's part of it, but the biggest reason is they can't compete in marketing. The big box retailer can come into town with a monthly multimillion-dollar marketing budget while the mom and pop stores gross less than a million in a whole year, if that.

It doesn't have to be that way. Today, with the billions of dollars being spent online, you can compete with the huge companies. On the internet, you can have the same presence they do. And because you are smaller and don't have the huge fixed expenses that the big guys have, you can compete head to head.

So today, successful guerrilla marketers begin by creating a list of their customers and prospects as well as having a system for turning their prospects into customers. The big idea is to create a list of people from the internet who are hungry to buy what you are selling so you can create a system that automates how you turn prospects into customers.

You can build a list like this very quickly, or you can move more slowly, depending upon how many visitors you get to visit your

THE ETHICAL BRIBE

Now don't get excited, there is nothing underhanded going on here. The ethical bribe involves offering a free report or other information to the visitor on your website in exchange for his or her email address.

Here is an idea of how this works.

I had a client in the mortgage industry. When people landed on his website, they were offered a free report titled "The Seven Mistakes People Make When Trying To Get A Mortgage, And How To Avoid Them." This type of information would be very useful and desirable for someone trying to get a mortgage, and they could receive it immediately if they would just provide first name and email address.

When you have had this on your website for a while, you will develop a highly targeted list of people who are most likely to want a mortgage, and you can market to them directly. When you supply them with education-based information, you have moved from a mortgage salesman to a trusted advisor, and you will be the first person the prospect calls when it's time to buy a home. Count on it.

On the internet, you can have the same presence they do; and because you are smaller and don't have the huge fixed expenses that the big guys have, you can compete head to head.

website. The speed at which you build your list is largely dependent on how much money you have to spend on marketing.

What costs money? You can drive an incredible amount of traffic to your site with pay-per-click (PCP) advertising using Google, Yahoo, and MSN search-engine advertising. Many people start with Google because the amount of traffic it can send you is exponentially higher than all the other search engines combined. That costs money, to be sure, but it is hardly an expense as much as it is an investment in mandatory knowledge.

chapter 33

FROM

Guerrilla Wealth

Co-Author Loral Langemeier

I N OUR MATERIAL WORLD, people tend to measure themselves by their wealth, but somehow money and finances are seldom discussed. The subject is taboo. We want to change that and get you into a wealth conversation. We want you to "live out loud" about your dreams, your hopes, the bills, investment opportunities, college funds, and gas money.

The Wealth Conversation

Creating wealth starts with a conversation. Unfortunately, the few conversations you have probably had about money use terms with negative implications. These old, Industrial Age terms impose limits that restrict how you think and act in regard to money and the creation of wealth.

If you seriously want to build wealth, discard the old, Industrial Age terms and their built-in limits. Come into the Information Age and replace that old language with a positive vocabulary that will expand your vision and your outlook about creating wealth. In the process, you'll be removing many of the roadblocks that have been preventing you from becoming wealthy.

Your Financial Baseline

Now it's time to clear out your financial mind and clean up your financial vocabulary. It's time to get a handle on your current financial picture. This is a point where many people simply stall out. And little wonder! Most people don't know what documents to keep or how to organize them, so they do nothing. Worse, they don't know how to use the information in the documents they have to make it easier to achieve wealth faster.

This is a key distinction between guerrilla wealth tactics and the Industrial Age model. We're moving decisively away from the old budgeting model, which was just dividing your money to meet expenses as best you could. Worse, as a concept, budgeting is deeply rooted in the scarcity mindset of skimping.

Now you're going to start living your life in a truly businesslike and professional way, which positions you to build wealth. To do that, we need to know where you stand financially now.

In the Information Age model, we start with something that looks familiar—financial papers—but then we use the information in those papers to create a personal profit and loss statement and a balance sheet. This provides the most useful financial baseline, which

If you seriously want to build wealth, discard the old, Industrial Age terms and their built-in limits and replace that old language with a positive vocabulary that will expand your vision and your outlook about creating wealth.

is foundational to the guerrilla tactics we'll be covering throughout this chapter.

Before you decide to ignore this step—and we know there's a big temptation to do that—you need to have a good reason to do it. An example will help.

Think of your financial baseline as a blueprint or financial fingerprint where you can see your financial condition in a glance. Once you know your financial baseline, you can get control of your money in a meaningful way. Only then can you begin growing your wealth and designing the life you want.

A personal profit and loss statement and a balance sheet provides the most useful financial baseline, which is foundational to guerrilla wealth tactics.

GET YOUR BEARINGS

Imagine if you parachuted from a plane into the middle of a desert. All you can see for miles and miles is emptiness, sand, and blinding sun. Your goal is to get to Lincoln, Nebraska. How would you start? Which way would you go? It would be absolutely critical to your success, and in this case, your life, that you first establish exactly where you've landed. Then, and only then, could you head in the right direction to get to Lincoln.

When you don't know where you are, there's no way to know what direction to take. No matter which way you go, you're guessing. It's easy to get lost.

You might get lucky and make all the right turns the first time, but would you really want to leave it to chance? We don't think so.

The exact same thing is true about your financial success. You must start with an accurate reading of where you are financially; you must take inventory. This is your financial baseline.

> *Think of your financial baseline as a blueprint or financial fingerprint where you can see your financial condition in a glance.*

We've learned in coaching others that this step has instant rewards for people. First, they relax—maybe for the first time in years. Even if their financial lives are in shambles, just knowing the truth of it is a relief. If you're currently in debt or your expenses seem to spiral out of control, not looking at your financial picture actually makes you feel worse, not better. Not knowing is a constant, under-the-radar stress you simply don't need in your life.

An unexpected surprise for many people is an almost automatic "course correction" that takes place when they see where they are and where their money is going. Many people are unconscious of the "leaks" in their money. Often just seeing it on paper gets them into action. "We spend how much on lattes every week?"

Another reward is a great sense of control. Suddenly you're no longer just drifting along. There's tremendous motivation in knowing you're beginning to model the behavior of the wealthy. Quite simply, one of their greatest tactics is being aware of where their money goes.

Be encouraged. Getting it all together the first time won't be nearly as hard as you imagine. And it truly will mark the turning point from "scraping by," "getting along," "doing pretty well," or even "doing better than most" to a well-charted course toward financial freedom.

THREE STEPS TO DETERMINE YOUR FINANCIAL BASELINE

1. Organize your financial filing cabinet.
2. Complete your personal/business profit and loss statements.
3. Complete your personal/business balance sheets.

33 / From Guerrilla Wealth

Your Financial Filing Cabinet

Relax. If your financial papers, unopened mail, bills, receipts, and statements are scattered throughout the house, stuffed in drawers or shoeboxes, you're not alone. For most people that's perfectly normal. But it's not normal for the wealthy. And since the whole point of this section is to propel you toward wealth, we're going to make this essential step as easy and painless as possible for you.

Since, despite your hopes, the papers never seem to miraculously organize themselves, roll up your sleeves and let's begin the process of building your financial filing cabinet.

> "First comes thought; then organization of that thought, into ideas and plans; then transformation of those plans into reality. The beginning, as you will observe, is in your imagination."
>
> —Napoleon Hill

Let's begin by collecting all of your papers. You may have to search through your desk and open all those unopened envelopes filled with statements.

Once you dig them out, spread them across the floor or across the dining room table. These pieces of paper may spark highly charged emotional reactions. Some may remind you that you made some foolish impulse purchases. Others may be evidence of your casual attitude toward reconciling your checking account.

Stop!

Disengage emotionally now. These are just pieces of paper you want to sort. If you let them, they'll make you feel so awful or so overwhelmed, you'll stop. It's possible that your past dealings with money just brings up too much guilt or remorse, if for no other reason than you haven't been as sharp about money as you could have been.

So, if you need to, take a minute to remind yourself, "That was then; this is now," and you're taking control responsibly.

The first part of this exercise is as easy as an elementary school game. Just divide all the papers into stacks with others like them in the following categories:

Banking Records
- Checking
- Savings
- Bank books
- Banking statements
- Certificates
- Safe deposit box keys
- Cash receipts

Bills, Payable, Expenses
- Credit card statements
- Utilities
- Phone
- Internet
- Cable
- Gardener

Legal Documents
- Powers of attorney
- Financial agreements
- Partnership agreements
- Living will
- Do-not-resuscitate order
- Will
- Trust agreements

Insurance Policies
- Life
- Health
- Disability
- Business continuation
- Homeowners
- Renters
- Natural disasters (flood, earthquake)
- Auto
- Employee benefit data

Group Insurance
- Pension plan
- Savings/profit-sharing

Investment Records
- Profit-and-loss statements
- Balance sheets
- Investment statements
- Buy and sell documents
- Stock certificates
- Bond certificates
- College education funds

Income Tax Records
- Current year backup
- Past year's records
- Yearly worksheets

Housing Records
- Improvements
- Property tax payments

- Mortgage payments
- Appliance warranties
- Repair and maintenance receipts

Now that you have all your documents in nice neat little piles, it's time for you to file them away.

GUERRILLA INTELLIGENCE

Store the original copies of important documents such as wills, trusts, deeds, and stock certificates in a safe, fireproof box or a bank safe deposit box. Make copies of each of those documents and place them in your financial filing cabinet. Inform key people in your life where the originals can be found.

Photocopy both sides of all your credit, identification, and membership cards and keep them in your safe deposit box, safe, or fireproof box, and in your financial filing cabinet. Do the same with your personal-information page of your passport and all vaccination certificates. When you travel, take a copy with you and give another copy to someone you trust at home.

Create a System

In the beginning, you'll have to organize and create a structure for your financial filing cabinet, so set up a system that's easy and intuitive to use. Create a system that's simple for you. Otherwise you won't be able to find information you need quickly.

WORRY

Fresh out of business school, the young man answered a want ad for an accountant. Now he was being interviewed by a very nervous man who ran a small business that he had started himself.

"I need someone with an accounting degree," the man said. "But mainly, I'm looking for someone to do my worrying for me."

"Excuse me?" the young accountant said.

"I worry about a lot of things," the man said. "But I don't want to have to worry about money. Your job will be to take all the money worries off my back."

"I see," the young accountant said. "And how much does the job pay?"

"I will start you at $85,000."

"Eighty-five thousand dollars!" the young accountant exclaimed. "How can such a small business afford a sum like that?"

"That," the owner said, "is your first worry."

In time you'll have the ability to hire others to keep your system in order. You can employ bookkeepers or assistants who specialize in doing this precise work. Often, they're experts who know shortcuts and can give you timesaving tips. One thing we do caution you about is that when you work with bookkeepers, accountants, or others, have them adopt your system. Don't feel obligated to adopt their systems or purchase a complex organizing system at the office supply store. It's no smarter to have a complicated, unworkable system than leaving your papers in a mess. Make it simple.

chapter 34

FROM

Guerrilla Marketing for Financial Planners

Co-Author Grant Hicks

What Is the Five Touch Guerrilla Marketing System?

If I asked you the name of a great marketing idea, you could probably name a few. However, if I asked you the name of a great marketing system for small business, could you name any? The five-touch guerrilla marketing system is exactly what the name implies, a system to develop five touches or contacts with new customers or prospects.

If I asked you to recommend a great financial advisor and you gave me a name I had never heard of, I might not feel comfortable going to see that person. But if I had heard of this advisor before, had seen his or her ads or marketing material, or had received a mailing, seminar invitation, or phone call from that advisor, I would feel more comfortable with your recommendation.

Here is another example. Imagine you are driving along a highway and your spouse turns to you and says, "We need to eat, but we don't have much time. At the next stop there are two restaurants: One is a familiar, food-chain operation, and the other is a local diner. Which one do you choose?"

Most people, when asked this question, say they would go to the recognizable name-brand restaurant if they were in a rush. They would go where they are going to be most comfortable. Now I did not say the chain restaurant would be the cheapest, have the best service, or offer the best value. Did I mention quality? No, none of these entered the equation, yet so many businesses try to market themselves as offering good value, good price, excellent service, or great quality.

The diner across the street from the chain restaurant offers great service, selection, price, value, and quality ingredients; yet day after day people pass by this restaurant and its operators wonder why.

Is the diner only for people who are not in a rush? Guess what. The whole world is in a rush. The owners thought they put the proper ingredients together to make a great restaurant, yet the parking lot across the street is full every day while theirs is empty. They have not learned the five touch philosophies of marketing.

How Do People Get to Know You and/or Your Business?

Use the law of familiarity to your favor. Successful marketers know that people want to know about your business before they will do business with you. How do they get to know your business? Through your constant marketing programs.

I (Grant) discovered that I was 80 percent more successful after the fifth contact. By then, people knew our business and were comfortable in choosing us. For example, I developed a system, which I will share with you, to develop five touches or contacts. I also discovered that most marketing programs or marketers stop or give up after three tries.

Why stop marketing after two, three, or four times when you are halfway there? Your chances of success can be greatly increased if you continue or develop a strategy to make five touches or contacts.

> *Successful marketers know that people want to know about your business before they will do business with you.*

Give People the Opportunity to Connect with Your Business!

At this point we have had five touches with them and we only have their name and contact information in a database. Often, a few weeks pass and we will get a call for an appointment. This is the fun part. Some strange person or couple has called in for an appointment. They know everything about us, possibly met us at the seminar or workshop. They are prepared to tell us everything about themselves and their financial problems; because they are comfortable with us and know who we are, they are usually prepared to invest their retirement savings with us.

Now think about it for a minute. Strangers call us, tell us everything about themselves in the first meeting, and are prepared to give up most if not all of their money to us. Weird concept, but that is how the five-touch system works. These "strangers" have had a minimum of five touches or contacts before they call us.

You can see that the system is designed for more than five touches, but it takes a combination of five touches to get the system going. Remember, it is not five mail drops, but consecutive marketing activities along with a combination of other actions that make up the five touches. It's five different touches, not five of the same marketing contacts or touches.

Once you have people call, email, or drop in on your company with their contact information, develop a drip system to capture these people over time. What we did was to send prospects a monthly email—if they

HERE ARE SOME TOUCHES

- They see a targeted advertisement or mail drop.
- They read an article or advertorial.
- They check out our business on our website.
- They phone a friend or colleague to find out more about us. Sometimes they ask their lawyer or accountant or other business professional.
- They call in or drop in to request one of our information kits.
- We mail out the kit.
- We make a follow-up call to see if they received the kit. (We do this also to make sure we have the right address and phone number.)
- They make a follow-up request for additional kits or a free one-hour consultation.
- We mail a seminar invitation.
- We make a follow-up call to see if they would like to attend the seminar.
- They attend a seminar.
- They receive additional follow-up requests (drip method).
- They email us with a question to see how we respond to them.
- We email a response.
- They call our office to book an appointment.

had email—to keep in touch. We also sent monthly one-page mailers about different financial errors we see retirees making. They also received future seminar invitations that were designed to be exclusive invitations, not just a mass seminar mailing, because we wanted a more personal contact at the workshops, not just a big seminar. We tried to restrict attendance to 20 people.

We then planned to put the prospects on a bimonthly marketing campaign to continue to attract them; however, we fortunately found we were so busy with people calling us that we did not have time for all of these additional people, so we just stayed with an email.

Do You Have a Prospect Follow-Up System?

Obviously there are several drip-marketing programs that we could also develop to keep in touch with these prospects or new customers. Over time, we found that some people would call in months after receiving the information package. We also found that following up with a phone call to make sure they received their information kit was critical to the program. This was one additional touch or contact.

Eventually we help another client solve their financial problems and all because we are persistent and have a marketing program that is based on five touches, not just mailing and calling. Remember these clients called us for the appointment because they wanted to come in and discuss their financial problems or challenge, not because we advertised about our products or services.

The five-touch system is all about developing trust and long-term relationships with you and your company.

The success we had with the system will help you follow up, establish trust, develop your customer relationships, and receive more referrals and new customers than you can handle.

The five-touch system is all about developing trust and long-term relationships with you and your company.

chapter 35

FROM

Guerrilla Saving

Co-Author Kathryn Tyler

FRUGALITY IS A PERSPECTIVE from which guerrillas approach every spending decision, looking beyond the easy, expensive problem solutions for more creative, low-cost answers. It is an attitude that is cultivated slowly, over time. A large part of saving money is getting in the habit of doing things inexpensively.

Frugality Is an Attitude

This chapter can help you learn to save money on specific items, but the most crucial lessons to learn are the philosophy of frugality and the importance of applying it in your business. This chapter covers some of the principles

> *A large part of saving money is getting in the habit of doing things inexpensively.*

> "You need to remember that frugal doesn't equal cheap."
>
> —Barbara Winter,
>
> author of *Making a Living without a Job*

of thrift so you can understand the rationale behind our cost-cutting methods. Because every business is different, it is vital to use these principles to begin examining your own circumstances to determine where you can start saving some hard-earned cash.

REASONS FOR SAVING

Before we start discussing how to save money, you need to consider why you might want to. Saving money in your business has many advantages, including the following:

- You do not have to earn as much to keep your business solvent. Failure to turn a profit causes thousands of businesses to fold every year. If your overhead is low, you can keep operating even if you are just starting out or have seasonal lulls.

- You have the option of working less. For instance, Jay has been working only three days a week since 1971.

- You can accept projects you enjoy that may not pay as well as others. When your expenses are few, you have the freedom to work when and on what you want.

- You can invest in expansion, improvements, or new markets. The less it costs your business to run, the more discretion you have for allocating funds in new areas or on new equipment.

- And, of course, you get to keep more of what you earn. The higher your profit margin is, the bigger salary you can take.

> "Evaluate all your options before doing anything. There is usually a way you can do it better or cheaper or get by with what you have."
>
> —Todd Weaver, Minstrel Music Network

Shopping 101

Two types of purchases exist in business: disposable purchases and investment purchases. Guerrillas recognize the difference between these two and decide which category a purchase falls into before they buy.

Disposable purchases are goods or services that you will use once. Staples and pens are disposable purchases. Purchases you will reap the rewards of or suffer the problems of again and again are investment purchases. A telephone is an investment purchase because you will use it every business day. A telephone answering service is also an investment purchase because a poor service may cause you to lose callers week after week, while a good service will impress your customers.

Two types of purchases exist in business: disposable purchases and investment purchases. Guerrillas recognize the difference between these two and decide which category a purchase falls into before they buy.

Paper could fall into either category depending on how you plan to use it. Copier paper for internal use would be a disposable purchase, whereas letterhead stationery would be an investment purchase—an investment in your image.

Once you know whether a purchase is disposable or an investment, then you can use that information to decide where to save money. If a purchase is an investment, you may be willing to spend a little more money for added features or slightly better quality. It is also worthwhile to shop around more, spending more time calling different vendors or driving to several stores. In contrast, disposable purchases should be bought at the lowest possible price with the least amount of effort. Therefore, you may want to drive to three stores to save $150 on a fax machine, but you would not want to expend that much effort to save 50¢ on sticky notes.

This point may seem obvious, but many times consumers do not consciously contemplate whether an item is disposable or an investment

BEFORE YOU SIGN THE CHECK, ASK THESE QUESTIONS

- *How will this purchase increase my profitability?* Whenever you're considering spending money, think about what would happen if you didn't spend it. Then try not to spend it. That way you avoid overbuying.

- *When do I need this?* The most important thing to employ when shopping is foresight. Think about it. The more expensive the item or the longer you will use it, the more you should think about it. You should buy something when not having it costs you money.

- *Which features do I need?* Which ones can I live without? You may need to track your usage for a month or so to really determine this.

- *Where can I get this?* Notice we did not say, "Where can I buy this?" By thinking in terms of acquisition, not consumption, you become more creative in thinking of where to obtain the item for free or how you can modify something you already have to serve a new purpose.

- *How much am I willing to pay for this?* If you decide you need to buy something, it helps to have a ballpark figure in mind before you hit the garage sales or the stores and become swayed by bells and whistles. If you do not have any idea how much an item costs, you might need to do a little research. Study sales fliers and newspaper ads. Call for mail-order catalogs. Ask around at association meetings.

before they buy. Instead, they rush, skimping on investment purchases and blindly spending too much on disposable ones.

Say, for example, you are considering Model X photocopier that costs $400 and Model Z copier that costs $475. All of the features are identical except that Model Z can make enlargements. You buy Model X because it is cheaper and think you have just saved yourself $75. But over the next two months, you make six visits to the local copy shop to make enlargements and spend $20 on each visit for a total of $120. According to this scenario, your decision to buy Model X cost you $45!

It is easy to see how equipment is an investment purchase, but do not overlook products or services that improve your image, such as a daily radio advertisement.

> "Learn to use your imagination more and your pocketbook less. The people who aren't in business a long time throw money at their problems. Those who are, are good problem solvers. Find imaginative ways to produce the goals you want. Figure out how to get the most mileage out of every dollar you spend."
>
> —Barbara Winter, author of *Making a Living without a Job*

Break Out of Your Comfort Zone

Even after you hear about a cheaper source for office supplies or a less expensive internet service provider, you may be tempted to continue to use old vendors. It is human nature. We grow accustomed to patronizing the same businesses or doing things the same way. It is easy, comfortable, and requires no effort. But it can be costly. After all, you will not save any money by continuing to do things the same way and buying the same things from the same people.

To trim expenses, guerrillas regularly test new methods and suppliers. They stretch a bit. They get out the map to find the new

> ### STEPS TO MAKE THE PROCESS A LITTLE EASIER
>
> - *Start small with something relatively inexpensive or easily replaceable.* Research new vendors thoroughly. Ask for references or call the local Better Business Bureau to ensure the company has a clean record.
> - *Take advantage of complimentary trial offers.*
> - *Pay by credit card.* If you are unhappy with the service or the supplier turns out to be less than reputable, you have greater leverage if you want to contest the charges.
>
> It may take some time before a new technique or supplier becomes comfortable. Keep experimenting!

print shop recommended by a friend or pick up the phone to call a new office supply company for a catalog.

Learn New Skills

Advertisements have convinced us that we must leave everything to the "experts." If we need our dog trained, we call a dog trainer. If we need a skirt hemmed, we call a seamstress. We, as a society, have become so specialized that we know how to do only one thing well, and we trade that skill for everything else we need. We are afraid to try a new task by ourselves, in case we make a costly mistake.

> "The best price is not always the best value. Service, durability, and reliability are components of value."
>
> —Shel Horowitz, author of *Marketing without Megabucks*

But many times, with the proper tools, guerrillas can do an even better job than the so-called experts. Why? Because we have a vested interest, we care more about the project than the person we are hiring. We know more about our own businesses. We know what we want done. And we are willing to take the time required to do it right. It is much more cost-efficient, in the long run, to become self-sufficient.

Get Organized

When was the last time you lost something? How long did it take you to find it? Did you ever find it? It is particularly important for home-based guerrillas to be organized because of the tendency for work and home life to blend together. Crayons get mixed with highlighter pens. Office supply catalogs lounge alongside copies of Lands' End and Eddie Bauer. In a traditional office, when you cannot find something, you only need to search one or two rooms. In a home office, when you cannot find something, you start in the office and then move to the rest of the house and, possibly, to the car.

Losing things is expensive. It costs money in lost work time and rework, if you cannot find what you want. It also costs when you buy more of what you already have but cannot find. For instance, when Kathryn moved her office from one spare bedroom to another, she lost a lot of things in the process. Even though she was only moving 10 feet, everything got boxed up and put in the basement until she had time to "organize it." The problem was, as you can imagine, she never set aside time to organize it and she kept trekking downstairs to look for things. When one deadline loomed, she lost two hours combing through boxes for plain manila envelopes. She finally bought more at the office supply store, even though she swore she had a brand-new box—somewhere.

If a purchase is going to make you more organized or save you significant amounts of time, it is usually worth the cost. Kathryn kept her files in cardboard boxes for three years. That worked for a while, but as she continued to accumulate research and copies of her work, the number of boxes quadrupled. Although they were a frugal solution, she eventually decided it was cheaper to buy a filing cabinet than to keep losing work time and energy shuffling papers and lifting boxes.

If you need help getting organized, it is usually because you have too much stuff to begin with. Start by throwing out the junk you do not use. Or donate it to charity and take a tax deduction. To assist you in your de-junking quest, we strongly recommend reading *Clutter's Last Stand* by Don Aslett.

Another way to become more organized is create systems for everything you do regularly in your business. Organizational failures occur when you leave things to chance. You need systems for tracking appointments, returning telephone calls, placing orders, replying to email, storing information that needs to be acted upon, updating web pages, backing up computer files, etc. For example, Jay answers his email immediately to keep it from piling up.

Manage Time, Manage Money

Workplace expert Alice Bredin says, "A few habits really differentiate the productive . . . business owners from those that seem to be struggling. One is the focus on viewing time as money. What I mean by that is a business owner who is continually asking himself, every few hours, 'Am I doing something that is going to earn me money? Move my business forward?'"

chapter 36

FROM

Guerrilla Breakthrough Strategies

Co-Author Terry Telford

Introduction to Joint Ventures

Working with joint venture partners gives you the freedom to accomplish twice as much in half the time. You can work on several joint venture projects at the same time with several partners and expand your business exponentially in ways you would never have been able to achieve on your own.

In the beginning, you'll be actively seeking joint venture partners, but as you become more and more recognized in the industry, the tables will turn and people will start approaching you with joint venture proposals. When you reach

> *Working with joint venture partners gives you the freedom to accomplish twice as much in half the time.*

this level, you don't have to prospect for new partners every day. You can wait for juicy joint venture opportunities to be presented to you. You can be selective and only accept the best of the best, which will help grow your business and take things to the next level.

Of course, you can still actively seek new joint venture partners, to accelerate your business expansion, but it doesn't have to be a major part of your workday any longer.

Let's start off with an example that shows the effectiveness of joint venture partnerships. If you contact 5 to 10 prospects a day, five days a week, and 10 percent of your prospects say yes, that's 1,300 to 2,600 new joint venture prospects a year. If each one of them sends you just two website visitors a day, that's 2,600 to 5,200 visitors to your site daily. If your website converts visitors to customers at an average rate of 1 percent, you'll be making 26 to 52 sales a day.

In reality, 10 percent of your joint venture partners will send you 90 percent of your traffic, but the numbers still work out approximately the same. You may end up with 130 to 260 partners that send you 20 visitors or more daily. When you see who's actively promoting your website, you can work closely with them to increase their effectiveness and you both win.

So let's dive right in. The strategies and tactics we're going to cover allow you to leverage the power of the internet to help you experience self-directed, exponential business growth. So strap in and let's get rolling.

Joint Venture Partnerships for Marketing

First, we'll look at joint venture partnerships for marketing. These partnerships are the easiest to set up and give you the opportunity to quickly test your partnership for compatibility. We'll also look at joint venture partnerships for product development and for running entire businesses.

We'll start off by taking a high-level overview of your business. You've got two ways to contact potential customers. You can contact them one at a time through conventional marketing and advertising, which requires a substantial investment of time, money, or both. Or you can leverage your time and money by contacting select groups of people who have large networks and let them spread your marketing message for you. The second marketing method is a true guerrilla marketing strategy because it allows you to leverage your time and capital.

> *Developing joint venture partnerships with industry leaders who introduce you and your products and services to the masses saves your business time, money, and effort.*

Developing joint venture partnerships with industry leaders who introduce you and your products and services to the masses saves your business time, money, and effort.

There's another benefit to working with industry leaders: borrowed credibility. If an industry leader recommends your products or services, that endorsement puts your company in a completely different light. Your credibility is elevated to a higher level.

Don't be afraid to approach anyone you want to work with. It makes no difference if you perceive the person to be 10 times more successful than you. Those are the people you want to be setting up joint venture partnerships with. They'll be the most difficult people to access, but since most entrepreneurs don't even try, you have a good chance of at least getting your prospect's attention. So give it a try.

What's the worst thing that could happen? The worst thing that can happen is someone chops you up into small pieces and eats you. But there's a 99.99 percent chance that none of the people you approach for a joint venture partnership will be interested in eating you. So don't feel afraid or intimidated to talk to anyone you want.

The worst thing they can do is say "no." And when you put that into perspective, a "no" is really not that bad.

What Makes a Joint Venture?

Joint venture partnerships have been a regular way of doing business for hundreds of years. Two companies or individuals join forces to build on each other's strengths or assets and produce a new company, product, or service that is stronger, more versatile, or able to capture a market that separately they didn't access.

Look around in your everyday life and you'll see joint venture partnerships abound. Sony Ericsson, Colgate-Palmolive, Verizon Wireless, and Nokia Siemens Networks are all the result of joint venture partnerships.

The simplest joint venture online is between a product owner and a database or list owner.

Online, joint ventures are often much simpler and take almost no effort at all. The simplest joint venture online is between a product owner and a database or list owner. The product owner offers the database owner a higher than normal commission per sale if the list owner will mail out an endorsement about the product. It's a pretty basic joint venture, but it works remarkably well. Many online businesses have seen tremendous growth using just this one type of joint venture.

The list owners win because they have an increased cash flow. The product owners win because they also have an increased cash flow, plus they acquire new customers, which is the biggest benefit of all.

Where Do You Find These List Owners?

Up until about 2003, electronic magazines or newsletters (e-zines) were effective and abundant. You could buy ad space in the e-zines and

Joint venturing with a publisher who has a private list that he or she doesn't sell ad space for is far more beneficial than spending money on advertising.

run your ad to thousands, sometimes millions for pennies on the dollar. But as spam became a bigger problem and e-zine readership dropped, the response rates to advertising in e-zines also dropped.

Today, there are only a handful of quality e-zines to advertise in. The majority of the "old-fashioned" e-zine publishers stopped selling advertising space in their publications and started paying attention to the quality of information they send to their subscribers. These personal lists are worth gold today, but you generally can't buy advertising space in

BENEFITS YOU MIGHT OFFER

Here's a list of some of the benefits you could offer your prospective joint venture partners. These benefits are the tactics you'll use to entice your prospective partners into accepting your proposal.

- Higher commissions
- A promotional mailing to your list or database
- Discount offer for your prospect's list
- Enhanced warranty only available through your partner
- Free bonuses for your prospect and their list
- Alternative payment options
- Delayed billing
- Contest
- Consulting or group coaching

them. But you can contact the publishers and form joint ventures with them, sometimes on a one-time basis and sometimes on an ongoing basis, depending on the relationship you develop with the publisher.

Joint venturing with a publisher who has a private list that he or she doesn't sell ad space for is far more beneficial than spending money on advertising. This is one of the notable differences between running an online direct-marketing business and an offline direct-marketing business.

Offline, direct-marketing companies rent their lists of prospects, subscribers, and customers using list brokers. Renting your targeted lists offers a secondary income that sometimes rivals your primary sales.

Online, large-list owners are very protective of their lists. They aren't rented, sold, or bartered. To get your product or service promoted to these large, personal lists, you need to develop a relationship with the list owner and put together a joint venture partnership. Even if it's only a one-time joint venture and it's as simple as the list owner mailing out an endorsement for your offer in return for higher commissions, it can be very profitable if your product is targeted to the list owner's subscribers' interests.

Joint ventures can literally happen in a few minutes. You phone your prospect, he or she agrees to your proposal, you set up the deal, and it's done. You could sit down beside someone in a conference, in a meeting, at lunch and start a conversation. By the end of the conversation, you could have a joint venture partnership. On the flip side, the deals can also take months or years to set up, depending on your business, the complexity of the deal, and the industry.

We're going to start off with a simple joint venture, but before we jump in, we're going to organize ourselves for success. First, segment your joint venture system into two components, strategies and tactics.

Your strategies are what you're going to do, and your tactics are how you're going to do it. So let's take care of the strategies first.

Strategies

Before you begin approaching your prospects, get a clear idea of what you want out of the deal and what you're willing to give your joint venture partner in return. Write a mini-outline so you have a reference when you're talking to your prospects. If you have an outline to look at when you're on the phone, it helps you keep your thoughts organized and the conversation on track, and impresses your prospects because you show them you have a clear understanding of what you're doing.

Tactics

Next, you want to consider your tactics. As we mentioned before, your tactics are the "how" part of your plan, or what you're going to give your partners.

THE DEAL

There are no limitations to the number or type of deals you can work with your joint venture partners. Here are a few examples:

- Product developers can give their joint venture partners a sample of their product in return for their partners' testimonial and sending a message to their lists.
- Service providers can provide services in return for marketing and promotion.
- Webmasters with membership sites can provide monthly or annual memberships in exchange for their partners' marketing efforts.

When you're working a joint venture partnership that creates a product, hundreds of variables are involved, so we're going to opt for joint venture partnerships that focus more on the promotion and distribution angle.

chapter 37

FROM

Guerrilla Multilevel Marketing

Co-Authors James Dillehay and Marcella Vonn Harting

Y OUR NETWORK MARKETING BUSINESS is crying out for help. You've exhausted your warm list. Prospects won't come to your opportunity meetings. Conference calls aren't inspiring your team to act. Ads are costing you money but not paying for themselves. You would quit except there's nothing much to give up.

Why Guerrilla Multilevel Marketing?

Despite the lack of vital signs in your business, you feel network marketing still holds a promise. It's just that some missing piece of the network marketing puzzle continually eludes you, prevents you from entering network marketing heaven.

> "It is impossible to win the race unless you venture to run, impossible to win the victory unless you dare to battle."
>
> —Rich DeVos, co-founder, Amway

That missing piece is the problem. It can be neatly summed up in the words: You don't know what you don't know.

What would it be like if you could discover what it is that you don't know but successful network marketers do and put that knowledge to work for you today?

Here's something almost everyone in the network marketing industry does know: The majority of newly enrolling distributors don't have a business background or a clear understanding of marketing. Nevertheless, recruits are still being urged to treat network marketing as a business.

Is it any wonder that new signups have a fear in the back of their mind? They don't really know what a business is or how to run one. How long will they linger before the fear tells them to run? Hint: 90 percent of new distributors quit their first year.

How many more distributors would stay with network marketing if they were confident in the beginning that they didn't have to know how to run a business in order to succeed at network marketing? What if you could present them with a system that was easy for anyone—even someone without business experience—to learn and teach?

Leaving Money on the Table

An obstacle for many distributors is the MLM culture of conformity—an expectation that everyone must follow the herd or be abandoned. A one-way-for-everybody attitude leaves a lot of money on the table.

The reality is that most people in network marketing do the business a little different from each other anyway. Evidence shows that you will earn more money by teaching a system that supports variety and is suitable to different personality types. Guerrilla multilevel marketing offers a way to support and enable distributors to thrive using tactics they can apply their personal strengths to.

In his best-selling book *The Wave 4 Way To Build Your Downline*, author Richard Poe cites a 50-percent boost in sales and a 15- to 20-percent increase in retention of people when offering downline members multiple ways of prospecting.

Guerrillas map out the coming months and years, which eliminates anxiety about what's ahead. How much more could you achieve if you could replace the fear of the unknown with certainty about your network marketing future?

The fastest way to clear up any confusion about what network marketing is as a business is for you to recognize that marketing is every communication you make about your product or opportunity.

Growing Your Warm List

Your upline wisely begins your entry into networking by encouraging you to make a warm list of everyone you know. They know from experience that by getting you started contacting people who know you, your first efforts at network marketing will be aimed at people who like and trust you.

Regardless of how many people you know, your initial warm list runs out. From then on, growth depends on consistently finding and bringing more people into your network. Your business requires an incoming flow of people—people with whom to communicate and grow relationships.

Guerrilla multilevel marketing tactics will generate streams of prospects. As a guerrilla, you'll learn ways to transform those prospects into new friends and then into lifelong customers and some into successful business builders.

Think Leverage

Network marketing lets you leverage your time and efforts by getting paid on the time and efforts of others. Guerrilla marketing magnifies the power of leveraging by teaching how to automate your lead gathering, reach hundreds more prospects, and even how to get prospects to pay you for your marketing.

Guerrilla marketing will work as a powerful leveraging tool for you when:

> *Network marketing lets you leverage your time and efforts by getting paid on the time and efforts of others.*

- You are using your company's products and are completely sold on their benefits.
- You are committed to network marketing as a business lifestyle.
- You are willing and eager to learn.
- You won't give up until you're dead.

Think Fun

Everyone desires fun, whether they acknowledge it or not. Play is worked out of us as we pass through school into the job market, but the desire for play never leaves. It just gets buried by fear that we won't be taken care of.

It's often difficult for new distributors to believe they can actually play for a living, but thousands of network marketers are living the proof every day. Guerrillas enjoy their business activities because they follow the guerrilla system, which takes away the confusion and uncertainty of what to do to grow.

Tactics for Meetings

Organized meetings provide a way to leverage your time by presenting to groups of people, rather than to individuals one by one. Speaking to crowds will help you achieve your goals faster.

TACTICS FOR WORKING WITH GROUPS OF PEOPLE

- Company conventions
- Opportunity meetings
- Home parties
- Lead group meetings
- Sizzle sessions

Company Conventions

There is probably no better tool for leveraging your efforts from a single activity than your company's convention. The advantages of getting yourself and everyone in your organization to your company's convention are listed below.

- *Meeting other distributors.* Social proof is a persuasive influence. By getting new and prospective distributors to a convention attended by hundreds or thousands of active members, you are proving that your opportunity is worth being involved in because all the other attendees agree that it is, or they would not be there. All you have to do is get there and bring all your people. The event does the rest.
- *Meeting the folks who manage and, in some cases, started the company.* MLM company founders are typically charismatic entrepreneurs who have attracted an experienced management team to help distributors grow their business. The marketing benefit to you comes from tapping into their authority as presenters of the event.
- *Receiving acknowledgement from people in your organization* who have demonstrated leadership and advancement in rank.
- *Getting exclusive offers and special savings* only available at conventions.

- *Being the first to learn about new products, contests, bonuses, and incentives.*
- *Expanding your knowledge through training sessions* on product usage and business development.
- *Acquiring the feeling of being connected to something bigger than you.* This fulfills a basic human desire for belonging.
- *Exploiting the opportunity to travel* to an exciting convention location and have fun.

Opportunity Meetings

Opportunity meetings have been one of the foundational building tools in network marketing. They are a venue for presenting a compelling call to action. Because of the presence of others, meetings invoke social proof and can also generate contagious excitement and enthusiasm.

Successful opportunity meetings are planned and have a flow that makes sense to the attendees. They come to a close in a way that leaves people longing for more.

Just because prospects don't show up at a meeting after you have invited them, don't write them off or you might miss enrolling your next superstar.

Home Presentations

When carried out in your home, an opportunity is often referred to as a "private business reception." The PBR is a comfortable setting in which to introduce your program because of the safe, at-home surroundings.

Advantages of Home Presentations

- Fun to do and attend
- Familiar, safe background
- Inexpensive to put on
- Can be planned on short notice

- Most likely to generate referrals
- Easy to do and to teach others to do

If you choose to have opportunity meetings in your home, set up displays of your products in visible spots and in easy reach throughout the house. Just as you would dress neatly for a meeting, clean and straighten up the yard to give the best impression.

Home Parties

Marketing through home parties has made companies like Tupperware and Avon into household names. Party-plan sales account for around $7 billion in direct-selling revenues.

Informal and relaxed, home parties make a fun way for people to socialize and for you to introduce your products and opportunity in safe and friendly surroundings to several people at once. Best of all, they provide a venue to put immediate cash from sales into your hands.

Hosting In-Home Parties
In-home parties follow a simple outline with these simple steps or variations that are appropriate to your product.

- Ask the hostess to introduce you.
- Have satisfied customers give testimonials.
- Pass some products around the room.
- Describe key benefits while people are seeing, touching, smelling, tasting, or hearing about your products.
- Play a company DVD or video.
- Briefly recap key benefits on the DVD / video.
- Talk about different ways to use the product.
- Describe the business opportunity.
- Have a drawing for door prizes (everyone should get something).
- Take orders.

It's no surprise that women dominate the party-plan area. Home parties are used to promote a wide variety of items women purchase, including household products, arts and crafts, toys, candles, cosmetics, jewelry, and many others. Enliven your home parties with games, recipes, and other tips on building a home-party business.

Lead Group Meetings

Lead groups for networking help their members by referring each other's services. They offer a way of building relationships and expanding one's base of prospects. Before getting involved, be clear about how you will be able to help refer potential clients or suggest useful tactics to other members.

Participating in a network group is a long-term social tactic, not an invitation to pitch your offer. After meeting your fellow members, make notes on their situations, so that when you come across a helpful resource, you can get it to them.

Be clear about the types of leads you are looking for in return. Are you looking for customers or for business builders? How do you define you ideal prospect? If you aren't sure, go to your marketing plan and use the guidelines there to describe your perfect client, not only to yourself, but also to those who are willing to refer people to you.

To get the most out of networking groups, attend meetings regularly. Get to know the people involved. Show up with the intention to grow relationships and you'll find your group is ready to support you with referrals.

One of the largest referral groups with chapters across the U.S. is BNI (http://www.bni.com). Websites like LinkedIn (http://www.linkedin.com) offer the possibility of locating online networking opportunities as well.

Sizzle Sessions

Sizzle sessions are informal meetings with distributors in small businesses who talk about what's going on for them and brainstorm ideas for growth. Excited distributors getting together generate contagious energy. Don Failla says in his book *The 45-Second*

Presentation That Will Change Your Life, "Your network marketing program is the steak and everyone knows that the sizzle sells the steak!" Sizzle sessions are about creating the sizzle.

Unlike most other types of meetings, sizzle sessions are free-flowing chats about products, the comp plan, and how business is going for each person. These sessions help distributors feel that they are connected as a team.

chapter 38

FROM

Guerrilla Networking

Co-Author Monroe Mann

NETWORKING DOES **NOT** mean meeting people. Actually, that definition is just plain wrong, and it's no wonder why so many entrepreneurs feel lost when it comes to networking—which should actually be very easy. You see, networking should be easy, and is easy. The key to your success simply lies in which definition of networking your subscribe to.

Guerrilla networking does not mean "meeting people." Actually, it means "becoming the type of person that other people want to meet."

For example, take some of the big movers and shakers in business, such as Bill Gates,

> *Guerrilla networking does NOT mean meeting people. It means becoming the type of person other people want to meet.*

Tony Hawk, and Sandra Bullock. They have taken the power of networking to its highest level: People want to meet them.

Ask yourself this question: Would people stand in line for hours to meet with any of these three people? Yes! Why? The answer is simple. They know how to network, for they became the type of person that other people want to meet.

This same networking principle applies to dating, friendship, and yes, small business. Why work your butt off to meet people when you can put that same energy into becoming an interesting person within your field, and then benefit by having the same people you want to meet come up to you?

Herein lies the power of this principle: You kill two birds with one stone. While your boring competition—who no one wants to meet—is out there desperately trying to meet people day after day, you, on the other hand, are actively putting your efforts into becoming as cool as humanly possible. By diversifying your offerings, by becoming a leader in your field, and by putting together a knock-out marketing angle, you'll end up taking your industry by storm.

The result: Your competition, the press, and customers all end up at your doorstep, trying to meet you.

To the uninformed, this public interest might appear to be a lucky fluke. You, however, would know that it was actually the result of your persistent, hard work, and the fruit of your foolproof networking plan finally reaping its reward: You became the type of person/business that other people wanted to meet and work with.

Meeting people can do nothing for you if you have nothing interesting to offer.

If you continually try to meet people, especially without changing and improving your marketing angle along the way, you're wasting time. Meeting people can do nothing for you if you have nothing interesting to offer.

Taken further, you might have noticed that no one wants you to tell them how wonderful you are; people want to discover and find that out for themselves. And therein lies another key to guerrilla networking: Your accomplishments are not as impressive if you have to tell people about them yourself.

Your accomplish-ments are not as impressive if you have to tell people about them yourself.

Bottom line: If you're playing your networking cards right, and are out there doing interesting things, people should be flocking to meet you. You should be receiving emails, phone calls, and letters from those who think you (and your company) are so cool that they want to do business with you. If not, it's because you're not memorable enough to warrant such action, in which case, you better re-evaluate your strategy immediately!

So remember: Networking does not mean meeting people; it means becoming the type of person other people want to meet. Become as cool as possible, get your brand out there as much as possible, and let us find out for ourselves how cool you are.

In other words, don't necessarily try to meet us; the idea is to make us want to meet you. And if you're reading this book, yes, you're probably someone we want to meet.

50 PROVEN WAYS TO GET PEOPLE TO COME TO YOU!

1. Write a successful book.

    TRADITIONAL NETWORKING: Spending your time reading books by others who you hope to meet one day.

    GUERRILLA NETWORKING: Spending your time writing books that are going to entice others to want to meet you.

2. Become the expert in your field.

    TRADITIONAL NETWORKING: Spending your time trying to meet and become friends with the experts in your field.

50 PROVEN WAYS TO GET PEOPLE TO COME TO YOU!

GUERRILLA NETWORKING: Spending some time working to become one of those very experts.

3. Become famous.

TRADITIONAL NETWORKING: Dreaming of meeting famous people.

GUERRILLA NETWORKING: Becoming a famous person so other famous people want to meet you.

4. Offer investment capital.

TRADITIONAL NETWORKING: Trying to meet money people.

GUERRILLA NETWORKING: Offering to invest in other people's projects, thus becoming a money person yourself.

5. Be a network hub.

TRADITIONAL NETWORKING: Working to discover who the network hubs are and desperately trying to connect with them.

GUERRILLA NETWORKING: Becoming a network hub yourself so others want to connect with you.

6. Get onto a TV show/radio show, or be written up in a newspaper/magazine.

TRADITIONAL NETWORKING: Trying to get media attention.

GUERRILLA NETWORKING: Doing such cool things that the media are vying for your attention.

7. Take matters into your own hands.

TRADITIONAL NETWORKING: Waiting for things to happen on the world's terms.

GUERRILLA NETWORKING: Making things happen on your terms.

50 PROVEN WAYS TO GET PEOPLE TO COME TO YOU!

8. Offer to help people.

   TRADITIONAL NETWORKING: Trying to get everyone else to help you.

   GUERRILLA NETWORKING: Offering to help someone else.

9. Introduce yourself to people.

   TRADITIONAL NETWORKING: People forgetting about you as soon as you leave.

   GUERRILLA NETWORKING: Everyone talking about you long after you leave.

10. Always smile.

    TRADITIONAL NETWORKING: Unconsciously seeking pity via your frowns.

    GUERRILLA NETWORKING: Consciously attracting alliances with your smiles.

11. Initiate conversations.

    TRADITIONAL NETWORKING: Hoping that everyone already knows who you are.

    GUERRILLA NETWORKING: Assuming no one does.

12. Become "cool."

    TRADITIONAL NETWORKING: Trying to hang out with the "cool" people.

    GUERRILLA NETWORKING: Becoming that cool person yourself.

13. Become noteworthy.

    TRADITIONAL NETWORKING: Trying to connect with noteworthy people.

    GUERRILLA NETWORKING: Becoming that noteworthy person yourself.

50 PROVEN WAYS TO GET PEOPLE TO COME TO YOU!

14. Do something radical.

TRADITIONAL NETWORKING: Playing it safe.

GUERRILLA NETWORKING: Understanding that breaking the rules often reaps rewards.

15. Become the go-between.

TRADITIONAL NETWORKING: Assuming that being a go-between is an unsavory position to avoid at all costs.

GUERRILLA NETWORKING: Realizing just the opposite.

16. Risk failure.

TRADITIONAL NETWORKING: Avoiding risk.

GUERRILLA NETWORKING: Realizing that being risky is often cool.

17. Send off an email.

TRADITIONAL NETWORKING: Assuming you'll never get a response.

GUERRILLA NETWORKING: Realizing that you never know!

18. Be creative.

TRADITIONAL NETWORKING: Believing that creativity is too hard.

GUERRILLA NETWORKING: Understanding that creativity is simply the opposite of mediocrity.

19. Write a spicy letter to the editor.

TRADITIONAL NETWORKING: Playing it safe.

GUERRILLA NETWORKING: Creating a controversy.

20. Write a press release.

TRADITIONAL NETWORKING: Trying to actually meet the editors.

GUERRILLA NETWORKING: Enticing them into wanting to meet you.

50 PROVEN WAYS TO GET PEOPLE TO COME TO YOU!

21. Hire a publicist.

TRADITIONAL NETWORKING: Doing it all yourself.

GUERRILLA NETWORKING: Using your limited time as effectively as possible.

22. Find their "sweet spot."

TRADITIONAL NETWORKING: Researching the person.

GUERRILLA NETWORKING: Understanding the person.

23. Take out an ad.

TRADITIONAL NETWORKING: Going to the prospect.

GUERRILLA NETWORKING: Encouraging the prospect to come to you.

24. Leave a voice mail.

TRADITIONAL NETWORKING: Insisting on speaking with someone.

GUERRILLA NETWORKING: Ensuring that they call you back.

25. Call them.

TRADITIONAL NETWORKING: Doing the bare minimum.

GUERRILLA NETWORKING: Doing whatever is necessary to make it happen.

26. Include them in your acknowledgements.

TRADITIONAL NETWORKING: Yearning for the day when you are acknowledged by someone else.

GUERRILLA NETWORKING: Acknowledge yourself.

27. Become their friend.

TRADITIONAL NETWORKING: Wondering why you don't have more friends.

GUERRILLA NETWORKING: Working to become the type of person other people want to be friends with.

50 PROVEN WAYS TO GET PEOPLE TO COME TO YOU!

28. Do them a favor.

    TRADITIONAL NETWORKING: Doing favors with an ulterior motive.

    GUERRILLA NETWORKING: Doing favors with a generous motive.

29. Let them do YOU a favor.

    TRADITIONAL NETWORKING: Not thinking highly enough of yourself.

    GUERRILLA NETWORKING: Realizing that you deserve some help!

30. Say thank you.

    TRADITIONAL NETWORKING: Hoping others will thank you.

    GUERRILLA NETWORKING: Thanking them first.

31. Become a success in your field.

    TRADITIONAL NETWORKING: Believing that you need to meet a certain person or be affiliated with a certain company in order to become successful.

    GUERRILLA NETWORKING: Realizing that the more things you can do to become successful, the sooner everyone in your field is going to want to work with you.

32. Help someone else become successful.

    TRADITIONAL NETWORKING: Waiting for someone else to help you become a success.

    GUERRILLA NETWORKING: Helping someone else become a success before you.

33. Invent something amazing.

    TRADITIONAL NETWORKING: Always thinking, "Hey, I thought of that!"

    GUERRILLA NETWORKING: Taking action on your thoughts.

50 PROVEN WAYS TO GET PEOPLE TO COME TO YOU!

34. Make our lives easier in some way.

TRADITIONAL NETWORKING: Wishing someone else would make your life easier.

GUERRILLA NETWORKING: Making your life easier yourself.

35. Get onto a TV talk show.

TRADITIONAL NETWORKING: Watching TV.

GUERRILLA NETWORKING: Being on TV.

36. Find a referral on your behalf.

TRADITIONAL NETWORKING: Desperately trying tactic after failed tactic to "meet someone."

GUERRILLA NETWORKING: Enticing someone else to introduce you to that very same person.

37. Get out of the house.

TRADITIONAL NETWORKING: Waiting for success to knock on your door.

GUERRILLA NETWORKING: Opening the door to allow opportunity in.

38. Tell people what you are going to do.

TRADITIONAL NETWORKING: Keeping your ambition to yourself.

GUERRILLA NETWORKING: Having the guts to tell the world.

39. Tell people what you've done.

TRADITIONAL NETWORKING: Thinking that you're bragging.

GUERRILLA NETWORKING: Knowing that it's true.

40. Tell people what you are currently doing.

TRADITIONAL NETWORKING: Keeping it to yourself so you don't jinx it.

GUERRILLA NETWORKING: Telling everyone so others can jump on board.

50 PROVEN WAYS TO GET PEOPLE TO COME TO YOU!

41. Thank them—AGAIN!

    TRADITIONAL NETWORKING: Being rude and insensitive.

    GUERRILLA NETWORKING: Realizing that no one can do it alone.

42. Do something that no one has ever done before.

    TRADITIONAL NETWORKING: Coloring within the lines on the piece of paper.

    GUERRILLA NETWORKING: Turning the paper into an airplane.

43. Do something BETTER than it's currently being done.

    TRADITIONAL NETWORKING: Stopping at good enough.

    GUERRILLA NETWORKING: Always striving to be better.

44. Partner up with a bigger name. Hitch your wagon to a star.

    TRADITIONAL NETWORKING: Going it alone.

    GUERRILLA NETWORKING: Gaining assistance.

45. Give them what they need.

    TRADITIONAL NETWORKING: Giving them what you think they want.

    GUERRILLA NETWORKING: Giving them what they actually need.

46. Solve a problem.

    TRADITIONAL NETWORKING: Coming up with the problems.

    GUERRILLA NETWORKING: Solving them.

47. Be useful.

    TRADITIONAL NETWORKING: Wasting time, energy, and resources.

    GUERRILLA NETWORKING: Not doing that.

50 PROVEN WAYS TO GET PEOPLE TO COME TO YOU!

48. Be the answer to their prayers.

TRADITIONAL NETWORKING: Praying for a solution.

GUERRILLA NETWORKING: Becoming the answer to someone else's prayer.

49. Name drop!

TRADITIONAL NETWORKING: Name dropping.

GUERRILLA NETWORKING: Strategic name placement.

50. Be a guerrilla.

TRADITIONAL NETWORKING: Meeting people.

GUERRILLA NETWORKING: Becoming the type of person other people want to meet.

The Bottom Line

- Guerrilla networking does NOT mean meeting people. It means becoming the type of person other people want to meet.
- Guerrilla networking does NOT mean who do you know or who knows you. It means who thinks highly enough of you to take your phone calls.
- Guerrilla networking does NOT mean schmoozing. It means becoming the type of person other people want to schmooze with.
- Guerrilla networking does NOT mean a huge Rolodex. It means becoming the type of person other people add to their Rolodex.

- Guerrilla networking does NOT mean getting out there. It means becoming the type of person other people invite out.
- Guerrilla networking does NOT mean handing out business cards. It means being so famous and successful that you don't need a business card.
- Guerrilla networking does NOT mean crashing parties. It means being the host of parties that other people want to crash.
- Guerrilla networking does NOT mean finding investors. It means developing projects that everyone else wants to invest in.
- Guerrilla networking does NOT mean dating. It means becoming the type of person that everyone else wants to date.
- Guerrilla networking does NOT mean becoming involved in others' projects. It means starting projects that everyone else wants to be involved with.

chapter 39

FROM

Guerrilla Public Speaking

Co-Author Craig Valentine

GUERRILLAS WHO ARE PUBLIC SPEAKERS always seek to make their audience members "TALL," which stands for Think, Act, Laugh, and Learn. Here are six strategies to make your listeners TALL.

1. Start with a Bang

The first 30 seconds of your presentation will either make or break you. That is all the time it takes for your audience to figure out whether or not they want to hear more. Do not waste this time on greetings such as, "I am so glad to be here" or "Thank you very much for giving me the opportunity to speak

The first 30 seconds of your presentation will either make or break you. That is all the time it takes for your audience to figure out whether or not they want to hear more.

Start with a bang by immediately going into a story or a major promise.

to you today." These are boring and predictable. Instead, start with a bang by immediately going into a story or a major promise.

For example, I (Craig) might start off with an irresistible story and then jump right into this promise: "In the next 45 minutes, you will learn how to keep your very next audience on the edge of their seats leaning on your every word. You will uncover the secret to generating more new customers with a one-hour speech than most entrepreneurs get in an entire month." Do you think that promise will grab audience attention more than the weather report most speakers open with?

2. Tell a Story and Sell a Process

The late, great Bill Gove (first president of the National Speakers Association) gave us the timeless advice to "tell a story and make a point." When people buy into your story and your point, you can sell them almost anything. Stories work because they evoke emotions, and people make decisions with emotions backed up by logic. As with any powerful tool, use this with the utmost integrity so that what you sell actually does what you promise.

Stories work because they evoke emotions, and people make decisions with emotions backed up by logic.

3. Cater to Your Visual, Auditory, and Kinesthetic Learners

This means you should use your words and gestures (and an occasional slide) to paint pictures for the visual learners. Speak clearly and with appropriate changes in your stress, rate, pitch, volume, and pausing for your auditory learners. Finally, include activities and other forms of interaction such as asking your audience members questions, physically moving out into your audience for their thoughts, and having them raise their hands occasionally to keep them kinesthetically involved. If you neglect to address any one of these learning styles, then you will find yourself speaking to only a fraction of your audience. This will severely damage your connection and your results.

4. Never End with the Question-and-Answer Period

This is a huge mistake most speakers make. Audiences remember best what they hear first and last, so make sure your strong message is the last one they hear. Do not leave it to chance. It is great to have a Q&A period— just as long as you follow it with a strong closing, which summarizes your main points and leaves your audience on an emotional high.

5. Do Not Give "Data Dumps"

It is much more effective to have only three major points that your audience can digest than to force-feed them 10 ideas that will overwhelm them, unless you want your audience to throw your speech out in the nearest trash can. In a paper, you can get away with 10 points. In speaking, you cannot. The old speaker proverb is correct: "When you squeeze your information in, you squeeze your audience out." Less is more.

> *It is much more effective to have only three major points that your audience can digest.*

6. Speak Conversationally with Your Audience

The days of oratorical Hyde Park-type lectures will not work for guerrilla speaking. Come out from behind the lectern, stand unguarded

> *Come out from behind the lectern, stand unguarded directly in front of your audience, and converse with them as if you are sharing stories and ideas with a friend.*

directly in front of your audience, and converse with them as if you are sharing stories and ideas with a friend. Remember that speaking is a dialogue, and your audience wants to be heard too. People buy into what they help create so find ways to make them part of your speech. The stronger you connect, the faster your business will grow! Visit http://www.craigvalentine.com for a free special report on "How to Keep Your Audiences on the Edge of their Seats and then Profit when they Get Up!"

One Final Thought

I completely agree with Jay Conrad Levinson that "Marketing is everything." Speaking is a piece of marketing, and, if you use these tools, speaking can become a huge slice of your profits. You will be thrilled at how fast new leads, customers, and profits come to you with each speech. The only thing you will be surprised at is how much other speakers are still leaving on the table.

chapter 40

FROM

Guerrilla Marketing for Writers

Co-Authors Michael Larsen, Rick Frishman, and David Hancock

WRITING A BOOK WILL HELP build your credibility in the marketplace and establish you as an expert in your industry and the authority on the subject you are writing about. Your book is the ultimate business card.

The goal is to sell books to big and midsize houses, and they want writers with a platform and a strong promotion plan.

How to Write a Book Proposal

Your plan will follow "The Author's Platform," a list in descending order of impressiveness of what you have done and are doing, online and off—including numbers when possible—to give you and the subject

Your book is the ultimate business card.

of your book continuing visibility with potential book buyers. A plan shows how you will leverage your platform to sell books. Editors will be wary of a plan unless it's a believable extension of what an author is already doing.

Your plan starts under the subhead "promotion" and begins like this: "To promote the book, the author will: . . . ." This is followed by a bulleted list in descending order of impressiveness of what you will do, online and off, to get books to the cash register and, when appropriate, how many books. Each item on the list begins with a verb.

The Parts of a Proposal

Most proposals range from 35 to 50 pages and have three parts: the overview, the outline, and a sample chapter.

The Overview

Your overview must prove that you have a marketable, practical idea and that you are the right person to write about the idea and promote the book.

- *Markets.* The types of readers and retailers, organizations, or institutions who will be interested in your book. This includes the size of each group and other information to show you know your audience and how to write the book for those readers. Other possible markets: schools, businesses, and subsidiary-rights markets such as film and foreign publishers.
- *The Author's Platform.* A list in descending order of importance of whatever will impress editors about your visibility to your readers. This may include the number of unique visitors or subscribers to your blog or website, your contacts on social networks, and online articles you've published. Your platform may include the number of articles you've had published in print media as well as the number of talks you give each year, the number of people you give them to, where you give them, and

INFORMATION TO SHARE

Provide as much ammunition about you and your book as you can muster. Examples include the following:

- The opening hook that will most excite editors about your subject
- The book hook
- The title and selling handle, up to 15 words of selling copy about the book
- The books or authors you're using as models for your book
- The suggested (or actual) length of your manuscript and when you will deliver it
- The book's benefits (optional)
- Special features (optional)
- Information about a self-published edition (optional)

your media exposure. Editors may not expect authors of quote books to have a platform; business authors must. For certain kinds of books, an author's platform is important for big and midsize houses.

- *About the Author.* Up to a page about yourself with information that isn't in your platform. Begin with the most important information.
- *Promotion.* A plan that begins: "To promote the book, the author will:" followed by a bulleted list in descending order of impressiveness of what you will do to promote your book, online and off, during its crucial two-week-to-three-month launch window and after. Start each part of the list with a verb and use numbers when possible. Publishers won't expect big plans from memoirists, and the smaller the house you'll be happy with, the less important your plan is.

- *Competing Books.* A list of the 10 or so strongest competitors for your book—not just best-sellers. In addition to basic info about each book (title, author, publisher, year of publication, page count, format, price, ISBN), include two phrases—each starting with a verb—about each competitor's strengths and weaknesses. List the competitors in order of importance.
- *Complementary Books.* A list of up to 10 books like yours that prove the market for your book.
- *Spin-Offs (Optional).* The titles of up to three related follow-up books.
- *Foreword (Optional).* A foreword by someone whose name will give the book credibility and salability in 50 states two years from now. Obtain commitments for cover quotes as well, if you can.
- *A Mission Statement (Optional).* One first-person paragraph about your passion or commitment to write and promote your book.

The Outline

Include a page called "Table of Contents" that lists the chapters and the back matter. Then offer one or two paragraphs in the present tense about every chapter, using outline verbs like describe, explain, and discuss. For an informational book, you can use a self-explanatory bulleted list of the information the chapter provides.

A Sample Chapter

Usually include one chapter that will excite editors by proving you will fulfill your book's promise to readers and make your book as enjoyable to read as it is illuminating. Include about 10 percent of the book, or about 25 pages. Memoirs should be finished, and agents and editors will request more chapters.

chapter 41

FROM

Guerrilla Business Secrets

Co-Author Steve Savage

R ATHER THAN REGALE YOU with tales of business secrets, a listing of the most important secrets seems most appropriate because you are a guerrilla and your time is valuable. These secrets have been gleaned from years of experience in the gift and fundraising businesses in companies large and small. They are battle-tested and proven successful. Simple as they may seem, some of these secrets have taken years to discover.

Quick Tips from Guerrilla Business Secrets

- Pick a hot product and target a market.
- Drive decision making downward.
- Make everyone feel important.

- Elevate your salespeople.
- Make your company easy to do business with.
- Make your business an adventure.
- Improve on someone else's idea.
- Be different.
- Use your wits not your money.
- Avoid lawsuits by friendly compromise.
- Help your local community.
- Hire consultants only when they can add value.
- Control your growth.
- Convert a disaster into a triumph.
- Don't be afraid to try again.
- Make it easy for the customer.
- Analyze the "typical" salesperson—and do the opposite.
- Use direct mail for dramatic growth.
- Hire salespeople from your target market.
- Diversify only when you have optimized your core product and territory.
- Don't let the lawyers be the only winners.
- Add new products cautiously.
- Rent as long as you can; build when you must.
- Place women in leadership positions.
- Work hard; work smart.
- Use telemarketing to boost sales.
- Sell before you peak.
- Test everything.
- The rollout must emulate the test.
- Increase the size of your tests before committing to a program.
- Hire professional managers when you reach your limits.
- Avoid bureaucracy; work out of your home.
- An easy sale is not enough; it's the easy delivery that counts.
- Sell your company; buy it back.
- Go international when you have fulfilled your domestic market.

41 / From Guerrilla Business Secrets

- Eliminate rules—every day.
- Don't ask for government permission.
- Hire a local manager you can trust.
- Open up other countries when you have a stable management in the first.
- Set up a distributorship when you can't justify a subsidiary.
- Work in countries where others fear to go.
- Jump in when the economic factors are right.
- Sell your company; buy it back; and sell it again.
- Abandon a country after you have tried everything without success.
- Learn the language.
- There is nothing more exciting than business.
- Love your business.
- Don't be afraid to fail.
- Just do it.
- Trust your gut.
- Get in the trenches.
- Take your job seriously, not yourself.
- Set the entrepreneur free.
- Greed and self-interest are the only honest ways to operate a business.
- International development takes time.

chapter 42

FROM

Guerrilla Marketing and the Human Ego

Co-Author Alexandru Israil

MARKETING IS PERFORMED BY HUMANS. Every human has an ego. Some of them are adequate, some too large. Ego influences human behavior more than we can imagine. The things people do in life are affected—even dictated— by their egos. People who make decisions in marketing are no exceptions—on the contrary, marketing and advertising are considerable ego magnets.

The end purpose of marketing—to bring a higher profit for the company—is sometimes sacrificed for ego reasons. The first step in bettering your marketing is to detect ego influence.

> *Marketing and advertising are considerable ego magnets.*

If you're in charge—the one directly interested in bettering the marketing process—your own ego should be examined first. Ask yourself how many times do you make decisions influenced by your own interpretation of the world, not questioning what your client might think, need, or desire. People tend to believe that the outside world is crafted under their personal paradigm of life. This is one of the biggest mistakes we can make, and its implications for entrepreneurs or people involved in marketing and sales are immense.

> *Ask yourself how many times do you make decisions influenced by your own interpretation of the world, not questioning what your client might think, need, or desire.*

Countless times decisions are made inside the box. Marketing departments vote for a main layout in a promotional campaign without asking their clients or the general public. Media vehicles are chosen according to personal feelings and preferences. Brand colors, backgrounds, photos, and casting characters are elected according to the decision maker's taste. No one is asking the clients what would persuade them best.

Tools to Escape Ego Influence

There are a couple of tools you might use while getting rid of the ego interference in your marketing. One is to talk to your people. Make them understand that the end result of their work is to bring profit for the company.

One other way to escape ego influence is to start thinking from your client's perspective. And the easiest way to do that is to ask. Ask your client. Do it through focus groups, questionnaires, surveys, cold calls, forums, social media tools. Be aware of what your client is thinking and you'll gain power. Come back with such data to the people

One other way to escape ego influence is to start thinking from your client's perspective. And the easiest way to do that is to ask. Ask your client.

involved in your marketing and show them how to think from your client's perspective. This way, their ego will shrink and the company's profits will expand.

chapter 43

FROM

Guerrilla Canvassing

Co-Author Ed Antle

C ANVASSING IS AN IDEA whose time has come—once again.

Numerous articles on the internet observe the growth—or reemergence—of door-to-door marketing. MSNBC recently published an Associated Press article with the headline, "A revival for door-to-door marketing." In it, the AP reported that "Now that the national do-not-call list makes it impossible to reach millions of potential customers, some marketing companies are returning to an old-fashioned alternative: door-to-door salespeople."

Some marketing companies are returning to an old-fashioned alternative: door-to-door salespeople.

Opportunity Knocks for Door-to-Door

Interestingly, another internet article says that door-to-door marketing has not only become more popular with businesses, but also with workers. "Things have changed," the article reports. "And now direct selling has become a very rewarding career . . . these days, door-to-door marketing has become a hot favorite job profile," especially with young workers.

Opinions about canvassing are changing. "While previously this medium has been portrayed as simple mass distribution, it is actually one of the most precisely targetable media there is. And with Direct Mail expenditure increasing by 118 percent in the last year . . . it is a medium that is impossible to ignore."

Door-to-door marketing, then, has grown in importance because it

- is one of the only ways left to reach every household in a company's market;
- is capable of delivering a highly targeted advertising message;
- is less expensive than other media; and
- has become more popular with those seeking employment.

Canvassing is also benefiting from the fact that other forms of advertising are not as effective as in the past.

Canvassing is also benefiting from the fact that other forms of advertising are not as effective as in the past. Direct mail is expensive, and the cost of postage is rising. Newspaper and radio advertising aren't what they used to be, and federal legislation killed cold call telemarketing several years ago.

WWW to the Rescue!

Of course, one of the reasons for the decline of the effectiveness of other advertising is that consumers are getting their news from the internet, which continues to grow as an effective advertising vehicle. Surprisingly, the internet has not kicked canvassing to the curb.

"It was first thought that the internet would do away with door-to-door salesmen forever," says an article on Edubook.com. "However, such concerns as National No-Call Lists and the overload of unsolicited email have brought back a situation where the old-fashioned knocking on doors to connect directly with people has once more become an important way for businesses to connect with potential customers."

The ability of canvassing to "connect directly with people" may be at the heart of the canvassing comeback. In marketing, the power of face to face can hardly be overstated.

The ability of canvassing to "connect directly with people" may be at the heart of the canvassing comeback. In marketing, the power of face to face can hardly be overstated. Most marketers—at least those who have done face to face and telephone sales—know this principle well.

Comparing canvassing to telemarketing, knocking on doors has always been more effective than calling in terms of converting contacts into sales. In other words, for every 100 potential customers a canvasser talks to, he produces more leads/sales than a telemarketer who talks to the same amount of consumers.

In the past, telemarketers compensated with the use of an automated dialer. A telemarketer on a predictive dialer could talk to more people—lots more. Now that legislation has limited the use of dialers, canvassers are running circles around telemarketers.

And telemarketing legislation has made some consumers completely inaccessible by phone. In a post-federal Do Not Call Law world, canvassing may be the only means a business can use to reach every household in a company's market.

This brings us back to the contrast between the internet and canvassing. The fact that the internet has not kept canvassers at home raises an interesting question: Why?

It's fairly easy to come up with at least one answer: While the internet can be very effective, it can also be one of the most

SOME FACTORS CONTRIBUTING TO INCREASE IN CANVASSING

- The death of the cold call
- The rising cost of postage and mail services, combined with their decreasing effectiveness
- The accelerating decline in newspaper circulation
- The decline in radio reach
- Decreasing attendance at trade shows and events
- Economic pressures on companies to get more impact from significantly reduced sales and marketing expenditures
- Economic pressures on consumers that make them less likely to contact companies to inquire about goods and services
- Rising unemployment pressuring workers to consider door-to-door sales positions
- The power of personalized, face-to-face marketing
- The ability of canvassing to use advertising dollars in a more targeted way
- The ability of door-to-door marketing to reach every household in a company's target market

impersonal types of advertising. Some consumers don't exactly get a warm, fuzzy feeling when they see email from an unknown sender. It can seem impersonal. Canvassing, it could be argued, is the most personal. The whole idea of canvassing is that someone from the company knocks on the door of potential customers to have personal conversations with them about their needs and how the company can meet those needs.

The revival of door-to-door marketing is not due to any one economic or advertising trend, but rather is the culmination of many factors working together.

---

43 / From Guerrilla Canvassing

Guerrillas Don't Go With the Flow

It is important to note that guerrilla marketers don't just go with the flow. In fact, they may be more likely to swim against the current. It may sound crazy, but if everyone else has stopped cold calling, maybe it's time to give it a try. If fewer companies are advertising on radio and in the newspaper, perhaps it's a good time to go bargain-hunting. Maybe there are cheaper, smarter ways to do direct mail.

Guerrilla marketers are always optimists—and opportunists. They see trends as opportunities to do something unusual, creative, against-the-grain. And they beat their competition with ingenuity.

Current economic trends have re-created the need for canvassing and other nontraditional advertising methods. Never before have guerrilla marketing and guerrilla canvassing been such a logical solution to the advertising needs of small businesses.

Today, opportunity knocks for door-to-door marketers.

To summarize, there are unique pressures on the advertising efforts of small businesses. Smart marketers will make the most of the situation by realizing that never was there a better time for guerrilla marketing techniques.

There are consumers out there who have money and are willing to spend it, but who are not being drawn into the market effectively by other means. The cautious cash simply needs to be coaxed out of the woods. Canvassing is just the kind of ultra-personal, face-to-face, targeted, and tailor-made approach that works best in this situation. But it is also a good time to take a nontraditional approach to traditional advertising such as newspaper and radio bargain-hunting.

Ready to get started?

Getting Out of the Car

A sales consultant once asked me, "What is the most difficult thing about canvassing?"

"Getting out of the car," I (Ed) answered.

Jay's best-seller, *Guerrilla Marketing*, has a very good chapter on canvassing. Canvassing "existed before any other marketing methods," Jay wrote. "In fact, the very first sale in history probably occurred when one caveman asked another, 'Want to trade me an animal skin for this fruit I picked?'"

He also noted that canvassing can be the most inexpensive marketing method of all. "In fact it can be free, except for the time you devote to it."

And Jay pointed out that canvassing is interactive. "There's little question that it was the first of all interactive media, if not the first of all media."

He outlined a three-step approach:

1. *Contact.* This is where you first meet your prospect and make the all-important first impression. Smile. Use the person's name. Try to establish a relationship.

2. *The presentation.* This varies widely in length depending on the product and the goal of the canvassing visit. But it always involves explaining the features and benefits of your product.

3. *The close.* "The magical moment when you complete the sale. . . . It doesn't really matter how good you are at the contact and the presentation. You've got to be a good closer to make canvassing work."

It can hardly be overstated: You must be a good closer to make canvassing work.

Canvassing isn't complicated. People skills and a willingness to work hard are all that is necessary. Add a working knowledge of a few door-to-door basics and you're good to go. Getting out of the car is literally the most difficult part.

But why is it hard to get out of the car? For most people, canvassing is intimidating because of the fear of the unknown. Who is on the other side of that door? Will the person who comes to the door be friendly or rude? Two-legged—or four-legged and baring teeth?

Any Excuse Will Do

Watch new canvassers in action. When they drive to a neighborhood, they stop for gas. Then they stop for food. Then they have to stop at Office Max to make copies of their flier. Then they have to drive around to pick out the perfect neighborhood. Before you know it, half their time is gone.

When I was canvassing for my own business, I would come up with every excuse in the book to delay going out in the field to canvass. And then I came up with every excuse in the world to come back early. The very thing that I needed to do—the very thing that had generated all of my sales—that was the thing I wanted most to avoid.

Canvassing is a lot like life. We often avoid doing what we are supposed to do. We don't always do what's in our best interests. So, if you are going out canvassing today, drive straight to the neighborhood and get out of the car. Once you get started, it is not nearly as bad as you expected.

Once you knock on a few doors and get a sale or a few leads in your pocket, you're on a roll. At that point it feels good to know you can do it. It feels good to be doing the right thing. It feels good to be productive.

On the way to the neighborhood, canvassing seems like the dumbest idea in the world. Once you've got your first lead, it's the greatest thing since God created doorbells. And on the way home, you feel like a hero coming back with the spoils of war.

Every day it is the same psychological battle. Every day the battle gets a little easier.

People worry about what to say at the door. The script is important; however, the conversation comes much more naturally than you think. And what you say isn't nearly as important as your enthusiasm, sincerity, and persistence. The hardest thing is getting out of the car. Remember that the first key to canvassing is to maximize the number of doors you hit—and therefore the number of leads/sales you generate.

If you have a large team of canvassers, remember that they will only manage their time wisely if you make them. You must—you absolutely must—create a culture that maximizes the door-knocking time of your team if you are going to be successful. Time away from canvassing—including transportation to and from the neighborhood, breaks, meetings, and pit stops—is waste and must be rigorously minimized. This point can hardly be exaggerated. Most canvass teams waste an obscene amount of time and money and don't even know it. Most solo canvassers do the same thing and don't want to admit it.

Canvass Managers

For these and other reasons, canvass managers should canvass. Most canvass managers don't canvass—to their own detriment. At least when they're starting out, canvass managers need to go to the field. They need to prove to themselves, their bosses, and their employees that they can do it. They need to be productive.

They also need to know what it feels like to knock on a door and not know what's coming at them from the other side. They need to know what it's like to canvass in the dark or in the cold. They need to know what it's like to be 75 percent of the way through the shift and be empty-handed and have to twist some arms to get a lead or sale. They need to experience this job.

However, it is important to realize that management and canvassing are two different jobs with two different skill sets. Sometimes the best manager is not the best canvasser. Suffice it to say that canvass managers may not canvass every day or produce more sales than anyone, but they must be able to grab the clipboard from one of their employees and show 'em how it's done. And job one for the canvass manager is to keep the team knocking on doors. If the team isn't knocking on doors, it's the manager's fault. There are many things we can't control. However, we can keep the canvassers canvassing!

It's a Numbers Game

The biggest reason to keep the canvass team focused on door-knocking is that canvassing is a numbers game. The more houses you hit, the more leads and sales you have. When asked to evaluate a canvass team, the first place I start is by evaluating how well they manage the clock. To get more leads, all I have to do is manage the clock more effectively.

I don't have to get different canvassers. I don't have to change the script. I don't have to change the company's reputation, change the economy, or change managers. If I can get the canvassers to knock on more doors every day, the leads/sales will increase. It is a mathematical fact.

Every team gets x number of leads/sales per house they hit. More houses mean more sales. It is the easiest thing to control. So start there.

A Few Rules Are in Order

It is important to remember that the delay tactics listed above often become bad habits, which then become part of the culture.

That is why it is important to put guidelines in place at the beginning of your canvassing program.

Time-saving rules set up at the beginning can pay huge dividends in the long run.

Some suggested rules:

- All supplies, maps, door hangers, pitch books, drinks, pens, etc. must be prepared ahead of time and ready when the canvassers walk in the door.
- There should be a minimal amount of meetings, usually no more often than once a week (every other week is better) and for a predetermined period of time. Also, it saves time to have

WHAT KEEPS CANVASSERS FROM CANVASSING

- Meetings
- Waiting for late-arriving canvassers
- Leaving the office late
- Leaving the field early
- Breaks
- Stopping for gas or supplies
- Picking out a neighborhood
- Picking out a street within a neighborhood
- Waiting for the manager to pick them up and move them when their area is complete
- Walking too slowly between doors
- Leaving the field to go to the bathroom
- Smoke breaks
- Cell phone calls during the shift
- Traffic on the way to the neighborhood
- Traffic tickets
- Waiting for the manager to get maps
- Waiting for the manager to get door hangers, fliers, etc.

If you want a longer list, just ask the canvassers. They can always come up with more! All of these things and more must be managed if you are going to maximize your canvassing operation's effectiveness. If this sounds petty, just remember time is money.

one long meeting every two weeks rather than lots of shorter meetings.
- Vehicles must be gassed up, cleaned, and maintained before the shift begins.

- There must be some type of consequence for showing up late to work (e. g. a late fine). And the team never waits for a late canvasser. To keep 15 people on the clock waiting for one late-comer is crazy! However, canvassers shouldn't be able to run a little late just to get a day off with no penalties. If the penalty is a reduction in pay, the employee must sign off on the penalty as part of their pay plan—consult your attorney!
- The canvass team must leave the office on time.
- Leaving the field early is a cardinal sin punishable by death or life imprisonment.
- The neighborhoods must be chosen before the shift starts. There must be enough area for an entire shift. Canvassers should be moved from one neighborhood or street to another as seldom as possible. Instead, give them enough streets for the whole shift. Upon arrival in the neighborhood, park the car or van and begin knocking immediately.
- Wasting time on the way to the field is unacceptable.
- During a short shift of four hours or less, breaks are usually unnecessary. Good canvass managers tell their workers to get their supplies, go to the bathroom, and get a drink before the shift starts. Providing water for canvassers can save time.
- Cell phone calls are allowed only on the way to and from the neighborhood—not while going door to door.

So rule number one for all canvassers is: Get out of the car. Job one for all canvass managers is: Keep the team in the field generating revenue. And priority one for all companies who want to canvass is: Focus on door-knocking. If you miss this one, nothing else matters.

chapter 44

FROM

Guerrilla Selling

Co-Authors Orvel Ray Wilson with William K. Gallagher Sr.

THE AD IN THE COMIC BOOK said, "Win A Bicycle." Well, I didn't know any better; I thought it was a sweepstakes. I tore out the coupon, sent it in. Got back this box of garden seeds, and these instructions: I was supposed to sell them door-to-door, for 25 cents a pack, even though you could buy them at Buddy & Lloyds for a dime. And they had this whole script, and all these rules: Never walk on the grass, always walk on the sidewalk, always step back from the door after you ring the bell. And always say "Yes, Ma'am," "No, Ma'am," "Thank you, Ma'am."

Well, I didn't know any better. I was 9 years old. I did everything exactly like they said. On a clear, cold, spring Saturday I dressed up in my Sunday best, went out, and rang every doorbell in our subdivision.

Then I crossed that street that my mother told me not to cross, and I rang every doorbell in that subdivision, and by about 2 in the afternoon, it was obvious that I had no future in sales.

You know how easy it is to give up when you're tired and hungry and exhausted. So I headed home taking the shortcut up the alley, and there was this lady out in her backyard, and she had her hair tied up in a dishtowel and she was wielding a shovel, just tearing up the dirt to beat the band.

So I yelled at her, "HEY LADY, YOU DON'T NEED NO SEED FOR THAT GARDEN DO YA?"

Well, she stopped her work, leaned on the shovel, and asked, "Whatcha GOT?"

"I've got EVERYTHING. Whatcha WANT?"

And of course, her next question was, "HOW MUCH?"

"TWENTY-FIVE CENTS."

"Twenty-five CENTS? I can buy seeds at Buddy & Lloyds for a DIME. WHY SHOULD I PAY TWENTY-FIVE CENTS?"

That's when I started to cry.

"Because I'm trying to win a BICYCLE, THAT'S why."

She bought nine dollars worth!

And what did I learn from that one transaction?

I learned that people who buy seeds buy seeds, and people who don't buy seeds don't buy seeds, and that's just the way the world works.

What I learned was: You don't go to the front door and ring the bell. You don't have time for that. You go up and down the alley and look in the backyard for that pile of dirt where they had last year's garden, and you go to the back door, and if they don't answer, you go back again, until you get a chance to tell your story.

I also learned that making a small change can make a big difference. One lady asked "How many for a dollar?"

Well, I thought that was a dumb question. I was only in the second grade, but I could do that math. "They're 25 cents each, or FOUR for a dollar."

"OK," she said, "I'll take a dollar's worth."

At the next house I changed the way I quoted the price, "They're 25 cents each or four-for-a-dollar," and instantly, miraculously, doubled my sales.

My prize bicycle was a red Huffy, with a banana seat and high-rise handlebars with streamers. I put so many playing cards in the spokes it sounded like a Harley going down the road.

And that, for me, was the beginning of what has been a lifelong love affair with sales and marketing. By the way, if crying works for you, fine.

In 1989, Jay Conrad Levinson invited me to co-write a sequel to his book *Guerrilla Marketing*, and that book became a classic. Together with the other books in the guerrilla series, it's helped millions of salespeople, small-business owners, and entrepreneurs just like you build success and wealth. In this *Remix*, we share some of the latest weapons and tactics that we've collected in 20 years of traveling the world, speaking and training, and coaching. The examples and stories are about people just like you who have fought the good fight and prevailed, despite the odds.

How to NaB &
CaPTuRe New Customers

The consonants in the acronym help us remember the six steps:

1. Need
2. Budget
3. Commitment
4. Presentation
5. Transaction
6. Reward

People ALWAYS follow these six steps WHENEVER they make a major purchase.

GUERRILLA PROSPECTING

Find people who already want, need, and have to buy your offering. Do they

- Have a need?
- Have a budget?
- Have the authority to make a commitment?
- Have a motivation to act now?

Five Steps in Finding Prospects

1. Identify your ideal prospects, those most likely to buy from you. Your headpin customer. Your best prospects are your competitors' biggest customers. Match your demographics.
2. Get out in the field.
3. Use an unusual, creative, or unexpected approach.
   - Message in a bottle
   - Carrier pigeon
4. Ask a lot of questions—the 38 magic selling questions.
5. Listen actively to the answers.
   - Maintain eye contact
   - Use verbal attends
   - Use nonverbal attends
   - Take visible notes
   - Ask for clarification
   - Paraphrase
   - Ask: "Who? What? When? Where? How?"
   - Don't ask "Why?"

The Iceberg Principle

In the psychology of customers' needs, it's the unspoken motivations that drive the decision-making process.

FIVE THINGS EVERY CUSTOMER NEEDS

1. The need to feel welcome
2. The need to feel comfortable
3. The need to feel important
4. The need to feel understood
5. The need to feel appreciated

Only 10 percent of an iceberg floats above the waterline. It's the part that you don't see that gets you into trouble.

What problems are your customers facing? What resources are available to solve that problem? What other solutions are being considered? Uncover at least one concern.

The 38 Magic Selling Questions

1. What is your main objective?
2. How do you plan to achieve that goal?
3. What is the biggest problem you currently face?
4. What other problems do you experience?
5. What are you doing currently to deal with this?
6. What is your strategy for the future?
7. What other ideas do you have?
8. What role do others play in creating this situation?
9. Who else is affected?
10. What are you using now?
11. What do you like most about it?
12. What do you like least about it?
13. If you could have things any way you wanted, what would you change?

14. What effect would this have on the present situation?
15. What would motivate you to change?
16. Do you have a preference?
17. What has been your experience?
18. How do you know?
19. Is there anything else you'd like to see?
20. How much would it be worth to you to solve this problem?
21. What would it cost, ultimately, if things remained as they are?
22. Are you working within a budget?
23. How do you plan to finance it?
24. What alternatives have you considered?
25. What benefit would you personally realize as a result?
26. How would others benefit?
27. How can I help?
28. Is there anything I've overlooked?
29. Are there any questions you'd like to ask?
30. What do you see as the next step?
31. Who else, besides yourself, will be involved in making the decision?
32. On a scale of 1 to 10, how confident do you feel about doing business with us?
33. What would it take to get that up to a 10?
34. Are you working against a particular deadline?
35. How soon would you like to start?
36. When would you like to take delivery?
37. When should we get together to discuss this again?
38. Is there anything else you'd like for me to take care of?

Eight Types of Closes

1. The Rx Close

   "Based on what you've told me, you're going to need . . ."

SEVEN CRITICAL PLAYERS GUERRILLAS ENCOUNTER WHEN PENETRATING A PROSPECT'S ORGANIZATION

1. *Gatekeeper.* Not authorized to say "yes" and trained to say "no."
2. *Influencer.* Evaluating your proposal from a technical or financial point of view.
3. *Purchaser.* Releases the funds.
4. *Decider.* Can say "no" even if everyone else says "yes."
5. *Users.* Have to live with this decision over time.
6. *Spy.* Someone who, for reasons of their own, wants to see you succeed.
7. *Saboteur.* Someone who, for reasons of their own, wants to see you fail.

2. The Action Close
   "If you can give me a P.O. number, I can start this today."
3. The Minor Choice Close
   "Did you prefer for them to start Monday, or is Tuesday better?"
4. The Question Close
   "What's today's date?"
5. The Add-on Close
   "Now you'll also need . . . I'd also recommend . . . "
6. The Bigger Order Close
   "There is a discount over $_____. . ."
7. The Assumptive Close
   "I'll stop by next Tuesday to see how they're progressing."
8. The Today Close
   "If you act now I can also include . . ."

Criteria Words

This is a very powerful concept. Every prospect has a set of criteria that the product or service in question must meet. Furthermore, they all have a specific vocabulary for describing those criteria. When you can isolate what those criteria are, and then use the SAME vocabulary to describe your solution, it makes it easier for prospects to understand, accept, and buy your proposal.

You might have 100 good reasons why they should buy from you; ultimately, their decision will hinge on the two or three reasons they feel are the most important.

Needs vs. Wants

1. *Universal criteria*: Pride, profit, need, love, fear
2. *Objective criteria*: Size, shape, measurable outcome
   - "What do you need in a _____ ?"
   - "What is your main objective?"
   - "Can you tell me more about that?"
   - "Are you working against a deadline?"
3. *Subjective criteria*: No mindreading!
   - "What do you want in a _____?"
   - "What problems have you had with that?"
   - "Why would you want to change?"
   - "What has been your experience?"
   - "Is there anything else you can tell me?"

The Most Powerful Reward You Can Give a Customer: Attention!

Follow-Up
- 48 Hours
  - Did it perform as promised?
  - Did it perform as expected?
- 7 Days, unanticipated problems arise
- 30 Days, ask for referrals
- 90 Days, offer supplies, accessories

AN ATTITUDE OF GRATITUDE, SENDING THANK-YOU NOTES

- Do it today
- It should be handwritten
- Write in the active voice
- Tell them what the next step will be
- Keep it short
- And of course, be sincere

- 6 Months, offer upgrades
- Annually thereafter, up-sell, cross-sell, and resell the company, the product, and yourself.

How to Get Customers to Pay More

Customers will pay more. You've done it. You buy a can of Coke out of a vending machine for 75 cents. If you order a Coke in a restaurant, it comes in a glass with ice and a straw, and it's $3.50. I wonder, are the glass and the ice and the straw really worth $2.75?

And do we whine and complain that it's too expensive? Of course not. Customers will pay more for all sorts of things.

There's a whole list here; check off the ones that you could use to add value for your customers.

- They'll pay more for higher *quality*. That goes without saying. The Maytag repairman isn't just lonely. He's old and lonely. Guerrillas translate higher quality to higher value. This justifies your higher price. "When you care enough to send the very best!"
- They'll pay more for superior *service*. Ask Nordstrom's.
- They'll pay more for *authenticity*, the real deal, the genuine article.

At the Musée du Louvre in Paris, you can gaze upon what is perhaps the most famous painting in the world, Leonardo Da Vinci's portrait of Lisa Gherardini del Giocondo, more commonly known as the Mona Lisa. For all the hype, it can be quite a disappointment. It hangs alone in a large hall in dim light. And it's small; only 21 by 39 inches. She's more than 500 years old and has not aged gracefully. The colors are cracked and smoky and faded. And she's cloistered behind thick plates of bullet-proof Lexan. However, scientists have analyzed the pigments and digitally recreated this masterpiece, just as it would have looked standing wet on Da Vinci's easel about 1506. It is aesthetically superior to the original in every way. In the gift shop, you can buy the poster-sized replica for only 20 Euros, while the original is still considered priceless.

- They will pay more for *company stability*: a company that's been in business since the landing at Plymouth Rock. Do you tell the story about how your Grandfather came from the Olde Country and started the business with his brother and cousin? Savvy customers will select a technically and financially sound vendor over one that's obsolete or on the brink of failure.

- They will pay more for *reliability*. Are you showing your customer that you're reliable? Does somebody answer the phone on a second ring? Do you show up for appointments exactly on time? Everything you do (or don't do) sends a message about your reliability.

- They'll pay more for *social or ecological values*. Do you recycle? Do you use recycled materials? Are you running alternative fuels in your vehicles? People routinely pay hundreds, even thousands of dollars for a knick-knack at a silent auction raising money for a scout troop, church group, or political cause. Many people select vendors who are socially, morally, and ethically responsible. Showing good intentions backed by good actions creates value for these customers.

- They'll pay more to deal with *knowledgeable salespeople.*
  We have this argument with clients all the time. "Oh, we can't afford training."
  "I'm sorry? What do you mean, you can't afford training?"
  "Well, what if we train 'em and they leave?"
  "What if you don't train them and they stay?"
  Buyers worry when a company rep doesn't know the product. It gets worse if your customer thinks you may have bad information. Neutralize this tough situation by being an expert on your products.

- They will pay more for your *reputation.* When your customer is uncertain of the market, they tend to select the vendor with the best reputation.

- They will pay more for *partnership.* Savvy buyers know that the best vendor becomes a partner in their mutual success. How can you create a partnership with your customer to create a larger opportunity?

- They will pay more for *consistency.* Consistent quality, delivery, service, and constant innovation create exceptional value. When your customer knows and trusts what to expect from you, it removes uncertainty, and you gain a fair advantage.

- They'll pay more for *customization.* Spend the second week of August at Sturgis and consider the land-office prices people paid for all those custom motorcycles.

- They will pay more for *authority.* Are you a respected expert in your market? Have you written a book or published articles?

- They will pay more for *popularity.* Remember the Beanie Baby craze? Many people are influenced by what's fashionable. They figure, "If it's so popular, I can't go wrong." They want to be part of the in crowd, so they choose the standard.

- They'll pay more for *exclusivity*; they just can't get it anywhere else. Guerrillas seek exclusivity as an advantage. What is the one thing that only you can do?

- They will pay more for *scarcity*.

  The DeBeers Company has huge vaults in South Africa filled wall-to-wall and piled to the ceiling with diamonds. They control the market because if the real supply ever actually came into the market, you'd buy a five-carat wedding ring for about $10.

  Anything that is considered scarce is considered more valuable, even when it's not more functional. A prime example is the "Beanie Baby" craze. Small stuffed animals that sold for $7 retail would resell for hundreds, even thousands of dollars after they were "retired" and no longer available. The waiting list for a Harley-Davidson motorcycle is now more than a year, and their used bikes sell for more today than they did when they were new.

- They'll pay more for *disposal*. Who's going to dispose of your old computer or your old mattress, your old tires?

- They will pay more for *miniaturization*. That's why computers have gotten smaller and smaller.

- They'll pay more for *ruggedization*. Timex "takes a licking and keeps on ticking." Your customer will pay more if what you offer has value at the end of its lifespan. This could be the scrap value, or the secondary market demand, or that you'll take it back with a guaranteed trade-in price when they upgrade.

- They'll pay more for *availability*. They want it yesterday.

- They'll pay more for *delivery*. This is why you pay $15 for FedEx instead of 44 cents for first-class mail. Remember, when you buy things for yourself, you want the best possible quality for the lowest possible prices, and you want it delivered yesterday. Isn't your customer the same? When you shorten delivery times you make it tough for your competitor.

- They will pay more for *expediting*. They want it out the door. You know, "Oh, we only have one left in inventory and it's over in our Fort Worth store. You want me to have them pull it off the shelf and have it waiting for you at the counter, or should I have one of my guys hop in a truck and meet you halfway?"

- They will pay more for *flexibility*. Easy to do business with is a guerrilla credo. Your customer will pay more to eliminate and avoid headaches.

- They will pay more for *financing*. Even *Time* magazine offers "three easy payments of $19.95." So, when you have a good customer who's shopping for terms, you can say, "Well, we can give you 2 percent net 30, or we'll give you 90 days net."

- They'll pay more for advanced *technology*. Can you say iPad?

- And they'll pay more for a product that *arrives in perfect condition*. If your competitor's product has ever arrived dented, dirty, or damaged, you've gained an advantage. Ask your customer if the competitor has ever short-shipped or back-ordered the product. When you can demonstrate that your products are guaranteed to arrive in perfect condition, you increase your value.

- They'll also pay more for problems to be *fixed quickly*. It's not product failure that causes problems. It's repair delays that cost money. A survey found that when a customer perceives that an organization responds instantly to a request, 95 percent of the time the customer will again do business with that organization. Rapid reaction reaps rich rewards.

- They'll pay more to do business with companies that are *environmentally friendly*. Seventy-eight percent of consumers said they would pay $2,000 more for a car that gets 35 miles per gallon. That makes pure economic sense only if gasoline is in the range of $4 a gallon over the life of the car. Meanwhile the Toyota Prius was voted Number One Most Ecologically Sensitive Product in the last decade. As companies become more sensitive to environmental issues, they tend to select vendors that conserve natural resources. Your customer may give you points for your environmentally responsible behavior.

- They'll pay more to *benefit a third party*. That's why you pay four bucks a box for Girl Scout cookies. They're good, but they're not that good. I was performing with my big band at a benefit for a local charter school and watched one of the parents bid $5,000 for an ordinary bottle of wine. Will some third party benefit from your transaction? Perhaps they're interested in you getting the business because their family owns stock in your company. Perhaps their purchase will trigger a donation to a favorite charity.

- They will pay more for *local sourcing*. Compare supermarket prices with those at your local farmer's market. Eighty-two percent of people surveyed have consciously supported local or neighborhood businesses. Trendy restaurants are going locavore, and charging more. There's a locally owned, two-pump gas station and two-car garage in our little mountain town in Coal Creek, Colorado: Carl's Corner. I've been buying gas from Carl for 20 years. And Denise is always giving me a hard time, "Why buy gas at Carl's when we can get it five cents cheaper at the Conoco in Boulder?" "Because we need more than just gas," I remind her. "We need Carl. You need him when you run out of propane for the grill, or you need to have a flat fixed or you have a dead battery or you need a tow truck. And if we don't keep his shop open, then we won't have a mechanic in the canyon at all."

- They will pay more for products *Made in the USA*. So, ask them, "Does it matter to you that it's made in the USA?" Try parking your Prius in a Pontiac plant.

- They'll pay more for *brand names*: Disney, Gucci, Levi Strauss. "Nobody ever gets fired for buying IBM."

- They'll pay more for *referrals*. They will pay extra to do business with a company they've been referred to by a trusted advisor because they already have confidence in you.

- They'll pay more for *reduced liability*.

- And they'll pay more to do business with a vendor who is more *fun*.

Now check off the rationales that YOU can use to justify your higher price. Many of these are things that you're ALREADY doing, but not taking credit for. Make certain that you explain ALL the aspects of your product or service that makes you more valuable to your customer. Focus on your uniqueness. It's better to be different than to be better.

chapter 45

FROM

Guerrilla Negotiating

Co-Authors Orvel Ray Wilson and Mark S. A. Smith

WELL-VERSED PRICE BUYERS use dirty tricks to get you to lower your prices. Keep your prices intact with these guerrilla tactics.

How to Avoid Price-Buyer Dirty Tricks

The Limbo

The buyer insists, "I won't pay any more than . . ." This is a game to see how low you can go. Guerrillas counter by asking, "Can you explain to me how you arrived at that figure? What did you take into account?" Ask them to itemize their calculation.

Well-versed price buyers use dirty tricks to get you to lower your prices.

"They're the Same (or Better) . . ."

The buyer insists, "They're the same (or better) . . ." This is easy for them to say and difficult for you to corroborate. Counter by asking for specifics. Gain an advantage by asking, "In what way are they better for your application? What do you like most about them? What do you like least about them?" When you understand what your customer likes and doesn't like, you can build a case for your desired outcome.

The First-Timer

The buyer insists that you should "give me a good deal on the first one." While this is tempting, it trains buyers to demand discounts. They'll want the same break next time, or more. Guerrillas resist this ploy, "While I could do that, I don't want to increase my delivery or cut my service on your first order, because when I cut price, I also have to cut somewhere else."

Moving Up the Launch

"Now we need it tomorrow . . ." This is a typical tactic. Your customer asks for a favorable price based on future delivery, then demands immediate delivery. Guerrillas counter this tactic with a rush charge. "I can do that, yet I'm committed to my other customers, and I will have to arrange for overtime shifts to meet their needs as well as yours. That necessitates that you pay a rush charge."

Stopping the Countdown

Some buyers will do the opposite, appearing to be a hot prospect, then stalling while they deal with some internal glitch. "Now that we know you can ship today, we don't really need it until next month." Now they want you to reduce your price. Guerrillas counter this tactic with the price increase. "I can do that, but our price increase goes into effect next month."

Excuse Me

"I'm sorry. I have to step out for a moment." A dirty trick from the old timers: They'll leave a competitive quote out on their desk, and then arrange to be called out of their office so that you can "discover" it. They want you to proffer a discount, whether they're seriously considering the competition or not.

Guerrillas will refuse the bait. If your customer is going to use the competitor's prices, let them bring them to the table where you can do battle.

One grizzled buyer would place a soda can over the numbers of a competitive quote and then excuse himself for a moment. The curious sales rep would lift the can, and BBs would flood out of the hole in the bottom of the can.

False Quote

With fax machines, scanners, and computers, it's easy for unscrupulous customers to falsify a competitive quote.

If you suspect that you're seeing a false quote, respond with, "That's interesting. I imagine that they must have a very good reason for selling at that price. But if prices were all the same, who would you choose?" If the buyer indicates that you'd be the choice, completely ignore the competitive document.

If they insist on using the competitive quote, say, "I think there must be a typo here. May I call them and double-check these numbers?"

Quota Time

"How's your quota looking this month?" They're looking to squeeze you! If you flinch and admit that your numbers are down, they've got you.

Guerrillas respond with, "Good question. How are your profit figures this month?" If they press you, "I'm sorry, that's not relevant to our discussion."

"Only Price Is Important . . ."

"I don't care about anything but price. Give me your best price or get out." You might be tempted. Instead, call their bluff.

"OK, here's the deal. Find the best price you can. I'll beat it by 10 percent, guaranteed! But I get to choose when I deliver."

"I don't think so," they'll retort.

"Alright, I'll beat the best price you can find. But I get to select the quality that we ship."

"Uh . . . no!"

"Hmm. So I guess price isn't more important than on-time delivery or quality after all?" You've made your point.

When You Should Discount

There may be legitimate reasons to offer a discount. Perhaps you want to reward a loyal customer or close a long-term contract. You may enjoy marginal increases in productivity at higher production levels and choose to pass that economy of scale on to your customer. Or you may have excess capacity and fixed costs and offering a discount brings in business that increases your overall profits.

You may wish to place a limit on the quantity you'll offer based on that discount or limit the time frame of its availability. A limited-time offer creates a deadline, motivating your customer to commit sooner rather than later.

In all businesses, a fraction of the price is reserved for marketing, research, development, and sales expenses. If your transaction doesn't require these costs, you may wish to offer that savings as a discount.

Guerrillas know exactly what they're giving away when they discount and adamantly refuse to give away profit.

"Mine's Better and It's Cheaper!"

A common position used to preempt price issues is, "We have a better product and it's cheaper, too." That argument isn't logically sound. Universal experience tells us that an apparently similar product at a higher price is perceived as being better. Higher quality = longer life = superior service.

When your customer observes, "You're expensive," the guerrilla will say, "Thank you!" And then proceed to help them understand the greater value.

When you do have a superior product for a lower price, you must offer a rationale for the price being lower. "Because of our unique technology, we can offer you a better solution, and because of the way we do it, we've lowered our costs, and we pass that savings on to you."

Tactics to Fight Price Cutters

Guerrillas aggressively protect their price. Guerrillas gain an advantage by resisting pressure to grant discounts. When they do lower their price, they do so only in exchange for a reciprocal concession.

These are guerrilla negotiating tactics to combat price concessions.

No Discounts

One tactic is to offer your price and stick to your guns. "This is the same price I charge everyone else. It wouldn't be fair if I charge you one price, and someone else pays a lower price. I can't do that to my other, loyal customers."

History

A guerrilla in Denver defends her advertising rates: "We've always charged more." There's no argument, and she gets to discuss the reasons why her customers think she's worth more.

The Swiss Army Knife Close

A guerrilla who has worked both sides of the negotiating table uses a prop to defend his prices. When he's done, he'll pull out his Swiss army knife, open it, and hand it to his customer. "Go ahead, cut my heart out. That's all I've got left to offer." It closes the deal.

Call Their Bluff

If your customers insist on you lowering the price, call their bluff. Stand and ask, "Does that mean we're done?"

While many are afraid to use this pointed question, the reply always reveals your customer's stance. If they say, "Yep, we're done," you know that price is the issue. If they say no, hang tough and keep your profits.

Act Busy

A commonly held belief is that you've got to be hungry to get the deal. Guerrillas know otherwise. Busy people are obviously doing something right: They and their products are in demand. If you aren't busy, act busy.

"We're Running Close to Capacity . . ."

Guerrillas use scarcity as a pricing weapon. If you have limited capacity to deliver, say so. It may be more profitable for you to hold your line and find another, more accommodating customer.

All Things Aren't Equal

Recapitulate how you'll satisfy their needs before you state your price. Build value by illustrating how your offering is superior to other opportunities. This tactic can backfire if you don't ensure that your proposition is of value to your customer.

Walk Away

If the deal isn't profitable, walk. The best way to drive your competitors out of business is to let them have all of the unprofitable business.

You've Earned It

When discussing discounts, guerrillas avoid the phrase, "I can give you a discount of . . ." This phrase implies that you can give them more and opens you up to price-cutting. It carries the implication that the discount is a gift, a gratuity, something that you can grant on your discretion. Instead say, "At this quantity, you've earned a 7 percent discount." This tactic sets the ground rule that if they want a deeper discount, they have to earn it.

No Round Numbers

If you normally offer a 10 percent discount, it's perceived that you've rounded the number, creating the opportunity for your customer to nibble at your price. When you formulate discount percentages, use odd numbers and decimal fractions, like 4.2 percent, 7.3 percent, or 9.9 percent, and you'll create the impression that you've used a sharp pencil to arrive at your numbers.

Take Ownership of the Price

When you relinquish the control of your price to a third party, such as your boss or your company, you open price to further haggling. You create an advantage when you take personal ownership of the price. "My price is . . ." is a stronger position than, "Our price is . . ." or "The price is . . . ." Asking you to reduce your price becomes a personal issue.

Guerrillas will make every discount a personal issue. When your customer requests a discount, let them know that the concession is coming out of your pocket. "If I do that, it comes out of my paycheck. Which of my two children should I not feed this week?"

Cuts Both Ways

In some cases, you will have to negotiate your price in order to reach an agreement but follow the rule of reciprocal concessions. Get tough by explaining, "When I cut price, I also have to cut somewhere else."

You can cut the price, but you have to withdraw the warranty. You can cut the price, but their order goes to the end of the shipping queue. You can cut the price, but you have to charge per call for technical support. You get the idea.

What's Too Expensive?

When your customer objects, "Your price is too high," the guerrilla will then find out what too high means with an about face. "Too high? When you say 'too high' what exactly do you mean? Too high compared to what?" Find out if you're two cents too high, $2 too high, or $200 too high.

MEMORIZE THE CATALOG

Chad Clay is the number-one salesman out of 16 for the Houston-based OilDry Company. It specializes in industrial spill clean-up materials, such as the stuff you sprinkle on the garage floor to clean up an oil spill. Chad brought in 41 percent of the sales. Orvel tailed Chad around to find out his amazing secret.

While driving in his car, Chad receives a call on his cell phone. "Our price is too high? Uh, do you have our catalog there? Great. Check page 7. . . lower right corner. Yes. See we ship 48 to the bail. Do you have the competitor's catalog there? Perfect. Turn to page 31. . . upper left. . . yes. Notice that they ship only 36 to the bail. Yes, that explains our price difference. You'd like to order two bails? Great! I'll call Houston and expedite that for you. I'll call tomorrow with a status report."

Orvel is amazed. "You've memorized your competitor's catalog?"

"We'll it's a pretty brutal business," admit Chad. "Actually, I've memorized all 16 of them."

Now Orvel is astounded. "What . . . are you some kind of a *Rain Man* guy?"

"Oh, no! I just travel a lot and instead of watching TV in the hotel room, I study my competitors."

When you know more about your competitors than they know about you, they're dead.

Combating Price Shopping

You may get calls requesting a price quote. If a person knows exactly what they want, they'll shop around for the best price. Guerrillas choose how they want to handle these requests.

"Call Me Last . . ."

When Mark was buying an electronic piano, he knew exactly what brand and model he wanted, so he called around for best price and delivery. One dealer refused to quote over the phone. "Call me last," he said, "and I'll see what I can do." Not only did this guerrilla match the best price Mark had found, but he threw in a free piano bench and delivery, locking down the deal.

"We'll Be the Most Expensive . . ."

A house painter was frequently asked to quote jobs. Although he put a lot of time into writing his estimates, very few of these inquiries actually bought. Now this guerrilla prequalifies his prospects with, "I'll be glad to give you a quote on painting your house, but I want you to know in advance that it will probably be the most expensive quote you'll get." Half of the people hang up on him. He chuckles, knowing that he's saved a lot of time, and that he's creating a reputation for being the most expensive painter in town. With the people who stay on the line and ask "Why?" he has an opportunity to explain his top-of-the-line approach.

"I'd Prefer Not to Quote Until . . ."

Guerrillas never give price quotes without finding out about the customer's problem. A guerrilla who sells copy machines often gets requests for price quotes. She asks, "Who else are you considering?"

"We've decided on the model and our company policy is to get three quotes," they'll reply.

The guerrilla responds, "I'm in business to help you get the best possible copier at the best possible price, and offer you the best possible service. I'm not in business to help you get a better price from my competitor. Instead of giving you a blind quote, I'd prefer to see how I can serve you best. May I come by to review your decision?"

What's Their Budget?

When you discuss your customer's budget, priorities, and expected payback, price issues will usually fade away. Budgeting includes more than just money. Following are some items to discuss.

Personal Agenda

What else do they have to take care of? Are there other issues that are more pressing, limiting the time that they have to get this job done? How can you help? Assist with their personal agenda and you'll score extra points.

Politics

Has their superior barred them from doing business with your competitor? Are you the preferred vendor for political reasons? Use your spies to get this information in advance.

Deadlines

Your customer faces a deadline and is motivated to keep the commitment or suffer the consequences. Impending deadlines increase demand for your product and reduce the pressure for you to cut prices. If you can deliver when no other vendor can, the deal is yours, at almost any price.

Special Occasions

If your customer is commemorating a special occasion, she or he may be motivated to spend more to celebrate. A couple who normally drives a Ford Escort will rent a limo for their wedding. A firm that customarily orders catering from the local deli will call the best caterer in town for a board meeting. A limited-edition production run requires highest quality materials. Guerrillas ask, "Are you celebrating something special?"

Cost to Buy

Negotiations incur some costs: the cost of time, the cost of research, the cost of lawyers, the cost of travel. Guerrillas ask their customers to examine the costs of acquisition. Guerrillas ask, "How can we reduce your requisition expenses?"

Tax Implications

Gain an advantage by researching the depreciation schedules and tax implications of the deal. Guerrillas will point out any favorable impact on the overall budget.

Shipping Costs

What will it cost to get the products delivered? If you are a regional supplier, you may be able to gain a geographical advantage. You may get a better break on your shipping costs then they can. If your customer needs the product now, guerrillas will include the additional charges for couriers.

Budget Distribution

Are there other pots of money that you can tap? If you need to charge a fee for training, you may find the money in the human resources department. If there are installation costs, see if there are funds in the facilities maintenance budget. If your proposal pares energy costs, prospect for cash in the utility budget.

Other Priorities and Opportunities

Can you kill two birds with one stone? When you can help your customer complete other commitments and exploit other opportunities, you'll come off with flying colors.

Financing

Can you offer financing? Can you help arrange financing? Can you work with a bank to set up a customer line of credit? Because financing is a cost of purchase, demonstrate how your favorable financing offsets your higher price. Or offer a discount when they take your more profitable financing package.

Space Considerations

When your customer's space is at a premium, your smaller installation may save them the cost of expanding their facility.

Power Considerations

If your customer has limited access to power, water, gas, or sewage services, your solution may be a better fit than the competitors'.

Training Costs

What procedures have to change? Does your customer have to retrain people? Training is expensive to deliver, especially when the participants are pulled out of production and trained on company time.

Operating Costs

How about costs to operate? What's the cost of raw materials, supplies, utilities, scrap, and quality control? Guerrillas will have these numbers prepared as they go into the presentation.

Downtime

What does it cost for your customer to be out of service? The price difference between the lowest-cost vender and the highest-priced vender is often less than the cost of workers standing around waiting for repairs for an hour. Guerrillas will guarantee up-time and charge a premium for it.

Maintenance

What about the cost of spare parts? Will they be available when needed? Can you stock spare parts onsite at no charge, sending an invoice when they're used? Calculate your lower costs of maintenance and have the figures available to justify your higher price.

HOW TO AVOID PRICE-BUYER DIRTY TRICKS

Well-versed price buyers use dirty tricks to get you to lower your price. Keep your prices intact with these guerrilla tactics.

Price-Buyer Dirty Tricks

- The limbo
- "They're the same (or better) . . ."
- The first-timer
- Moving up the launch
- Stopping the countdown
- Excuse me
- False quote
- Quota time
- "Only price is important . . ."
- When you should discount
- "Mine's better and it's cheaper!"

Tactics to Fight Price Cutters

- No discounts
- History

- The Swiss army knife close
- Call their bluff
- Act busy
- "We're running close to capacity. . ."
- All things aren't equal
- Walk away
- You've earned it
- No round numbers
- Take ownership of the price
- Cuts both ways
- What's too expensive?
- Memorize the catalog

Combating Price Shopping

- "Call me last. . ."
- "We'll be the most expensive. . ."

HOW TO AVOID PRICE-BUYER DIRTY TRICKS

- "I'd prefer not to quote until. . ."

What's Their Budget?

- Personal agenda
- Politics
- Deadlines
- Special occasions
- Cost to buy
- Tax implications
- Shipping costs

- Budget distribution
- Other priorities and opportunities
- Financing
- Space considerations
- Power considerations
- Training costs
- Operating costs
- Downtime
- Maintenance

chapter 46

FROM

Guerrilla Marketing for Franchisees

Co-Author Todd Woods

WHAT IS THE FORMULA for franchise success? Before we share it with you, let us warn you that it takes several steps and could involve some attitude adjustments along the way. But you obviously want help or you wouldn't be reading this chapter, so hang on and get ready to take your game to a whole new level.

Develop the Proper "Success" Mindset

It's interesting the number of people I (Todd) meet who either want to own their own business or do own their own business. The other interesting thing I see is this: Out of those who own their own business, many

Out of those who own their own business, many seem to be run by it; meaning, their business runs their life.

THE FORMULA FOR FRANCHISE SUCCESS INCLUDES THESE STEPS

- Develop the proper "success" mindset.
- Become a lifelong student of marketing and business development and be teachable.
- Own your success.
- Do the work of a CEO, not a "chief executive opener" who spends all his or her time behind the counter or working IN the business.
- Execute and TAKE ACTION.

seem to be run by it; meaning, their business runs their life. They don't seem to have much time for themselves or for their family. Instead of them owning the business, the business owns them. Many I run into are struggling and not enjoying it. Getting out of this rut starts with two key success principles.

Visualize, with Absolute Clarity, What You Want

You need to create a way to make money while you sleep. There are two ways to do that. One way is to invest your money into good investments so that it is earning you interest in your sleep, and the other way is to own your own business.

Become a Lifelong Student of Marketing and Business Development

Starting and growing a business usually takes twice the money, three times longer, and four times the amount of effort and stress than expected.

Effective marketing can be the difference between having a decent franchise business and having an incredible franchise business. Marketing can be one of the most enjoyable parts of your business, especially if your marketing efforts make your business more profitable. This means that, if you aren't already, you need to become a lifelong student of marketing and business development.

Successful Franchisees Own Their Success

In many cases, success boils down to the principle of responsibility and accountability and/or the lack of execution.

Marketing can be one of the most enjoyable parts of your business, especially if your marketing efforts make your business more profitable.

The Buck Stops Here

It is easy to point fingers at everyone and everything:

- *Corporate.* My franchisor: It was their fault. After all, isn't it their job to market my store?

TYPECASTING

There are three types of people when it comes to learning from others.

1. The first type includes those with great big egos. They make mistakes and don't learn from them. This type of person is invincible and "knows everything."

2. The second type learns from their mistakes and tries to avoid making them again in the future.

3. The third type, and the wisest in our opinion, learns from others' mistakes and successes and uses that knowledge to capitalize on successes while minimizing mistakes. This type will, of course, still run across challenges they didn't anticipate. However, the businessperson armed with knowledge of what works and what doesn't will, in almost every case, be more successful.

- *Bad locations.* I would have been successful had I been in better locations.
- *The weather.* If only it were warmer or colder.
- *Not enough product offerings.* Yes, that was it. Our menu was too limited.
- *Bad employees.* Man, it's tough to get good employees these days. It's their fault.

The Accountability Factor

I'm sure you've heard the phrase, "If it is going to be, it is up to me!" Well, in the franchise business, as in life, it is true! One of the biggest challenges in owning your own franchise business is feeling out of control. The extent to which we accept accountability determines the extent to which we are in control. And generally, those franchisees in control are usually more successful. Where do you fall in the accountability factor? If you are not where you need to be, take action now and get there as quickly as possible.

> *"If it is going to be, it is up to me!" Well, in the franchise business, as in life, it is true!*

Taking Action

Local Store Marketing

Let's start by focusing within the four walls of your business. First of all, it is absolutely crucial that you DO NOT increase traffic into your store or location until you can create an excellent customer service experience. No marketing can compensate for poor performance by employees once prospects or customers are in the store. No marketing campaign can succeed without killer execution on the customer service side. If you are not ready with the employees and the experience, HOLD ON! Don't do any more marketing until you nail that one.

Remember, to deliver killer customer service you must train for it. Not just once, not just twice, but continually—at a minimum, monthly. Those companies that are truly successful have customer service training weekly. The meeting is sometimes as simple as "one-minute meetings" with management teams. But they have them.

It is absolutely crucial that you DO NOT increase traffic into your store or location until you can create an excellent customer service experience.

Internal Customer Marketing

Before we market to our external customers we need to market to our internal customers, our employees. If our employees aren't behind a marketing campaign, it will flop. Hands down! We need to get our employees involved as much as possible in our marketing and marketing campaigns. Employees are our greatest asset. They are the front lines. The more excited they are about your marketing and marketing initiatives, the more successful everyone will be, including you. Before thinking too much about marketing outside your location, remember, your employees are your first priority.

Hire the Right People

When it comes to employees, mistake number one for most businesses is not taking enough time to get the "right" people. You can be sure that if you can consistently hire the right employees, you have won half the battle. You should be recruiting constantly. Give employee referral incentives, and even customer referral incentives. Hold weekly open interviews. Get your key employees involved. Let them help in the process. Have employees hold "auditions." The employees only hire about 4 out of every 100 applicants. They need to hire actors, very into performing and very friendly. Make no exceptions; make great profits.

Employee of the Month Programs

These programs are very underrated. In all the studies I've seen, money is not the most important part of employees' jobs. The most important thing is recognition for a job well done. It doesn't cost money to recognize and highlight star performers.

Team Unity

Team unity is built by spending fun times together outside of work. Successful franchise companies have company picnics, go bowling together, go boating, or even just meet occasionally at the movies. Assign someone on your team to be in charge of these activities or have a committee to plan them. Employees love this. Just like a tight athletic team, the better your employees know each other—understanding how individuals operate and what makes them tick—the better they perform on the field, so to speak.

Encourage Employees to Come Up with Promotional Ideas Themselves

Perhaps you've noticed, as have I, that most people think "their idea" is the best. It's human nature to want our ideas implemented. Ideas that come from within the ranks of your own employees will often get much better "buy-in." Why? Because it is "their" idea, and they therefore take more ownership of it. Also, before rolling out marketing ideas or campaigns, get feedback from employees on how it might best be rolled out. If you use an employee's idea, you will be amazed at how they will get the entire staff charged up about it.

Constantly Share Marketing Results with Your Staff

Use graphs or charts in the back room to help them get a visual understanding of how things are working. They will be able to see at a glance what is working and what is not. Again, information is power. The more you empower employees, the more buy-in you get.

Marketing Training

Make marketing a part of new employee training. Train employees from day one that they are the company's ambassadors and it is part of their job to help increase your sales and profits.

Friends and Family Discounts.

Give out family discount cards for employees' family and friends. After all, they are your customers too. Plus, this is a nice way to show your thanks and add more "perks" to the job.

Friends and Family Night

Building on the idea above, once per quarter have a night that friends and family can come in for a special discount. It's a great opportunity for you as the owner or manager to meet the family and see just why their kid turned out the way they did. No, really, it's a good way to show the friends, family, and employees that you care. Everyone wants their employer to give more. This is a simple way to do it.

Employee Discounts

Many franchise locations give employee discounts. Restaurants give food discounts. Clothing stores give discounts on clothing. Some companies offer a discount during the employee's shift. Seriously consider giving them the discount during "off the clock" times as well. Why? Because most people will bring friends in with them and they will spend money while they are there.

Employees Hand Out Fliers/Coupons to Neighbors, Friends, Etc.

Make it a contest occasionally (if your employees hang out with your target market of course) to have employees hand out promotional vouchers or coupons, and give awards for the most redeemed. It is a way for employees to earn extra cash while giving your business great exposure.

Again, there are tons of ways to motivate employees, and we have just touched on a few. Try some of these and your sales will increase, guaranteed.

Database Marketing

This is, by far, one of the most effective things you will ever do: Build a customer database. If you are in a business that collects customer information as part of your business, it's a piece of cake; just be sure to market to them on a regular basis. If you are in a business that doesn't get customers' information, BEGIN IMMEDIATELY. These are customers who have come to you. Capture their information and market to them. How? Simple—just ask them to join your mailing list. Preferably collect their email addresses and let them know you will be sending them quarterly or monthly special offers. Let them know you will not be giving their information to anyone else and be sure to honor that promise. If it's a rainy day and you have a business that is slow on those days, send out an email with a coupon valid on that day only. If you don't do this now because you don't have the time to enter the information or don't have the resources to manage it, there are companies out there that do it all for you.

Mobile Marketing

"Eighty million customers have used text messaging. In June 2005, cell phone customers sent 7.2 billion messages using the text feature built into most phones." —Brand Republic, 25 Oct 2005

"A survey found that 79 percent of businesses that used SMS, Short Message Service, said it was more effective than other marketing channels or loyalty tools." —Brand Republic, 25 Oct 2005

Community Center

Create a community board or even a community wall. Although franchise businesses are successful because they look alike and are

‡||||||||||||||||||||||||||||||||||||||||||||||||||||||||||||||||||||||||||||||||||||||||||||||||||||||⊥

NUTS AND BOLTS OF MOBILE MARKETING

- Build a database to send incentives or periodic promotions by text message. Imagine sending an instant coupon on a slow day to drive traffic.
- Build an email database to announce new products and promotions.
- Track all advertising (print, radio, billboards, in-store, etc.) for effectiveness with text. It promotes an immediate response.

⊤||||||||||||||||||||||||||||||||||||||||||||||||||||||||||||||||||||||||||||||||||||||||||||||||||||||⊤

generally well-known brands, people like to know they are locally owned and operated. This is one way to create that experience.

Some Things You Can Put on a Community Board

- Pictures of you and your family with the caption, "Locally owned and operated by the _____ family."
- Pictures of your team members with their names and their favorite movies, or their favorite songs—something to personalize them so customers can connect.
- Past successful fundraiser information as well as new fundraisers coming up.

Customer Wall of Fame

Take pictures of "regulars" and list the favorite items they purchase while patronizing your business. Have them sign their picture to make them feel even more important.

Trivia Question of the Day

This is something team members can have a blast with. If you have a location near a movie theater, they could be movie trivia questions. If it's during some sporting playoffs, the questions could be geared toward that. Whatever your trivia promotion, you may want to consider giving a discount to customers when they get it right. Of course, you don't need to give a discount because it's just a great way to create fun and more loyalty from your customers.

Always a Party

I like to live by the theory that "commotion equals promotion." You've seen how many people slow down to look closely when there is an accident on the freeway. It's because it's human nature to look at a crowd and wonder, "What's going on?" The same thing happens when you create commotion around your store. Besides, just about everyone can use more fun in their day. Occasionally blow up balloons and put them outside on your front door, or patio, and throughout your store. People may ask what's going on. Your answer is simple, you are celebrating the fact that they are there, or you are celebrating your great products, etc. Have some fun with it. You'll find this one also helps with visibility. People who generally may just pass by will stop and look.

Game On

If you are in a high walk-by traffic location, create a wheel (like on *Wheel of Fortune* but much smaller; perhaps out of a dart board). Let people spin it for a prize. Make sure everyone gets at least a coupon to use in your store. You may also give out T-shirts, promotional mugs, and other accessories with your logos on them. Again, this follows the "commotion equals promotion" idea.

Become an Art Gallery

The Wildflower Restaurant in Phoenix displays art from local schools for a week or so at a time. Why? You guessed it, the kids bring their parents in to see their "famous" picture proudly displayed on the wall of the restaurant. And yes, very likely, the family will eat while they are there as well. You know, one gets hungry looking at great artwork. This also shows people that you are involved in the community and giving back whenever possible.

Give Out Promotional Items

Jack in the Box even sells them. Maybe you've seen the "Jack" for the antenna of your car. You can sell promotional items for a nominal amount or simply give them away. The only rule here is to make sure it has your logo on it. Key chains, lanyards, Frisbees, blow-up beach balls, mini footballs, antenna balls, etc.

Offer Free Popcorn, Drinks, Ice Cream, and More

If you are NOT a food establishment, especially if people need to wait in a line or for a product to be repaired, it can be very classy to offer waiting customers a soft drink or more.

Good-Neighbor Marketing

Start with businesses around your location. If you have a location within a retail center, create a "good neighbor" discount card and give it to all the businesses to give to their employees to use in your business. This is a captive audience. They are there nearly every day of the week. Get them as customers. As you provide excellent service for them, they will talk about you and actually send people your way.

The best yet was with our Jamba Juice stores. We gave a "good neighbor" discount to Office Max a few doors down. When they had a "customer appreciation day" they asked if we wanted to come down and give out free samples to hundreds of their customers.

And we said what? Of course it was a resounding "YES." Do you see how a small thing like a "good neighbor discount" can snowball into some great things?

Free Day or Discount Day for Employees

If you are near businesses, pick one a week and invite them in (generally through the human resource department) for a freebie or a great deal. Get them hooked on your product. Whether the invited business comes over on that particular day or not you have exposure in their store.

Business to Business

This can be a blast! Get a team of two people together to go building to building and hand out free promotional items. If you deliver or accept fax orders, let them know. If you own a smoothie business, dress up like a banana and have some fun with it. If you own a cell phone store, dress up like a big cell phone. People will remember it. If they haven't had your product before, give them an aggressive discount. If they are a regular customer, perhaps you have a different coupon that isn't quite as aggressive. This is an ongoing process. Get a map (even a hand-drawn one) of the businesses you hit and the date you do it. Start close to your store and work your way out up to a mile or two. It works. In fact, it is far more effective than any print advertising you will ever do!

Sample Within and Outside Your Business

It's no secret that when you have a great product and you get people to taste it or to use it, they will very often become a customer. Not only will they become a customer, but you may also create some buzz. The key to product trial is that you must have a quality product; otherwise it will backfire. For that reason, the sample itself must be outstanding.

Logo Mania

Everywhere you go, wear your company shirt. It's amazing how effective this is. I see many franchise owners who perhaps are tired of wearing the company uniform, so they don't. Wear it proudly. It will help you strike up conversations and give you the opportunity to talk about your business. Wrap your car or at least get your company logo put on it. Build your brand wherever you go.

chapter 47

FROM

Guerrilla Marketing on the Front Lines

Co-Authors Alex Mandossian and Mitch Meyerson

G UERRILLA MARKETERS KNOW HOW important taking action is. This chapter, in a sense, gives you a multitude of ways to take action, for we know that if we take action, things happen and our business grows. But there is a difference between taking action and taking smart action.

I'm no stranger to taking action. From 1993 to 2000, I (Alex) worked on Madison Avenue. While I was there, I worked like an animal. There is no other way to look at it. I felt like I was in the galleys rowing, like in one of those old movies about the Vikings or the Romans.

> *There is a difference between taking action and taking smart action.*

I was a chief marketing officer of a company on Madison Avenue, and I worked 16-hour days. Why?

> "Inaction breeds doubt and fear. Action breeds confidence and courage.
> If you want to conquer fear, do not sit home and think about it.
> Go out and get busy."
>
> —Dale Carnegie

Not only did I want to keep my job, but I also wanted to make more money, and the only way I could do that was to get a promotion. I didn't get a pay raise every month like I do now, and I had very little time for freedom. In fact, if I had continued at that place, I would have most likely lost my marriage and would not have had the two beautiful kids I have now. That is definitely not taking smart action.

Guerrillas Are All About Action

What I'm about to give you are the seven secrets of action management, secrets that I use every day in my business, and if you apply even one or two of them to your business, you will find that you are able to manage all your marketing and production actions much more effectively. And once I give these secrets to you, they will become strategies that will enable you to get 16 hours worth of work done in an eight-hour day, triple your revenue, and quite possibly double your time off. Ready to get started? Here's the first one.

Action Step 1: Create Your Master To-Do List

We all know the importance of having a "to-do" list, and it is vital to any action-management plan. Now, I (Alex) don't use a Palm Pilot or Outlook for this. I use a physical, master to-do list. I physically write out the action items that I want to accomplish. I use a junior legal pad that's about 5 inches wide by 7 inches tall, with 50 sheets on it. It's yellow and has about 20 lines on it. No matter what kind of pad you use, it's very important you physically write it out because this is the way that works. I've tried it other ways, and it hasn't worked; it was too overwhelming.

> *Write down no more than 20 actions per day.*

I use this small pad because I like to fill it up. The 20 lines allow me to write down no more than 20 actions per day. I typically complete anywhere between 15 and 20; I have found that's all that's humanly possible. Furthermore, when I fill up my junior legal pad, I feel like I'm doing something, and that sense of accomplishment gives me a positive boost.

I have also found that it works better to write out your action management in advance—at least a day before. Sometimes I write mine a few days before. Whenever you do it, however, doesn't matter so much as writing your master to-do list for the future. Why? Because it's easier to come to a desk that's clean and has a master to-do list already sitting on it. This way, you can start your first prime-time hour by attacking that list and crossing things out. Isn't that a lot easier than trying to invent things to do?

As I go through my day, I execute each action item and cross out those suckers with a red felt-tip pen I bought specifically for that purpose. Do you know why I do that? I get to see all I've accomplished. I feel so good when I write those things down and then cross them out with a red pen because they're done.

At the end of the day, what happens? You often have items that weren't finished, and so the third element of creating your master to-do list is to take the items left over, flip the page, and put those items on a new list. Once I have started my new "to-do" list for the next day, I cross those items I just moved off the previous days. If I didn't finish three items on, say, a Tuesday, I flip the page to Wednesday's list, write them down, and then cross them off Tuesday's list. I'm going to flip the page. Make sure you flip the page. Also, if you have 12 left over, you didn't have a very well-managed day, but you have 12 things to start out with tomorrow. So you resolve to do better and move on. I can't tell you how satisfying it is to cross out every single one of those actions.

Once I have everything crossed off, I rip out the sheet of paper from that day, scrunch it up, and throw it in the wastebasket. That day is officially over, and even though I may have more for the next day, that next day hasn't started. I get to start my day fresh, every day, using this strategy.

> *Always do the things that are going to be the most fun first because if you get to do something fun first, that puts you on a positive note for the rest of the day.*

Now, you may be wondering if and how I prioritize my list. When I'm creating my to-do list, I prioritize. I have to, but not in the way that you might think. Guerrilla marketers, listen up. The fun first. Fun first. Sometimes, the fun is easy; sometimes, fun is hard. But I always do the things that are going to be the most fun for me because if I get to do something fun first, that puts me on a positive note for the rest of the day.

Action Step 2: Block Out Your Daily Prime-Time Hours

This is very important, as important as creating the master plan for your day. What is a prime-time hour? A prime-time hour is anything you control 100 percent of that is going to generate revenue for you now or sometime in the future. Now, you can have just one prime-time hour a day or two a day, even four a day. I have four. I don't think you should have more than four, and if you're skeptical about that number, just know that most people don't have any.

Think about this. If you only have one prime-time hour a day and you work five days a week—many of us work many more than that—that's 225 work days per year. How many prime-time, revenue-generating hours are you giving yourself as a gift for the year? You are giving yourself 225 hours. As a guerrilla marketer, don't you think you can generate some revenue with that? I think so. In fact, aren't we robbing ourselves if we don't give ourselves prime-time hours?

I would like you to block off one prime-time hour a day starting next week. When you're considering which hour to block off, go for the most important hour of the day, the first one. Why? You are fresher in the morning than you are after having been beaten down by the events of the day. When you have your first, fresh hour of the morning in which to produce, you start with the positive.

> *A prime-time hour is anything you control 100 percent of that is going to generate revenue for you now or sometime in the future.*

Think about it, what is the first thing that you typically do when you get in front of your computer? Check email. Is that an interruption? Yes. And worse, it can start your whole day off badly. What if you wake up and see an email from someone asking for a refund or telling you they're not happy with your services? Doesn't that put you into some type of emotional tailspin which you don't want to be a part of? Now, rather than checking your email, generate revenue for one full hour first and see how good you feel about yourself. You've already crossed out some things on your master action to-do list and so that makes handling any bad news a little easier. See what I am saying? There's also another reason why I don't start with emails with their potentially bad news, and it has everything to do with intention. When people get bad news first, they concentrate on that bad news, not the good news. When you start with good news, it is not so bad afterwards.

So start with good news so that you have positive intentions to take you through the rest of the day. Start your day with a revenue-generating activity. And if you only have one prime-time hour, make sure that hour is in the very beginning. Eventually, you want no fewer than two hours a day that are prime time. Oh, and prime time is always during the day: 9 to 5, 8 to 5. Your choice, but it's not in the middle of the night.

Another element of prime time is to focus only on revenue-generating activities you can control. I think everyone knows what that means, and to do that, always avoid the daily interruptions you cannot control, like email. Just turn email off. Also, during your prime time, don't listen to your voice mail and don't take phone calls. That's why you have voice mail (but don't listen to your voice mail either during prime time). Don't open your letters. Tell your family it's prime time and get their support by agreeing that they cannot enter the office or call you (unless, heaven forbid, it's an emergency).

By setting prime-time hours, and starting with a revenue-generating activity, you will feel great about yourself and you will be much more able to manage your actions throughout the rest of the day.

Action Step 3: During Prime Time, Put Pressure on Yourself—Use a Timer

In order for me to perform better, I put pressure on myself. I give myself deadlines, in a way, and I use this next technique to keep myself accountable. This technique is something different, and I really want you to at least try it. Since I can't manage time but I can manage actions, I put myself on a timer. I use a kitchen timer that cost $9 at Bed, Bath & Beyond. What do I do with this timer? I set it for 47 minutes (I'll tell you why that is in a minute), and I put it where I can see it, right next to my computer screen. As I work, I hear it ticking. Does that put pressure on me or what! It will do the same for you—put pressure on yourself to really put your head down and perform.

Now, when the beeper goes off, stop everything you're doing. It's incredibly important because you've got to give yourself a break. I give myself breaks. This is why I set my timer to 47 minutes because I like to have a 13-minute break. I am greedy with my time off. However, I recommend you initially set your timers to 50 or 55 minutes. I started with 55 minutes and gave myself a 5-minute break and worked my way up to the 13-minute break. This break is very, very important because it allows you to step back into a highly creative space, and that's where some pretty magical things happen. This is the essence of secret number 4.

Action Step 4: Be Prepared—Capture Your Big Ideas Digitally

Guerrilla marketers are good Girl Scouts and Boy Scouts because we know how important it is to be prepared. You see, when you take a break from the task at hand, your mind will still be going on what you were doing. If you were brainstorming a new idea, if you were talking to a joint venture partner, it doesn't matter. Whatever you were doing, your mind is going to keep going, and this is where the magic happens. So the bottom line is to be prepared to record that magic.

Set your timer to 55 minutes to start, and give yourself a five-minute break. This break is very important because it allows you to step back into a highly creative space, and that's where some pretty magical things happen.

Here's what I do from 6:30 A.M. to 7:30 A.M. I'm in prime time—not for the whole hour, but for 47 minutes. When that beeper goes off, I go downstairs and either do some sit-ups, pushups or grab a glass of water or a cup of coffee. During that time, I have a digital recorder with me. It's one I got from Radio Shack, for about $60. You deserve to give this to yourself, so spend 60 bucks. Don't buy one that has two hours on it, or even 60 minutes. Buy one that only gives you 15 minutes or at the most 30 minutes. I'll explain why in a moment. Keep that recorder next to you at all times because then you can record your big ideas the moment they pop into your head. And once they're recorded, you don't have to think about them anymore. You can purge them from your mind, freeing your mind to come up with more. Also keep your recorder handy during nonprime-time hours so you can record everything you think of as you think it. Try

Keep a recorder next to you at all times to record your big ideas the moment they pop into your head.

this, and once you've digitally recorded five or six ideas, then I want you to write them down in an idea file—whether that is a notebook or a Word document, it doesn't matter. What does matter is that you've transcribed these ideas from the voice recorder. This is why I don't want you to have two hours worth of recording time.

If you have two hours worth of ideas on your recorder, you're never going to transcribe them. There's also another reason why I like to write things down. When you type or write, it's a different activity than speaking; it really is a different modality of learning. So as you speak into your recorder and then write down the ideas, you have engaged the tactile, the kinesthetic, and the auditory parts of learning. The more modalities you can use, the more the idea sticks. Heck, if there were a scratch and sniff part to this process, I would do that too!

Action Step 5: Offer One Free Consultation Per Week or Per Day

I don't care what you are good at or what you're selling. It could be coaching, mentoring, writing, publishing, or developing software. Whether you're an author or a service provider, you're going to have customers who have questions. These questions can turn into potential sales. Knowing this, I offer one 30-minute free consultation per day for someone who wants information from me.

People really like getting something for free, but the trick is to keep a tight lid on that 30 minutes. So my free consultation has a twist. The clients know, up front, that at the end of the consultation, if they want to work with me, they are going to pay up. At the end of their 30 free minutes, I ask them if they'd like to proceed. If they say yes, they then owe me for my time—all of it.

Let's say my hourly fee is $450, and our consultation lasted 30 minutes. They know before we set the appointment for the call that if they want to continue with me at some point in the future, then they will give me their credit card for $225 at the end of the call. Now if they want to continue for the full hour, great. If they want to go two hours, great, because that has become revenue-generating for me, right? If they say no, then we hang up, and the consultation is free—but with a caveat. While there are no obligations, no commitment, no further expectations on my part or theirs, they don't get to talk to me again.

It really is a conditional free consultation, but it keeps everyone honest. Many coaches and service providers give free consultations, but they don't put their people on the hook. You have far fewer free consultations if you tell potential clients they will pay for it if they are satisfied. Also, make sure you have your free consultations during nonprime time.

Set aside a block of maybe 40 minutes and call it gifting on your yellow pad. You are giving back to your clients, so you are giving them a gift, but believe me, if that "gift" becomes revenue-generating, that is also a gift for you. It's a win-win because you gave them something valuable and they gave you a gift—their business.

Each week, I also have one hour every Tuesday at noon (3 P.M. EST) when I do a guerrilla marketing seven-step plan that Jay Conrad Levinson taught me. But I don't do it alone. Everyone who receives my MarketingWithPostcards.com auto-responder series gets to be a part of this on day seven. You can be part of this, too. All you have to do is send a blank email to Teleclinic@ThatOneWebGuy.com.

Now, what did I just do? I just pitched you a free teleclinic, and I did it on purpose. This is one of my best-spent hours because I get customers from these teleclinics. I also get email addresses that will go into a sublist. That sublist is a teleconference list, and teleconferences are a huge source of revenue generation.

So everyone who has given me an email address for the teleclinic then gets emailed for the teleconference. The teleconference is also free, but I have built a list of very active subscribers by offering them free teleconferences, and very active lists are huge revenue generators, believe me.

Just like the free consultations, I do that teleconference during nonprime time. I even plan for it in nonprime time, but that doesn't take much time because when you have a free teleconference class each week, you just use the exact same curriculum week after week. Don't worry about repeating yourself.

Guerrilla marketing is about building and maintaining relationships, and the more people listen to you, the higher level of intimacy they create with you. More intimacy equals better relationships and better relationships equal higher revenue. So what I am doing here with free consultations and free teleclinics and teleseminars is that I'm playing a trick on myself. I am finding ways to convert nonprime time into revenue generation. It is action oriented, and when you think about it as a gift that you're giving yourself—for all the reasons I just gave you—it keeps you motivated to stay in action the rest of the day.

Now, there is something that you need to know about this gifted time. With whatever amount of time you want to gift to yourself and your clients, or potential clients, figure out what you are going to do and then do it religiously. It might be that you just do the one free consultation per day and not the teleseminar, or vice versa. Or, you may decide to model what I do and do them both. Whatever you do, however, think of it always as a gift—never, ever as a pitch. When you gift your time to help educate people, you will have access to more people wanting to listen to you. Don't promote yourself, just give them something they can use. But do tell them what your fees are and what your services are, especially when they are listening to you in context of what you're ultimately selling. If you want to see what this all looks like, just send a

When you gift your time to help educate people, you will have access to more people wanting to listen to you.

blank email to Teleclinic@ThatOneWebGuy.com or opt-in to http://www.7StepActionPlan.com.

Action Step 6: Find a Mutual Coaching Buddy

It's great when you can give something to somebody and they can give something back. What I like to do is find a mutual coaching buddy. Here's how you do this: Hunt for an expert in the field you want to master. Make sure you have something of equal or greater value to share with that expert. Use one hour of nonprime time for the mutual coaching, and set a deadline for the number of coaching sessions you have. Agree on maybe four or six of these sessions and see how it works. Don't do it forever because you'll feel awful if you want to stop. Test it.

Hunt for an expert in the field you want to master.

Understand, I am trying to get you guerrilla marketers to do work that generates revenue, and using one nonprime-time hour a week, every other week, or even once a month for a mutual coaching buddy is probably one of the best hours you'll ever use.

Action Step 7: Set Your Revenue Quota Every 90 Days

Every good, productive action is attached to a plan, and my seven secret steps are no exception. While a 90-day revenue quota might sound daunting, it isn't. This is what you do. First, figure out what you can make in a year, then divide that into weekly goals. Make sure it's realistic, but at the same time make sure that you're not selling yourself short either.

Now, I like weekly goals because they're easy to measure. You can graph your progress or simply keep the numbers in a journal. However

> *Once you have established what your weekly goals are, you write down every week if you made it or not.*

you keep track isn't as vital as actually doing it. The most important point is that once you have established what your weekly goals are, you write down every week if you made it or not. Then, every 90 days, review how you did and adjust it either up or down.

This is how I do it. I set my quota and then do the least amount of work possible to get there. When I reach my weekly quota, believe it or not, I stop working. I'll still take phone calls, but I will stop working. It doesn't always happen. I don't always meet it. But when it does happen, it sure is fun! I remember making it on a Tuesday once, and I went on a little mini vacation. It took me about a day to plan, and from Thursday all the way through the following Sunday, I went on a vacation with call forwarding. I laughed the whole time, and I was laughing at time. I managed my actions, and I made it work to my favor that week. Fortunately, I did get that revenue, but I did something most don't. I rewarded myself for it. Most people don't reward themselves; they just work more. But why do that? You are robbing yourself of the nectar of living. Isn't the whole purpose of work to play?

So there you have it. The seven secrets to action management. They will help you organize your enterprise online or offline. These tactics will help you complete 16 hours of worth of work within an eight-hour day, as well as triple your income and double your time off. You don't even have to follow every step. You can start by following one or two of them, and I bet you'll be very surprised. And if you want to learn more of my secrets to success, make sure you check out my blog at http://www.AlexMandossian.com and sign up for the free audio e-book, *5 Secrets To Making Change Now*.

One final note: When I tell you my secrets, I do it selfishly. Because if I am espousing it, I better follow it. I admit I don't always follow it. I do run amuck sometimes. So by stating this in a major marketing publication, it will force my self and every cell in my body to remember to focus on this and get even better at it. I don't know if this is for the sake of embarrassment or because I am putting myself on the spot, but ultimately it doesn't matter. I am giving you my seven secrets selfishly because I want to be able to master action management.

GUERRILLA ACTION STEPS

1. Create your master to-do list
2. Block out your daily prime-time hours
3. During prime time, put pressure on yourself—use a timer
4. Be prepared—capture your big ideas digitally
5. Offer one free consultation per week or per day
6. Find a mutual coaching buddy
7. Set your revenue quota every 90 days

About the Authors and Co-Authors

Jay and Jeannie Levinson

Jay Conrad Levinson fell in love and married Jeannie the day he met her. After living near San Francisco for 35 years, they recently sold their house and traveled the United States full time for more than six years in their luxury motor coach—visiting grandkids and exploring national parks. On the road, they completed a major update of their classic book, *Guerrilla Marketing*, and co-wrote several other books. While giving seminars and workshops about marketing to small businesses and major corporations throughout North and South America, Asia, Europe, and Australia, they have learned the ways of successful marketing guerrillas worldwide.

Jay and Jeannie Levinson are the authors of the best-selling marketing series in history, *Guerrilla Marketing*, plus 58 other business books. Their books have sold more than 21 million copies worldwide, and their guerrilla concepts have influenced marketing so much that their books appear in 62 languages and are required reading in MBA programs worldwide.

Jay was born in Detroit, raised in Chicago, and graduated from the University of Colorado. His studies in psychology led him to advertising agencies, including a directorship at Leo Burnett in London, where he served as creative director. Returning to the U.S., he joined J. Walter Thompson as senior vice president. Jay created and taught guerrilla marketing for 10 years at the extension division of the University of California in Berkeley.

A winner of first prizes in all the media, he has been part of the creative teams that made household names of the Marlboro Man, the Pillsbury Doughboy, Allstate's good hands, United's friendly skies, the Sears Diehard battery, Morris the cat, Mr. Clean, Tony the Tiger, and the Jolly Green Giant.

Jeannie was born in Orlando, Florida, and raised in Daytona Beach. She is the president of Guerrilla Marketing International and co-founder of the Guerrilla Marketing Association and The Guerrilla Marketing Business University. She is the co-author of *The Startup Guide to Guerrilla Marketing* (Entrepreneur Press) and several other guerrilla books. With decades of sales and marketing experience, she is a sought-after consultant and seminar and workshop leader.

Together Jay and Jeannie have eight children, 26 grandkids, and two great-grandkids and now live near most of them in their home on a lake outside Orlando, Florida.

Today, *Guerrilla Marketing* is the most powerful brand in the history of marketing, listed among the 100 best business books ever written. Now this latest book, *Guerrilla Marketing Remix*, is considered the best they've ever written. The new stuff here—the thinking, technology, mind-bending marketing tactics, and actual new laws of marketing—are explored in "Part 1" by Jay and Jeannie Levinson and in "Part 2" by the gifted guerrilla co-authors. Get it before your competitors do. To receive FREE guerrilla marketing tips and become a guerrilla yourself go to: http://www.gmarketing.com.

Let's Hear It for the Guerrilla Co-Authors!

The guerrillas who submitted the wisdom in this Part 2 of *Guerrilla Marketing Remix* are far beyond awesome. We've mined the most salient insights from a number of these guerrilla co-authors, but there are many others awaiting you to read what they can impart.

You could grow your business substantially just by knowing the gems they wrote that we had to cut. We laud their books to the skies and invite you to contact them if you want to learn more or allow them to contribute to your own further success. Contact information for the co-authors appears with their biographical notes up ahead.

Ideas from their books and timeless perceptions are updated in this *Remix*. Sometimes, we took those nuggets from their books; sometimes they wanted to create things from scratch—proving that you can indeed reinvent the wheel. We've reinvented it to the best of our abilities right here. The proof of those abilities will be reflected in your bank account.

This *Guerrilla Marketing Remix* can remix your company's profits if you do it right. This book tells you how to do it right.

The Guerrilla Marketing Hall of Fame

There are so many Hall-of-Fame guerrillas in the world that we've devoted a special website to listing them. You can find it at http://www.gmarketing.com/halloffame.

We invite you to contact any of those Hall of Famers—many of whom still answer their own phones and respond to their own emails. They can help you as they have helped us. Not all of them are guerrilla co-authors. But every last one of them is a world-class, proven-in-action, battle-scarred (even with victory come ow-eees and scars) mentor and role model.

I wish I had known a blue-ribbon panel of guerrillas when I embarked upon my journey.

We will continue to update and add to our Hall of Fame. We want you to know not only how to do it but where to go for help. Now that you know, we hope you'll pay a click-visit to the Hall. I remember the sense of awe I felt when I first walked into the Baseball Hall of Fame in Cooperstown, New York. I feel the same in our own Hall of Fame.

Its doors are open to you now that you're a thoroughly remixed guerrilla.

Biographies of Co-Authors

(Listed Alphabetically)

Frank Adkins

Frank Adkins is the co-author of *Guerrilla Marketing for Nonprofits* with Chris Forbes. Frank is a National Board Certified Teacher. His experience with fundraising and nonprofit organizations comes from the many years he has volunteered with causes he believes in. He has studied directly from Jay Conrad Levinson. As a certified guerrilla marketing coach and guerrilla marketing master trainer, Frank Adkins is vice president of special projects for Guerrilla Marketing International. He has helped companies by providing them with research and insight on how they too can reach more people with guerrilla marketing tactics. His latest venture involved co-authoring *Guerrilla Fundraising* with Jay Levinson and Chris Forbes. Frank holds a Bachelor of Science degree from the University of Central Florida. He lives in Orlando with his wife and three children. Visit his website at: www.FrankAdkins.org; email: coachfda@aol.com.

Ed Antle

Ed Antle is the co-author of *Guerrilla Canvassing*. He knocked on his first door 20 years ago. Since then he has generated millions in revenue for various companies across the United States—all through door-to-door marketing.

He has helped companies build profitable canvassing operations in San Diego, Virginia Beach, Louisville, St. Louis, Minneapolis, Chicago, Richmond, and many other cities. He has worked with 50-person canvass teams, and he has canvassed alone.

Ed is a traveling consultant and guerrilla marketing trainer. He does extensive work with internet marketing, direct mail, trade shows, and TV advertising, but canvassing is his first love. His no-nonsense, bare-knuckled, door-knocking techniques will help any organization generate revenue, make leads, get votes, or just get the word out. With a bachelor's degree in journalism, he has a conversational and pithy writing style that makes information easy to digest. His hands-on experience ensures no words are wasted on wishful thinking.

Ed Antle is past president of Sudden Impact Marketing. While the marketing director of a $27 million home improvement company, he developed canvassing, direct mail, and event-marketing programs that produced more than 100 leads a day at a cost of 12.6 percent over a 10-year period.

Contact Info: Sudden Impact Marketing, 400 Lazelle Road, Suite 20, Columbus, OH 43240; phone: (614) 515-5090; fax: (614) 515-5082; email: info@simarketing.net; website: http://www.simarketing.net.

Stuart Burkow

Stuart Burkow, known as "The King of Profits," is the co-author of *Guerrilla Profits*. He is a serial entrepreneur, marketing rainmaker, and a high-caliber, business profits expert with more than 35 years of hands-on, "in the trenches" experience, starting with his first business when he was just 14 years old. He has owned, built, and operated successful businesses in retail, wholesale distributing, manufacturing, publishing, marketing agency and services, direct sales, and mail order—and is president of Guerrilla Profits International.

Stuart has worked directly with the legends in business training, growth, motivation, and marketing such as Jay Abraham, Dan Kennedy,

Robert Allen, Brian Tracy, Denis Waitley—and of course, Jay Conrad Levinson—and has joint-venture partners around the world.

He can be reached at: http://www.kingofprofits.com. For information about the book *Guerrilla Profits*, go to: http://www.guerrillaprofits.com/book.

James Dillehay

James Dillehay is the co-author with Marcella Vonn Harting of *Guerrilla Multi-Level Marketing*. He reached diamond level in his network marketing. James is author of nine books and numerous articles that have helped readers of the *Chicago Tribune, Bottom Line Personal, Family Circle, The Crafts Report, Better Homes & Gardens, Working Mothers, Country Almanac*, and many more including *The Wall Street Journal*. He is also a co-author of the new book, *Guerrilla Marketing on the Front Lines*, which hit #1 best-seller in Entrepreneurship category on Amazon.

James has been interviewed on *Entrepreneur* Radio and appeared as a featured guest on HGTV where he shared marketing advice with more than three million viewers. He serves as a member of the advisory boards to the National Craft Association and ArtisanStreet.com and has been listed in the *Who's Who of American Entrepreneurs*. James' book, *Overcoming the 7 Devils That Ruin Success* has been published in 18 countries.

He recently produced a series of webinars for the state of Alaska to help local artists and craft makers learn more ways to market their creative products.

James is passionate about helping others develop fulfilling careers profiting from their creativity. He has presented workshops around the United States, including events for the National Association of Independent Artists in Atlanta and the Bootcamp Marketing for Artists and Craftspeople in Santa Fe, New Mexico. He operates and provides content for Craftmarketer.com, and he started and published *Natural Awakenings* magazine in Colorado.

As a certified guerrilla marketing coach, James has helped individuals and organizations learn how to leverage their existing assets into bigger profits using guerrilla strategies. See http://www.GMMLM. com for more details about the program. If you are looking to reach higher levels of income, contact James to learn how he can help you with marketing, public relations, internet sales, or business coaching at email: 4jamesd@gmail.com; website: http://www.jamesdillehay.com.

David T. Fagan

David T. Fagan is the co-author of *Guerrilla Rainmakers* and a former CEO of Guerrilla Marketing who currently owns Cutting Edge Ventures, Icon Builder, Guerrilla Rainmakers, and Cash Club for Kids. David is an author, in-demand speaker, and business development consultant. He is director of special projects for Guerrilla Marketing International. David's Icon Builders program and *Guerrilla Rainmakers* book and marketing package are based on Jay Conrad Levinson's guerrilla marketing concepts. David has taken these marketing concepts further by developing products and services enabling an entrepreneur to make profits rain. To contact David, call (480) 370-4442; email him directly at dfaganbusiness@gmail. com; visit his website, http://www.davidtfagan.com; or write to him at 1555 E. Southern Ave., Suite #208, Mesa, AZ 85204.

Chris Forbes

Chris Forbes is co-author with Frank Adkins of *Guerrilla Marketing for Nonprofits*. He is a certified guerrilla marketing coach specializing in nonprofit and political marketing. Chris helps nonprofits, politicians, and other leaders effectively reach people of all kinds with astounding results. His varied background of work in marketing includes extensive experience in the faith sector.

Chris Forbes is a 20-year veteran of communications, ethnographic research, and nonprofit marketing. A slightly frustrated, ex-standup comedian, Chris writes and speaks about nonprofit marketing. Through his humorous and unique perspective, he makes learning about nonprofit communications fun, interesting, and practical. He helps people become better at marketing.

About the Authors and Co-Authors

He has developed contextualized marketing and media strategies on five continents and today uses his skills as a contextual marketer to help advocates, influencers, and anthropreneurs make more impact with the people they want to reach. He has helped nonprofits, politicians, and business leaders effectively reach people of all kinds with astounding results.

He has pioneered multiple global and national media initiatives in internet, public relations, radio, and TV while working as a ministry communication strategist and marketplace researcher with various organizations and ministries within the Southern Baptist Convention.

He lives in Edmond, Oklahoma, with his wife and three daughters. See http://ChrisForbes.org for contact information.

Rick Frishman

Rick Frishman, a co-author of *Guerrilla Publicity* and *Guerrilla Marketing for Writers*, is the founder of Planned Television Arts and has been one of the leading book publicists in America for more than 30 years. Rick also serves as publisher at Morgan James Publishing in New York. Rick has appeared on hundreds of radio shows and more than a dozen television shows nationwide, including *Oprah*, *Bloomberg TV*, and *Fox Business*. He has been featured in the *New York Times*, *The Wall Street Journal*, Associated Press stories, *Selling Power* magazine, *New York Post*, and scores of publications. He is the co-author of eight books. Contact information: website, http://www.rickfrishman.com; email, rick@rickfrishman.com; 1225 Franklin Avenue, Suite 325, Garden City, NY 11530; phone, (516) 308-1524.

David Garfinkel

David Garfinkel, co-author of *Guerrilla Copywriting*, has worked with businesses in more than 100 industries and has helped thousands of people around the world become better copywriters. Some of the sales letters he has written for businesses have brought in more than $1 million for each business. He is president of Overnight Marketing in

San Francisco. The firm specializes in results-driven direct marketing for entrepreneurial businesses, helping them get more sales from the advertising they do. As a marketing consultant and master copywriter, David has worked with businesses in 81 different industries.

He's an established teacher of business writing skills with a long list of successful clients in the corporate, entrepreneurial, and professional services arena. David's "Money-Making Copywriting Course" is the only such course endorsed and recommended by the National Mail Order Association.

David's clients include such well -known companies as IBM, United Airlines, Pacific Bell, Time-Life Books, and MCI. Today, most of David's clients are smaller, prosperous businesses that want to increase sales quickly and sustain the increase at the lowest possible cost. David still works in many industries, but most of his clients are in the seminar, software, and financial services businesses.

David is the co-author of *Effective Sales Management and Guerrilla Marketing for the Imaging Industry*. He is one of a small group of experts on Bank of America's website. In his early career, David was an award-winning business journalist. He completed his journalism career in 1985 as McGraw-Hill Magazines' San Francisco Bureau Chief.

Today David is frequently sought out by the media for his expertise on marketing, and has been featured in *The Wall Street Journal, USA Today, Fast Company, Home Office Computing*, and dozens of other newspapers, magazines, and trade journals throughout the United States.

Contact David at Overnight Marketing, 236 West Portal Avenue, PMB 255, San Francisco, CA 94127; phone: (415) 564-4475; fax: (415) 564-4599; email: Garfinkel@aol.com; website: http://www.davidgarfinkel.com.

Shane Gibson

Shane Gibson is an international speaker and author who has addressed more than 100,000 people over the past 18 years on stages in North America, southern Africa, and South America. He is in high demand as a keynote speaker on the topics of social media and sales performance.

Blogging since 2002, and podcasting since 2004, Shane drives the majority of his business from social media and social networks. He is the author of three books: *Sociable! How Social Media is Turning Sales and Marketing Upside Down* (with Stephen Jagger); *Closing Bigger: the Field Guide to Closing Bigger Deals* (with Trevor Greene); and *Guerrilla Social Media Marketing*, co-authored with Jay Conrad Levinson.

Shane works with clients providing everything from enlightening keynote seminars on social media to in-depth social media launch plans for large organizations. Shane's excitement about social media comes from the fact that today anyone with a blog, video camera, and Twitter account can reach millions of customers in true guerrilla style. It doesn't take millions of dollars or hundreds of hours. All you need is imagination, knowledge, innovation, and community.

Shane shares his insights and teachings online across a vast network of social media sites. Connect with him as follows. Blogs and websites: http://closingbigger.net, http://guerrillasocialmediahq.com, and http://socialized.me; Twitter account: http://twitter.com/shanegibson@ShaneGibson; Facebook: http://facebook.com/shane.gibson.author and http://facebook.com/guerrillasocialmediamarketing; LinkedIn: http://linkedin.com/in/shanegibson; YouTube: http://www.youtube.com/user/shanegibsonvan; Skype: knowledge.brokers; or email: shane@guerrillasocialmediahq.com.

Seth Godin

Seth Godin is a blogger, author, and entrepreneur. Find out more and read 3,900 free blog posts at sethgodin.com. Jay considers Seth to be the best nonfiction author in the world. If he wrote fiction he'd be the best at that, too. Just check his name and books on Amazon.com!

Seth's contact information: 45 Main Street 3R Hastings on Hudson, NY 10706; http://www.sethgodin.com; http://www.squidoo.com/seth; and http://www.amazon.com/Seth-Godin/e/B000AP9EH0. Subscribe to his blog at http://feeds.feedburner.com/typepad/sethsmainblog.

David Hancock

David Hancock is the co-author, along with Mike Larsen and Rick Frishman, of *Guerrilla Marketing for Writers*, the *The Entrepreneurial Author* with Frishman and Jay Conrad Levinson, and *Guerrilla Marketing for Mortgage Brokers* with Levinson. He is a certified marketing coach and the founder of Morgan James Publishing and was recognized in 2008 by NASDAQ as one of the world's most prestigious business leaders. He was also named a finalist in the Best Chairman category in the 2006 American Business Awards. David is the founder of the Entrepreneurial Author University and the founder of the Ethan Awards, the only international, all-encompassing, entrepreneurial author awards for business authors. David sits on the advisory board of the Mark Victor Hansen Foundation and on the executive board of Habitat for Humanity Peninsula. David and his wife, Susan, live in Hampton Roads, Virginia, with their two children. David can be reached at: (516) 522-0514; http://www.DavidHancock.com; Twitter.com/DavidHancock; and Facebook.com/DHancock.

Paul R. J. Hanley

Paul Hanley was a friend, a guerrilla marketing master trainer in the United Kingdom, and the co-author of *The Guerrilla Marketing Revolution: Precision Persuasion of the Unconscious Mind*. After taking enormous strides for guerrilla marketing in Russia and the Middle East, Paul died in the crash of the plane he was flying. He left behind a son, Kieran, a sister, Maria, and his parents, Brian and Julie, who reside in North Hampton, England. The words he wrote in *The Guerrilla Marketing Revolution* have helped many guerrillas around the world.

Donald Hendon

Donald Hendon, co-author of *Guerrilla Deal-Making*, has valuable information that nobody else in the world has. He has given several thousand seminars and consulted for firms in 36 nations on six continents—from Saudi Arabia to Australia. He has made deals with executives from 54 nations, using more than 300 tactics in his repertoire. Each nation has a unique negotiating style, and Dr. Hendon knows these styles intimately—the specific tactics used the most by executives in those countries when they buy and sell, when they wheel and deal. Don trains his clients <u>THOROUGHLY</u>. He gives them the power to win big—and to win often—when they negotiate with people from these nations. Contact him and become more powerful when *you* make deals. He lives near Las Vegas, Nevada. He's at donhendon1@gmail.com.

Grant Hicks, CIM, FCSI

Grant Hicks is the co-author of *Guerrilla Marketing for Financial Advisors*, president of Hicks Financial, and one of Canada's leading authorities on marketing financial services. He is a dynamic and entertaining speaker with an amazing ability to motivate audiences to achieve more. The average attendee writes seven pages of notes and is captivated by his brilliant marketing ideas. Grant is a Fellow of the Canadian Securities Institute and a retirement planning specialist.

Grant played professional hockey in Europe before starting a career in financial services. His background includes recruiting 60 representatives as a manager of a financial planning firm in less than three years and building a clientele from $1 million in assets to more than $40 million in less than two years. Grant was also a top producer with the BC Credit Union Financial Planning Association.

Grant has been an invited speaker by many organizations, including TD Bank, Manulife Financial, Standard Life, Malaspina University, Advocis, Federation of Canadian Independent Deposit Brokers, RBC Dominion Securities, Scotiamcleod, AIC Group of Funds, and the Guerrilla Marketing Association.

He runs his retirement planning practice, speaks, and writes, and manages http://www.financialadvisermarketing.com, a website for financial professionals from his offices in Parksville, British Columbia, on beautiful Vancouver Island, Canada.

Chet Holmes

Chet Holmes is the co-author and co-creator with Jay Conrad Levinson of the *Guerrilla Marketing Meets Karate Master: Business Growth Seminar and Home Study Course*, which consists of live events, books, workbooks, CDs, and DVDs. Chet has developed 75 training products selling in 60 countries, and he was top producer in every position held. He is a best-selling author with the number-one sales book on Amazon for four years running: *The Ultimate Sales Machine*. In April of 2010, he founded Business Breakthroughs with Tony Robbins, a string of 12 companies that provide a roster of services all designed to help companies grow. To take an introductory seminar on his material, go to http://www.howtodoublesales.com, or see http://www.BusinessBreakthroughs.com for all the services offered by Chet Holmes and Tony Robbins to help businesses grow.

Shel Horowitz

Shel Horowitz is the co-author of *Guerrilla Marketing Goes Green: Winning Strategies to Improve Your Profits and Your Planet*. He is an international speaker/marketing consultant/copywriter who specializes in win-win green, ethical strategies that lower costs, boost profits, and attract potential customers. Five of his eight books have won awards, sold foreign rights, and/or made at least one Amazon category bestseller list.

Shel also writes the Green And Profitable and Green And Practical columns, helps turn unpublished writers into published authors, is starting an international trade association for green marketers, saved a local mountain, and has been both a marketer and environmental activist since the 1970s.

Contact Shel in a number of ways: Twitter: @shelhorowitz; email: shel@greenandprofitable.com; website directory: http://shelhorowitz.com; phone: (413) 586-2388 (8 A.M.–10 P.M. Eastern time).

Alexandru Israil

Alexandru Israil is the co-author of *Guerrilla Marketing and the Human Ego*. He has been in the business of marketing since 1996, operating from his home in Romania. He worked in Europe, for brands like Compaq, IBM, Bosch, Xerox, Ariston, Yellow Pages, Siemens, and Microsoft. His long practiced credo, to offer unconventional, consistent, and effective marketing solutions for his clients, was fulfilled in 2007 when he trained with Jay Levinson and became a guerrilla marketing master trainer.

He is now representing Guerrilla Marketing International in Europe, providing training, coaching, and consulting in marketing and sales. His declared mission is to inspire his clients in finding and implementing optimal, realistic, and effective strategies in sales and marketing, focusing on profits and bottom-line results.

Alexandru is the owner of MarketMinds Co., a company gathering independent consultants employed on project basis. They offer inspirational, analytical, and functional solutions to companies willing to improve their results in marketing and sales. As a speaker and trainer, Alexandru has inspired thousands of business professionals in their search for better performance and results. His articles on sales and marketing appear in various online and print publications. He is also hosting the Guerrilla Marketing Association Weekly Teleclass, interviewing key professionals in sales and marketing around the world.

Find out more on http://www.gmarketing.ro. Or contact: via email: alexandru.israil@gmarketing.ro.

Robert Kaden

Robert Kaden is the co-author of *Guerrilla Research*. He has lived in Chicago all his life and has been married to Ellie for more years than either like to admit. He is the father of Hilary and the grandfather of Samantha. Bob has degrees from Lincoln College in Lincoln, Illinois, and from Columbia College in Chicago. He has been in market research his entire career, spending 10 years in the research departments at various Chicago advertising agencies and then, in the early 1970s, becoming president of Goldring & Company. In 1992, Bob started The Kaden Company and continues to serve his market research clients. He has been involved in more than 3,000 focus groups and survey studies and has pioneered many unique quantitative and qualitative market research approaches. Bob also devotes a considerable amount of time to The LeRoy Street Band, a rock and roll cover band, where he is the conga player and percussionist. Bob can be reached at The Kaden Company, 6725 N. LeRoy Avenue, Lincolnwood, IL 60712; (847) 933-9400, or at thekadencompany@sbcglobal.net.

Loral Langemeier

Loral Langemeier is the co-author of *Guerrilla Wealth* and one of today's most dynamic and pioneering financial strategists. A *New York Times* best-selling author and a leading motivational speaker, Loral has spurred thousands across the country from dazed apathy and fear of finance to millionaire status by giving them the simple tools to launch innovative businesses that generate cash and build wealth.

Born and raised on a farm in Nebraska, Loral Langemeier started from scratch. Growing up, she had neither money nor connections. She created her first business at 17, and by the time she was 34, had established a multimillion-dollar portfolio. Loral has built a number of businesses in a variety of industries, several of which have grossed millions.

Loral is the author of the national best-seller *The Millionaire Maker* and two *New York Times* bestsellers, *The Millionaire Maker's Guide to Wealth Cycle Investing* and *The Millionaire Maker's Guide to Creating a Cash Machine for Life*.

In addition to hosting her sold-out Millionaire Maker® events, Loral currently acts as a financial expert on the *Dr. Phil Show*, mentoring families in financial crisis. She has appeared frequently on CNN, CNBC, and Fox News Channel; been featured in *USA Today*, *The Wall Street Journal*, and the *New York Times*; and appeared on the web at ABCNews.com, Forbes.com, and BusinessWeek.com. She has been a weekly guest columnist on Gather.com and for TheStreet.com, an in-depth financial analysis and news website co-founded by CNBC Mad Money host, Jim Cramer.

She is the creator of "The Millionaire Maker Game," a board game that teaches people how to build wealth through asset generating ventures.

After creating her own financial freedom and reaching a net worth of $1 million, Loral decided she would start a coaching and seminar company to provide a catalyst that would allow others to reach this same level of success. The company started small with one office in Novato, California, in 2002; and within five years it grew to a $19 million company. During that time, the organization expanded to its current size, which includes locations in Novato and South Lake Tahoe and Carson City, Nevada. Find Loral at: http://lorallangemeier.com; phone: (888) 262-2402.

Michael Larsen

Michael Larsen is the co-author of *Guerrilla Marketing for Writers* and *How to Write a Book Proposal*. He is a literary agent, and he and his wife own Michael Larsen-Elizabeth Pomada Literary Agents. He has been helping writers launch careers since 1972.

Michael is a member of the Association of Authors' Representatives; he handles prescriptive nonfiction, and he and Elizabeth have sold hundreds of books to more than 100 publishers. They are also the co-founders of the San Francisco Writers Conference and the Writing for Change Conference.

Find Michael at http://www.larsenpomada.com; 1029 Jones Street, San Francisco, CA 94109; (415) 673-0939.

Al Lautenslager

Al Lautenslager, the co-author of *Guerrilla Marketing in 30 Days*, is an award-winning marketing/PR consultant, direct-mail promotion specialist, author, speaker, and entrepreneur. His knowledge has helped hundreds succeed in their own businesses. He is the principal of Market for Profits, a marketing consulting firm in Chicago, and the former owner of a small business, The Inkwell, a commercial printing and mailing company. Al recently appeared on radio as a marketing expert to review Super Bowl commercials.

Al has started up businesses and closed them down. He has walked the walk of a guerrilla marketer. He is a multiwinner of Business of the Year awards from various organizations. His articles can be read on more than 100 online sites, including that of *Entrepreneur* magazine (http://www.entrepreneur.com), where he serves as a marketing expert and coach.

Al speaks to audiences about low or no-cost marketing tactics. His leadership has extended to community involvement as a member of the board of directors of numerous nonprofit organizations, including two chambers of commerce. Al is also a certified guerrilla marketing coach and can be reached at al@allautenslager.com; website: http://www. market-for-profits.com; Market For Profits, 297 Rice Lake Square, Wheaton, IL 60187; phone: (630) 740-1397.

Jill Lublin

Jill Lublin is the co-author along with Rick Frishman of *Guerrilla Publicity*. With more than 200 speaking engagements across the globe each year, Lublin, a master publicity strategist, consistently wows audiences across the world with her highly entertaining, interactive keynotes, seminars, and special programs on how to be influential and gain the attention of the media.

Praised as a modern-day Dale Carnegie for her lessons on how to be influential, Jill Lublin has empowered and inspired more than 100,000 people through her best-selling books, national and international speaking tours, and strategic consulting engagements.

She has been featured on Tony Robbins' stage and has also appeared with T. Harv Eker and has spoken at various events with Jack Canfield, Mark Victor Hansen, and Richard Simmons. Jill is the author of the bestselling book *Get Noticed. . .Get Referrals* (McGraw-Hill).

She is also the co-author of two national best-selling books, *Networking Magic*, which rose to number one on the Barnes and Noble charts for three weeks, and *Guerrilla Publicity*.

In the past 20 years, she has worked with ABC, NBC, CBS, and other national media, and knows what the media wants. Jill has been featured in the *New York Times*, *Woman's Day*, *Fortune Small Business*, *Inc.*, and *Entrepreneur* magazine, and on ABC and NBC radio and TV national affiliates.

Deeply committed to public service, Jill founded GoodNews Media, Inc. and hosts the TV program, *Messages of Hope*, as well as the nationally syndicated radio show, Do the Dream. Jill is thrilled when the stories she shares encourage and inspire people to follow their dreams, especially when a crisis has stopped them in their tracks.

Website: http://www.JillLublin.com; phone: (415) 883-5455; email: info@JillLublin.com.

Alex Mandossian

Alex Mandossian is a contributing co-author in *Guerrilla Marketing on the Front Lines*. Since 1991, Alex has generated more than $300 million in sales and profits for his clients and partners via electronic marketing media such as TV, infomercials, online catalogs, 24-hour recorded messages, voice/fax broadcasting, teleseminars, webinars, podcasts, and internet marketing. He has personally consulted for Dale Carnegie Training, New York University, Nightingale-Conant, Super Camp, Trim Spa, and many others. He is a certified guerrilla marketing coach and has hosted teleseminars with many of the world's top thought leaders such as Mark Victor Hansen, Jack Canfield, Stephen Covey, Les Brown, Brian Tracy, Harvey Mackay, T. Harv Eker, Lisa Nichols, Loral Langemeier, Michael Gerber, Jay Abraham, Donald Trump, and others.

He is the founder and CEO of Heritage House Companies—a boutique electronic marketing and publishing company that "repurposes" written and spoken educational content for worldwide distribution. He is also the founder of the Electronic Marketing Institute.

He has trained more than 15,000 teleseminar students since 2001 and knows that any entrepreneur can transform annual income into a weekly income once they apply his principle-centered, electronic marketing strategies.

Alex lives in the San Francisco Bay area with his wife, Aimee, and two children, and enjoys more than 90 "free days" each year. Visit: http://www.AlexMandossian.com for more information.

Monroe Mann

Monroe Mann is the founder of Unstoppable Artists, the world's only business, marketing, and financial strategic firm for established (and up-and-coming) actors, directors, authors, and artists. He has helped his clients sign with major agencies, publish books, star in their own films and plays, play in their own bands, and in general, just become really successful. Students/clients have appeared in/on *People* magazine, *Inside Edition, Entrepreneur, Entertainment Tonight, CNN, ABC News, Variety, Hollywood Reporter, Backstage, Boston Globe, Glamour, Keith Ablow, New York Times*, and the list goes on. Monroe is also the CEO of Loco Dawn Films; a graduate of Hollywood Film Institute and Digital Film Academy; an actor listed on IMDb; the lead singer of a seven-piece band; the screenwriter/executive producer/co-star of the upcoming wakeboarding feature film *In the Wake*; a certified guerrilla marketing coach; the recipient of a business degree from Franklin College in Switzerland; a graduate student at Lubin School of Business, Pace Law School, and Western Carolina University's Master of Entrepreneurship program; and a combat veteran of Operation Iraqi Freedom. He is also the author of a number of critically acclaimed books, including *The Theatrical Juggernaut—The Psyche of the Star; Battle Cries for the Underdog; To Benning & Back*; and the upcoming *The Artist's MBA*. Finally, he is also the founder of the exclusive networking action group called "The Juggernaut Club," and the founder of the American Break Diving Association. For those who are completely obsessed with success, he is available for private business coaching internationally—please feel free to contact him to set up a free, 20-minute career consultation. More info: phone: (646) 764-1764; email: monroemann@aol.com; website: http://www. UnstoppableArtists.com.

Mitch Meyerson

Mitch Meyerson is the co-author of *Guerrilla Marketing on the Front Lines* and—with Mary Eule Scarborough—of *Guerrilla Marketing on the Internet*. He is a speaker, trainer, and consultant and coauthor of nine personal and business development books including *Mastering Online Marketing, Six Keys To Creating The Life You Desire, When Is Enough Enough?, When Parents Love Too Much, Success Secrets of The Online Marketing Superstars*, and *World Class Speaking*. His books appear in 26 languages, and he has been the featured expert on *Oprah*.

Since 1999 Mitch has cofounded four groundbreaking internet-based programs: The Guerrilla Marketing Coach Certification Program with Jay Conrad Levinson, which has certified more than 300 guerrilla marketing coaches worldwide; The 90 Day Product Factory; The Online Traffic School; and Master Business Building Club. Mitch is also an accomplished jazz musician/songwriter and lives in Scottsdale, Arizona. Contact him through email at www.mitch@ gmarketingcoach.com.

Roger C. Parker

Roger C. Parker is the co-author of *Guerrilla Marketing Design*. Well before the start of this century, Roger C. Parker has been exploring and sharing the DNA of writing for branding success with guerrilla marketers around the world. His goal is to help business owners translate their expertise into brand-building blogs, books, and e-books.

Roger's background includes writing 39 books that have sold more than 1.6 million copies around the world. His latest is *#Book Title Tweet: 140 Bite-Sized Ideas for Compelling Article, Book, and Event Titles.*

Roger has interviewed more than 500 best-selling authors and marketing authorities for the Guerrilla Marketing Association and http://www.PublishedandProfitable.com. His blog shares more than 1,000 blog posts with ideas, tips, and examples of writing and branding success.

Learn more at http://www.publishedandprofitable.com. Submit your questions about writing and personal branding to Roger by mail: Roger C. Parker, PO Box 697, Dover, NH 03821; or by phone: (603) 742-9673.

David E. Perry

David Perry is the co-author of *Guerrilla Marketing for Job Hunters*. He is a veteran of almost 996 executive search projects, with a 99.8 percent success rate. Called "The Rogue Recruiter" by *The Wall Street Journal*, he is a student of leadership and its effect on organizations, ranging from private equity ventures to global technology corporations.

David is the author of *Guerrilla Marketing for Job-Hunters: 400 Unconventional Tips, Tricks and Tactics to Land Your Dream Job* and *Career Guide for the High Tech Professional: Where The Jobs Are and Where to Land Them*.

David graduated from McGill University in Canada in 1982 with a bachelor's in economics and industrial relations. As a commissioned officer, he graduated first in his class and was awarded The Sword of Honor. He has been recognized as one of the "Top 40 Under 40" entrepreneurs. He lives in Ottawa, Canada, with his wife and business partner, Anita Martell, and their four children. He recruits globally.

He can be reached at david@perrymartel.com. Check out his free job resources at http://www.GM4JH.com Code 613-236-6695.

Steve Savage

Steve Savage is the co-author of *Guerrilla Business Secrets*. Steve, a sales guru, is an energetic and dynamic speaker who motivates people in keynotes, workshops, and seminars. His presentations are not based on abstract theory; they flow from a life of work as an entrepreneur.

Steve and two partners took a company from zero to $60 million in six years—and sold it to Colgate-Palmolive. He conducts business seminars all over the world and delivers motivational keynote addresses.

He grew up in Ecuador and is 100 percent bilingual. Much of his focus is in Latin America, delivering speeches in Spanish to packed audiences from Mexico to Argentina. Businesses report dramatic sales increases after Steve works with their sales forces. He's at email: savage@stevesavage.com; website: http://stevesavage.com; and blog: http://savagebusinesssecrets.com.

Mary Eule Scarborough

Mary Eule Scarborough is the co-author along with Mitch Meyerson of *Guerrilla Marketing on the Internet*. She is an award-winning speaker, writer, and certified guerrilla marketing coach who draws upon her real-life experiences as a Fortune 500 marketing executive; founder of two successful small businesses; AdWords advertising expert; and independent marketing consultant to help businesses grow their profits.

She is also the co-author of two other business and marketing books: *The Procrastinator's Guide to Marketing* and *Mastering Online Marketing*.

Mary currently spends most of her time teaching pay-per-click mastery webinars (http://www.GuerrillaPPC.com) and managing AdWords campaigns for her clients.

She has a BA in English/journalism from the University of Maryland and MS in marketing from The Johns Hopkins University. You can email Mary at maryeulescarborough@gmail.com; visit her website at www.strategicmarketingadvisors.com; or call at (480) 264-3646.

Mark S. A. Smith

Mark S. A. Smith is co-author of *Guerrilla Trade Show Selling*, *Guerrilla TeleSelling*, and *Guerrilla Negotiating* and *Guerrilla Selling in Tough Situations* along with Orvel Ray Wilson.

An internationally renowned speaker and writer on trade show selling, Smith has been writing, producing, and delivering seminars on sales skills topics for many years. He edits a monthly newsletter and has published more than 50 articles on various marketing topics. He is a contributing editor to Business Tech International, and is featured regularly in *Cintermex*, a Latin American trade show journal.

Mark has self-published two books: *How to Be Your Best at Trade Show Selling*, and *49 Ways to Be Your Best at Trade Show Selling*, two videocassettes (*How to Get the Most Leads From Your Trade Show* and *The Ten Things Most Companies Do at Trade Shows that Don't Work, and How You Can Fix Them*), and three audiocassette programs on the subject of trade-show selling, including one targeted at volunteer and nonprofit organizations.

Although he graduated with a degree in electrical engineering, Mark went straight into sales support for Hewlett-Packard. His training style has evolved from years of working with audiences, including three years with European groups. Mark markets his training and consulting services through direct marketing, telesales, referral, and media relations.

Mark is a past president of the Colorado Speakers Association and on the adjunct faculty at Front Range Community College of Denver, in the Applied International Management program. He is a certified professional consultant, and a member of the Trade Show Bureau. He is also president of The Valence Group, a company committed to excellence in training and personal development, and a partner with The Guerrilla Group, Inc., conducting The Guerrilla Selling Seminar for audiences worldwide.

For more information see his blog at http://marksasmith.com; website at http://oceinc.com; or contact him at Outsource Channel Executives phone: (800) 743-4349 or (719) 323-6100.

Wendy Stevens

Wendy Stevens is the co-author of *Guerrilla Marketing to Women* and *Local Guerrilla Marketing*.

What do you do when you're a struggling single parent on the verge of losing your house? Whatever it takes. In early 2000, a bitter divorce wrenched Wendy Stevens from her life as a comfortable

Nashville socialite, leaving her an unemployed single mother on the verge of losing everything. Like so many baby boomer women, necessity forced her to launch a second career. But Wendy not only launched a second career, she drew upon her experience as an athlete and coach to succeed beyond her wildest imagination.

In 1980, a devastating head-on collision with a drunk driver robbed Wendy of her rocket tennis serve, causing her to lose her tennis scholarship to the University of North Carolina. Undaunted, she enrolled at the University of Maryland and took up lacrosse. Maryland was building a dynasty, packed with All-American players, and Wendy had never even played the sport before. But through ability, tenacity, and determination, she not only walked onto the team, but became an All-American as well as captain and Most Valuable Player for the national champion 1986 University of Maryland women's lacrosse team.

Today, Wendy coaches budding entrepreneurs around the world as a much sought-after keynote speaker, trainer, success coach, and mentor. Her greatest satisfaction is reproducing the financial success she has achieved in the lives of others. Wendy Stevens splits her time between Franklin, Tennessee, and Fort Lauderdale, Florida, and is the proud mother of Bo and Haley. For more information, see Wendy's website: http://www.coachwendystevens.com.

Terry Telford

Terry Telford is the co-author of *Guerrilla Breakthough Strategies: Triple your Sales and Quadruple Your Business in 90 Days with Joint Venture Partnerships.*

In his own words, Terry says, "I come from the marketing and advertising world. In 1991, I graduated from the advertising program at Loyalist College in Belleville, Ontario, Canada. Immediately after graduating I started an advertising agency with a partner. Six months later, I sold the agency to my partner and moved to the 'big city'—Toronto.

"In 2001, I hopped onto the internet with the hopes of expanding my mail-order business. At first glance it seemed pretty simple. The upside of online marketing was it cost next to nothing. The downside was, I was getting very little response. I did a lot of experimenting with ways to advertise effectively online. I tried everything and anything. Although I was experiencing minimal success online, I could see it was the future, so I sold my offline mail-order company and started working online full time. But I still hadn't connected the dots. It took me three years before I had my epiphany.

"My big AHA moment happened when I suddenly realized my online business was actually a direct marketing company. Exactly the same as what I had been running offline, but with a lot more advantages. As soon as I started running my online company the same as I'd been running my offline company, my business started growing.

"When I discovered the power of joint ventures, it started growing exponentially. I've been very fortunate to meet hundreds of wonderful people like Jay, and I have dozens of joint venture partnerships and strategic alliances with fantastic people all over the world. I'm just an average guy, if I can do it, so can you. I wish you all the success you deserve now and in the future. Contact me at: http://www.TerryTelford.com."

Kathryn Tyler

Kathryn Tyler is the co-author of *Guerrilla Saving: Secrets for Keeping Profits in Your Home-Based Business*. She has been a homebased freelance writer since 1993 and a homeschooling mom since 2002. Kathryn has also written the e-book *Convince Your Husband to Homeschool*, available from Pear Educational Products.

Kathryn has written regularly for *Human Resources Management* magazine for 18 years and has written for *Home Education* magazine, *Your Money, Woman's Day, FamilyFun, The Rotarian, Good Housekeeping*, and others.

In addition to writing, she has taught at the University of California, San Diego; San Diego State University; Oakland Community College; and in the private sector. Kathryn received her BA in English-American literature from the University of California, San Diego, in

1992 and graduated with an MA in English literature from San Diego State University in 1994. To contact Kathryn, visit her website at http://www.kathryntyler.com.

Elly Valas

Elly Valas is the co-author along with Orvel Ray Wilson of *Guerrilla Retailing* and the past president of the North American Retail Dealers Association. An internationally renowned author and speaker, she has worked with retailers worldwide on family business planning, management, sales, and marketing.

She is a regular contributor to *The Independent Retailer* and the Consumer Electronic Association's publication *Visions* and has received the Editorial Excellence award from the American Society of Business Press Editors.

Reach her at Valas Consulting Group, LLC, phone: (303) 316-7569; website: http://www.EllyValas.com.

Craig Valentine

Craig Valentine is contributing co-author of *Guerrilla Speaking* in the compilation book *Guerrilla Marketing on the Front Lines* and the 1999 Toastmasters International World Champion of Public Speaking.

As president of the Communication Factory, he has helped thousands of up-and-coming speakers in seven countries and 44 U.S. states using his process to enhance their presentations and increase their profits. Using this special process, Craig has sold more than $12 million in educational earning resources and received a U.S. Congressional achievement award for "Excellence in Communications." He is the author of the book *The Nuts and Bolts of Public Speaking* and the producer of several training courses designed to turn presentations into huge profits.

Contact him by email: Info@CraigValentine.com; through his website: http://www.CraigValentine.com; phone: (800) 682-5063; (410) 262-9577; fax: (410) 381-8417.

Marcella Vonn Harting

Marcella Vonn Harting is a co-author along with James Dillehay of *Guerrilla Multilevel Marketing* and an internationally recognized author, speaker, facilitator, and entrepreneur. Since 1992 Marcella has built two highly successful network marketing distributorships with more than 200,000 representatives worldwide.

Marcella has achieved the highest rank in her network marketing compensation plan and is one of the top earners in her company. Marcella teaches how to achieve network marketing success in the U.S., Canada, Australia, Japan, and throughout Europe.

In network marketing, she demonstrates how creating a residual abundant income centered in health and wealth can empower balance and purpose in one's life. Marcella is an inspirational mentor in manifesting and teaching how to achieve one's highest goals with grace, ease, and fun. She resides in Paradise Valley, Arizona, with her husband, daughter, and son. For more information, see her website: http://www.marcellavonnharting.com; or contact her by email: marcella@marcellavonnharting.com; or phone: (480) 443-3224.

Orvel Ray Wilson

Orvel Ray Wilson is the co-author of *Guerrilla Selling: Unconventional Weapons and Tactics for Increasing Your Sales*, with Bill Gallagher; and *Guerrilla Trade Show Selling, Guerrilla TeleSelling, and Guerrilla Negotiating* with Mark S. A. Smith.

Ray is the president of The Guerrilla Group, Inc., an international training and consulting firm serving clients worldwide. An internationally acclaimed author and speaker on sales, marketing, motivation, and management, Ray's speaking career has taken him to more than 1,000 cities around the world. His articles appear regularly in dozens of industry and trade magazines. He also edits the *Guerrilla Selling Tip of the Week* e-zine distributed by email to thousands of subscribers worldwide.

He started his career early, selling garden seeds door-to-door when he was 9 years old, and founded his first company at 19. Twenty-five years of real-world sales experience ranges from encyclopedias to advertising, from used cars to computers. He's taught closing techniques to Xerox field reps and job search skills to Indochinese refugees.

In 1980, he founded the Boulder Sales Training Institute, and his client list has since grown to include industry leaders like AT&T, W. F. Gore Associates, and Microsoft. He has taught in the management development programs for the University of Colorado and the University of Denver and created innovative business courses for Harbridge House, the University of Toledo, the Spring Institute for International Studies, and Australia's Canberra College of Advanced Education. He has even pioneered workshops on capitalism for the Tyumen School of Management in the Russian Republic.

Orvel was elected president of Colorado Chapter of the National Speakers Association in 1986 and served two additional terms on its board of directors. In 1997, he was awarded the highest earned designation in the field of professional speaking, the Certified Speaking Professional (CSP) conferred by the National Speakers Association. Fewer than 300 professional speakers worldwide have achieved this distinction.

Contact Orvel Ray Wilson through The Guerrilla Group Inc., phone: (800) 247-9145; fax: (303) 642-7617; website: http:www. GuerrillaGroup.com.

Todd Woods

Todd Woods is a guerrilla marketing master trainer specializing in *Guerrilla Marketing for Franchisees*—also the title of a book he co-wrote with Jay Levinson. He is a successful businessman, primarily through his ownership of several Jamba Juice franchises. He's a graduate of the University of Utah and lives in Anthem, Arizona, with his wife, Michelle, and their five children. You can find Todd on Facebook and LinkedIn. Or contact him at Todd@gmstrategies.com or twoods@ gmarketingstrategies.com.

Index

content
  creating a map for, 192
  credibility and, 237–238
  substance and, 43
  transparency in, 109
  value-added, 110
content maps, 192
convenience, 46
conventions, 332–333
copywriting, 196–202
creativity
  in advertising, 85–86
  memes and, 116–119
  profits and, 136
credibility
  in advertising, 93–94
  authoring and, 353–356
  content and, 237–238
  joint ventures and, 322
  in online presence, 237
  social media marketing and, 239
  specificity and, 191
  third-party feedback and, 224
criteria words, 380–381
cultural diversity, 209
curiosity, 106–107
customer relations
  competitive edge and, 155–156,
    172
  customer retention and, 71
  during economic downturns, 126
  five touch system for, 307–311
  follow up and, 50, 229
  guerrillas and, 136, 141–142
  importance of relationships,
    282–283
  market research and, 208–216
  in social media marketing, 235–240
  transparency in, 109

customer service, 36, 45, 108, 124,
  155–156, 406–407
customers
  budgets and priorities of, 398–401
  copywriting and, 196–197
  price buyers as, 389–393
  price cutters as, 393–396
  price shoppers as, 397–398

D
database marketing, 410
deal-making, 173–179
deciders, 380
decision making
  deciders in, 380
  internal dialogue and, 70–72
  unconscious mind and, 72–76
department stores, 169
dependence, 50–52
descriptive business names, 163
Dillehay, James, 433–434
direct mail, 12–13
direct response marketing, 224–225
dirty tricks of buyers
  price buying, 389–393
  price cutting, 393–396
  price shoppers, 397–398
discovery, 236–237
Disney, Walt, 9
Disney World, 9
disposable purchases, 314–316
door-to-door marketing. See
  canvassing

E
edge advantage, 155–158
educational-based marketing,
  262–263
ego influence, 360–362